Praise for *The Magick of Food*

"Gwion takes us on a rich and witty journey through our Pag[...] brings us bang up to the present day and current Pagan practice... With [...], amusing anecdotes, practical, down-to-earth advice, and dozens of recipes from rolled date bites to midnight margaritas, this is a feast of a book."

—Anna Franklin, author of *The Hearth Witch's Compendium*

"Wildly original and a feast for both the body and the spirit, Gwion Raven has created the must-have tool for witches who love food, magick, and combining the two. *The Magick of Food* is fun, fascinating, and incredibly comprehensive. This book is delicious!"

—Deborah Blake, author of *Everyday Witchcraft*

"This book reads like a wonderful deep conversation with a dear friend who not only covers a wealth of great recipes, but also branches into history, magick, and the power of community. There is a great deal of wisdom within these pages... Above all, this book is a celebration of life, which I feel serves an important need in the magickal community and should be in every witch's home."

—Michael Furie, author of *Supermarket Sabbats*

"*The Magick of Food* is your travel guide through thousands of years of culinary myth and history, from ancient Sumer right up to the present day. With a generous portion of wit and wisdom, Gwion Raven escorts us through exotic lands and delicious dishes to delight the senses and inform the soul, all while grounding the experience with practices and exercises to help us make a deeper connection with the food we eat, the land from which it was made, and each other as we share our sacred meals."

—Storm Faerywolf, author of *Forbidden Mysteries of Faery Witchcraft*

"Kitchen witches could not possibly be better represented than they are in the pages of this delightful and informative book. Gwion has perfectly captured the love and magick of food and serves it up in a spectacular multicourse meal for the spirit."

—Katrina Rasbold, author of *Crossroads of Conjure*

the

MAGICK

of FOOD

© Marina Avila Photography

About the Author

Gwion Raven is a tattooed Pagan, writer, traveler, musician, cook, kitchen witch, occult shop owner, and teacher. Although initiated in three magickal traditions (Avalon Druid Order, Reclaiming, and Gardnerian Wicca), Gwion describes his practice as virtually anything that celebrates the wild, sensuous, living, breathing, dancing, ecstatic, divine experiences of this lifetime.

Born and raised in London, England, he now resides in Northern California and shares space with redwood trees, the Pacific Ocean, and his beloved partner.

To Write to the Author

If you wish to contact the author or would like more information about this book, please write to the author in care of Llewellyn Worldwide Ltd. and we will forward your request. Both the author and publisher appreciate hearing from you and learning of your enjoyment of this book and how it has helped you. Llewellyn Worldwide Ltd. cannot guarantee that every letter written to the author can be answered, but all will be forwarded. Please write to:

Gwion Raven
℅ Llewellyn Worldwide
2143 Wooddale Drive
Woodbury, MN 55125-2989

Please enclose a self-addressed stamped envelope for reply,
or $1.00 to cover costs. If outside the U.S.A., enclose
an international postal reply coupon.

Many of Llewellyn's authors have websites with additional information and resources. For more information, please visit our website at http://www.llewellyn.com.

the MAGICK of FOOD

Rituals, Offerings & Why We Eat Together

GWION RAVEN

Llewellyn Publications
Woodbury, Minnesota

FIRST EDITION
Second Printing, 2020

Book design by Samantha Penn
Cover design by Shira Atakpu
Editing by Annie Burdick

Llewellyn is a registered trademark of Llewellyn Worldwide Ltd.

Library of Congress Cataloging-in-Publication Data (Pending)
ISBN: 978-0-7387-6085-8

Llewellyn Worldwide Ltd. does not participate in, endorse, or have any authority or responsibility concerning private business transactions between our authors and the public.

All mail addressed to the author is forwarded, but the publisher cannot, unless specifically instructed by the author, give out an address or phone number.

Any internet references contained in this work are current at publication time, but the publisher cannot guarantee that a specific location will continue to be maintained. Please refer to the publisher's website for links to authors' websites and other sources.

Llewellyn Publications
A Division of Llewellyn Worldwide Ltd.
2143 Wooddale Drive
Woodbury, MN 55125-2989
www.llewellyn.com

Printed in the United States of America

This book is dedicated to Phoenix, Angelica, Andrew, Amy, and Trinity, without whom there would be no reason to cook or make magick.

Contents

List of Recipes   xiii

List of Rituals, Spells & Things to Try   xv

Disclaimer   xvii

Acknowledgments   xix

Foreword by Kristoffer Hughes   xxi

Introduction   *1*

How to Use This Book   5

SECTION I
———— A Brief and Incomplete ————
History of Food and Ritual

Chapter 1: Sumer   *11*

Civilization Started as a Drinking Game   12

We Know the Gods Liked to Eat, but What about the People?   15

Let's Talk about Beer and Ninkasi   17

A Dinner Party Four Thousand Years in the Making   18

Chapter 2: Greece   25

So Much Food, but Not a Gyro in Sight   26

Three Meals a Day   28

Vegetarians and Demeter   30

Athena's Gift Most Useful   34

Dionysus, the Wildest of Gods   36

Chapter 3: Rome   41

Apicius: The First Rockstar Chef   42

Street Food   44

Pop Round to My Place Later for a Convivium   45

The Lares and Penates   46

Chapter 4: The Isles of the Mighty   51

A Dark Age for Cuisine   52

The Importance of Feasting   55

A Table for the Gods   56

What's That Witch Cooking?   57

SECTION II
—— Food, Magick, and Rituals for Today ——

Chapter 5: Food and Magick   61

A Little Bit of Time Magick   68

A Collection of Old Bowls   78

Sing to Your Food   81

Chapter 6: Food and Sex   *85*

Why Aphrodisiacs Work   86

Colour and Taste   87

Making the Magick Just Right   91

Chapter 7: Food and Healing   *101*

Spice Is the Variety of Life   106

Pickle Everything   110

Wisdom from the Community Pantry: Offerings to Preservation   *112*

The Magick of Chicken Soup   118

There's No Place Like Home   123

Wisdom from the Community Pantry: The Long Tale of Industrial Agriculture   *124*

Magick in the City   127

Chapter 8: Food and Grief   *131*

A Place at the Table   132

Riding the Food Train   133

A Meal to Heal and Say Goodbye   135

Ancestor Dinners   136

What Is Remembered Lives   138

Wisdom from the Community Pantry: Willo Soup   *140*

Chapter 9: Food and Community   *143*

Don't Wait for Cakes and Ale   143

Wisdom from the Community Pantry: Imbolc Baking Day   *145*

Eat Your Way through a Ritual   148

The Incredible Edible Harvest Altar   155

Wisdom from the Community Pantry: The Fast and the End of the Fast   *157*

The Dude Who Always Brings a Roasted Chicken   158

If Everyone Brings Something, We All Eat Well   163

Wisdom from the Community Pantry: Cabbage Is My Favourite Vegetable   165

Chapter 10: Food and the Kitchen Witch   169

A Witch's Kitchen Tool Kit   170

A Few Words about Cauldrons   176

Cooking with Intention and Attention   179

Sharing Leftovers with the Earth   181

Three Speedy Food Spells   183

Food Blessings   187

SECTION III
—————— All the Recipes ——————

Chapter 11: Everyday Food Magick   191

Chapter 12: Magick Potions   199

Cocktails   201

Mocktails   205

Magickal Libations   211

Chapter 13: Food Magick for Special Occasions   215

Eating with the Gods   217

A Year of Food Magick   227

Four Ridiculously Good Aphrodisiacs   247

Conclusion: Time to Clean the Kitchen   255

Bibliography   257

Index   259

Recipes

Tuh'u Broth: Lamb and Arugula Stew   20

Simple Flatbread   21

Rolled Date Bites   22

Modern-Day Tiganites   29

Kykeon   33

Super-Quick Bonus Recipe for Apicius's Libyan Shrimp   43

Pottage from the Dark Ages   54

Super-Quick Bonus Recipe for Warmed Figs   88

Super-Quick Bonus Recipe for Chocolate Fondue and Strawberries   90

Super-Quick Bonus Recipe for Wine-Soaked Fennel   105

Super-Quick Bonus Recipe for Gwion's Red Onion Pickle Bliss   117

A Starter Recipe for Chicken Soup   121

Willo Soup   140

Super-Quick Bonus Recipe for Potluck Mac & Cheese   162

Super-Quick Bonus Recipe for Magickal Pancakes   185

The Salmon of Wisdom: Salmon with Hazelnut Topping   192

The Thermos of Gratitude: A Spell with Bone Broth   194

Keep 'em Sweet: Honey Shortbread for Love   197

Gin and Cthonic: An Underworld Cocktail   202

Baba Yagatini: A Sorting Cocktail   203

Cerridwen and Cassis: A Spell for Transformation   204

Melon Pomona: A Spell for the Joys of Summer   206

Metamorphoses Mojito: A Spell for...   208

Midnight Margaritas: A Spell for Hangin' with the
    Coven or Other Magickal People   209

Hot Toddy: A Libation for Health   212

Mulled Wine: A Libation for the Gods   213

In Praise of Inanna: A Modern Take on a Traditional
    Sumerian Recipe   218

Goat for a God: Roasted Goat Leg with Grape Molasses   220

Demeter's Vegetarian Feast: Lentil and Olive Salad with
    Cabbage and Carrot Slaw   222

Boar for Bacchus: Boar Tacos with Spicy Berry Salsa   224

Brigid Bread: Bread Pudding and Whiskey Sauce   228

Equinox Eggs: Fresh Vegetable Frittata   230

Summer Passion: A Flummery of Fresh Fruit   232

A Slow Solstice Supper: Slow-Braised Pork with Fruit and
    Onion-Bacon Jam   234

High Summer's Bread: Garlic and Herb Focaccia   237

A Bowl Full of Autumn: Butternut Squash and Ginger Soup   239

Samhain Pot Roast for One   241

A Winter's Feast: Shepherd's Pie to Live For   244

Breakfast in Bed: New York Strip, Arugula, and a Poached Egg   248

Aphrodite on the Half Shell: Oysters with Fennel   250

Hot and Sweet: Chocolate Pots   252

The Platter of Seduction: A New Way to Look at Finger Foods   254

Rituals, Spells
& Things to Try

A Ritual for Inanna   23

A Devotional for Athena   35

A Feast for Dionysus   38

Inviting the Lares and Penates to Your Home   47

A Feast for the Gods   56

The Best Meal You Ever Had   67

Reverse Menu   68

An Enchanted Cup of Tea   70

The Magick of Dining Out   71

The Buffer Zone   77

Taking Stock of Your Kitchen   80

Shopping with Your Senses   91

A Feast for the Senses   93

A Perfect Date for One   96

Calm Home Spell   107

Love Spell   107

Get Outta Here Spell   107

Vitality Spell   108

Healing Spell   108

House Protection Spell   108

No Trespassers Spell   108

Prosperity Spell   109

Prosperity Spell II   109

Avoiding Exhaustion Spell   110

Another Love Spell   110

A Ritual with the Elements   127

A Ritual with Grief   132

An Eating Ritual   149

Invoking Air   151

Invoking Fire   152

Invoking Water   152

Invoking Earth   152

Invoking Center   153

The Magick I Bring   160

Serving the Spirits of Place   182

A Classic Love Potion   183

Calming Tea   184

Magickal Pancakes   185

Disclaimer

I believe a big component to cookery and witchery is practicing common sense and common care. With that, I offer this advice: If there's an ingredient in a recipe that you are allergic to, please don't use it. Just because this is a magickal book with magickal recipes and exercises, doesn't mean your food allergies will disappear when you cast a circle. Likewise, if you've been instructed by a medical professional to avoid, cut out, or otherwise abstain from eating or drinking certain ingredients, please, please, please follow their advice.

I strongly recommend adhering to food safety guidelines, understanding that consuming undercooked and raw foods can pose severe health risks. Here's a chart with recommended cooking temperatures.

Most chefs will tell you that the best temperature for steak and lamb is rare to medium-rare. A rare steak should have an internal temperature of 120–125 degrees Fahrenheit. Medium-rare steaks should be cooked to 130–135 Fahrenheit. However, according to foodsafety.gov, beef, lamb, and pork should be cooked to at least 145 (or above if desired). Keep in mind that the lower temperatures in the chart for rare and medium-rare meat are not recommended by the USDA.

The following chart includes temperatures for meat, poultry, seafood, eggs, casseroles, and leftovers.

Meat	Temperatures
Steak/Beef	
Rare	120 F–125 F (48.9 C to 51.6 C)
Medium-rare	130 F–135 F (54.4 C to 57.2 C)
Medium	140 F–145 F (60 C to 62.8 C)
Medium-well	150 F–155 F (65.5 C to 68.3 C)
Well done	160 F (71.1 C) and above
Lamb	
Rare	135 F (57.2 C)
Medium-rare	140 F–150 F (60 C to 65.5 C)
Medium	160 (71.1 C)
Well done	165 (73.9 C) and above
Other	
Chicken	165 F–175 F (73.9 C to 80 C)
Turkey	165° F–175 F (73.9 C to 80 C)
Pork	145 F (62.8 C)
Ham, Fully Cooked (to reheat)*	140 F (60 C)
Ground Poultry	165 F (73.9 C)
Ground Meat	160 F (71.1 C)
Fish and Shellfish	145 F (62.8 C)
Eggs and Egg Dishes	160 F (71.1 C)
Casseroles	160 F (71.1 C)
Stuffing, Dressing	165 F (73.9 C)
Reheated Leftovers	165 F (73.9 C)
Holding Temperature for Cooked Food	140 F (60 C)

Acknowledgments

My name appears on the front of this book. I'm the author. That means I wrote the book. But no book is ever really written by a single person. There are so many people that made this possible. First, I'd like to thank the person or persons I've forgotten. I'm going to list a lot of other people in a minute, but invariably there will be someone I leave out. This is for you. Whatever you did, however you supported this project, I couldn't have done it without exactly what you contributed. Thank you.

Everyone at Llewellyn has been amazing. Thank you to my editors who gave me excellent notes and prompted me to explain myself more clearly and made this a much better book than I could ever write by myself. Elysia Gallo, I owe you a shot of palinka and so much more.

To Stephen, Megan, Tegan, Elizabeth, Jill, and Carin, thank you for your contributions and for sharing your passion for food and your stories with me. Many thanks to Gwydion, Helen/Hawk, Sayre, Dorian, and Nora for constantly inspiring me to try new recipes and share food generously. A special note of thanks to the entire butcher's department at Oliver's Market, in Cotati. They tracked down goat purveyors and duck suppliers, and put up with all sorts of other odd meat requests. It's rare to see bankers thanked in a book about food and magick, but the folks at the Cotati branch of Exchange Bank have suffered through the creation of this book every step of the way. They even suggested a recipe, which I went home and cooked, then included.

To the estate of Diane Wolkstein for allowing me to excerpt portions of Ms. Wolkstein's work. Likewise, Carin McKay for letting me republish the recipe for Wilo Soup. Carin, you are my hero and your impact is great.

I send oodles of deep gratitude to Anne Newkirk Niven and Jason Mankey, who believed in my writing and encouraged me to keep at it. Special thanks to the members of a secret writing support group; you know who you are. Without the PPI and your encouragement and snark, this book might well never have happened.

As ever, I thank my teachers and my teachers' teachers. I owe you all a debt I can never repay. To Roy Hudd, who once said, "Watch that boy, he's going to be something special." It took me a while to remember. There's a group of about one hundred witches, attendees at a workshop at Pantheacon 2018, that joined me in a spell and chanted, "Gwion, write that book." Promise kept. Magick works.

And to my partner in all things, she who reminds me to write and eat and enjoy the moment. My dearest Phoenix, thank you for simply everything.

Foreword

I love food. I think that statement must be made at the beginning of this short discourse and praise for the book that you now hold in your hands. Restraint is one quality that cannot ever be associated with my love of food, and whilst greed may be seen as an errant fault, I find in certain circumstances that it can also be a fine and just motivator. The love of food has taken me to local and far-flung locations in search of the delicious. The topographical nature of our planet—at least in my mind—is not defined by contours of terrain, but by the gargantuan diversity of food. Food provides a map that sings of connection to locales and the people and creatures that inhabit them. I am quite able to recall towns, cities, parties, events, and countries by the food that I have eaten there. When I am happy, I eat; when I celebrate, I eat; I eat when I am sad; I eat to express emotions and also to suppress them. I imagine that those statements are not alien to those who have found their way to this book.

Food and drink do not simply sustain and nourish the body; they have long been associated as sustainers of the spirit, family, and community. As a Druid, food plays an important function in the expression of my spirituality. The Celts are renowned for holding hospitality as a vital attribute, made the more wondrous and fulfilling by special foods and beverages taking center stage in any hospitable act. The cauldron plays an important role in the symbology of Druidry and within the greater Pagan movement, a symbol that embodies hospitality, mystery, sustenance, and nourishment. It is no accident that a cooking vessel finds itself amidst the mysteries, for surely they all serve to feed.

To invite another into one's home or sacred space and to then offer them the fruits of your edible labours is to give something of yourself, your community, and your foundation of hearth and home. It is perhaps the feast that usually follows a sacred observation that instils and reaffirms the communal aspect of my Pagan practice, which delight-fully is a common trait in any denomination or tradition of spirituality. I anticipate that feast—I long for it.

The food we eat connects us to a multiverse of relationships; they tell the story of growth, of the quality of soil and water. Food acts as a bridge between us and the very land that we walk upon. Growing our own food, even if only some potatoes in a bucket on an apartment windowsill, expresses an action that, as humans, we have participated in for countless millennia. This magick of connection articulates a mystery that binds us to all the people who have gone before us, for nothing on our planet vanishes completely, but merely changes its form. Its energetic component remains. All the food that our ancestors ate, all the fine beverages that they inspirited with their celebrations, all their rituals and their emotions are still here and held by the organism of our biosphere. We take in, we give back, we live, we feast, we die, and the circle begins again. All our food arises from the amalgamated wisdom of all things that have found their way to the birth-ing ground of soil.

If I was able to articulate one human emotion associated with the act of eating and drinking, it would undoubtedly be joy. It is this quality that fills the pages that follow; Gwion has succeeded in imbuing the words of this book with the joy he gleans from food and drink. He has succeeded in combining not only a sense of the celebratory, but also deep thought and a joyous articulation of the history and complex magickal traditions surrounding food. This is not just a book of recipes, albeit they are plentiful, but there is also a lot to surprise you in this book, and a magickal view that may well transform your relationship to food.

Whilst Gwion and I share a common heritage and foundation in Great Britain, per-haps what we mostly have in common is our love of food. Regardless of cultural dif-ferences, tradition, or worldview, the delightful act of feasting will always bring people together.

And with that, feast and rejoice in the words that dance from the following pages.

Kristoffer Hughes
Head of the Anglesey Druid Order, author of *From the Cauldron Born*, *The Celtic Tarot*, and *The Book of Celtic Magick*

Introduction

Ever since I can remember, I've been completely fascinated by food. I grew up in Southeast London, which exposed me to an eclectic mix of cultures and cuisines. The food my mum and grandmothers cooked was solid, hearty, standard English fare. There was a veritable parade of steak and kidney pies, full English breakfasts, mince tarts, and trifles piled high with cream and strawberries. However, the meals I ate with my friends were completely different, because their families emigrated from Cyprus, Pakistan, Jamaica, India, Turkey, and even Scotland. I learned that while many meals require knives, forks, and tables, other dishes were meant to be scooped up between fingers and thumbs, plucked from skewers, or eaten from shared platters served on the floor.

As I began to travel through Europe and the United States, my love of food continued to blossom. Each new place I would visit had distinct flavours and wonderful foods accompanied by stories that conjured tantalizing combinations of ingredients. Every food story transported me to faraway places, oddly enough all called "home."

And years later when I began cooking, I realised the meals I served up were full of stories too. My food tells the story of my ancestors, the counties and countryside they traveled through, and the ones they eventually settled in. I cook dishes that recount my journey with magick and the practices I've learned along the way. Every chapter and recipe in this book has stories baked into it. That's how I view cooking: stories on a plate that we all get to taste and share.

I learned to cook because I had to eat when there was no one else to cook for me. Then I became a parent, and later a single parent, and all the household food preparation fell squarely on my shoulders. I've worked in restaurants and bars, pulling pints and firing food on the line. For a brief period, cooking was my primary source of income, and I still miss the adrenaline of being in the middle of a busy service when everything is going just right.

When I realised that cooking could be an act of devotion and service and not just a means to an end, everything changed. That's when I started to call myself a kitchen witch. Although I make magick in lots of different ways, my primary practice, my "go to" method, nearly always involves food. I might have a cup of tea with a friend to discuss what's ailing them. I've been known to spread out a blanket and work magick with a cucumber sandwich while listening to folks tell me their heart's desire. I've walked through a supermarket with people, trying to recapture a part of their soul they misplaced, only to find it hidden in a file box filled with family recipes.

Practicing food magick, consciously preparing meals, has shaped who I am as a witch, while at the same time providing nourishment for myself and others. Kitchen witchery, magickal cooking, Pagan pantryfying (okay, I made that last one up) is simultaneously delicious, fun, ridiculously practical, and profoundly satisfying. And let's speak plainly here for a moment. We all must eat. We might as well make it a magickal act, right?

It's an obvious statement to make, but we all eat food. It doesn't matter which decade we were born into or what geographic space we currently inhabit. If you are reading this right now it means that you've eaten enough food in your lifetime to survive to this moment. Every human being living today eats food to survive. And in that one way, with that one singular need, we are truly all the same. At some point, every one of us has chewed, slurped, and swallowed food.

Religion may inform us how to prepare the meals we eat or which foods we should avoid eating altogether. Familial enculturation exposes us to different combinations of ingredients, flavours, and preparation techniques. Political rhetoric and policy have an ever-increasing impact on just who has access to food and what even gets classified as food. Social status determines much about the quality and frequency of which foods are available to us. Being an omnivore, carnivore, vegan, freegan, or vegetarian defines the types of food we choose to ingest. And of course, millions of years of evolution and the genes that have been passed down to us through the ages impact what we're allergic to, which foods make our lips tingle, which ones cause us to retain too much water or get really bad heartburn.

There's an inherent question in the title of this book: Why do we participate in rituals, make offerings, and eat together? The answer is astonishingly simple. We gather in rituals, make offerings, and eat together because we're not dead. Over the next few hundred pages you'll discover all sorts of rituals and exercises you can incorporate into your magickal practice. You might find new ways to make offerings, and you'll certainly find recipes you've never considered. The food witchery practices are designed to bring you closer to the foods you eat, the kitchen magick you create, and the people you share your food and life with. But, and this is a big but, you can only do all of this because you are alive.

Regardless of whether we grow and cook our own food, buy prepackaged, prepared meals from the local grocery store, order ingredients online, eat at the world's very best restaurants, frequent fast food joints, or cook for other people by choice or vocation, every one of us eats. Food sustains our lives. We simply cannot survive without it. On one level, food is basically minerals and vitamins and nutrients. Viewed another way, food is the literal stuff of life. The animal flesh you might choose to consume was once alive, so too the radishes and oranges and leeks. We are alive because we eat Life. That is some powerful magick to contemplate.

But there's something else we all have in common when it comes to food, and that's the act of sharing food together. There's a good chance that at some point in your life, a parent, a caretaker, a nurse, a friend, a lover, or a neighbour has shared a meal with you. And in that sharing, certain agreements have been made; we repeat these in all sorts of social situations. We've learned to ritualize food. If you've blown out the candles on a birthday cake and made a wish, you've ritualized food. If you've brought someone breakfast in bed or been lucky enough to have someone else bring you breakfast, you've taken part in a food ritual. Practically every personal rite of passage, public celebration, national holiday, or communal tragedy throughout history, right up to the present day, is commemorated with food.

From a specifically Pagan perspective, there's a rich history of combining food, magick, offerings, and ritual. We only need to read a few lines of most myths and magickal tales to find cauldrons that are ever full, pomegranate seeds that bind us to the Underworld, and apples that confer immortality. There are goddesses and gods whose sole job is to ensure a successful feast or plentiful harvest. And fortunately, many polytheistic and Pagan societies from the past have bequeathed us rituals and recipes and directions, albeit not always complete directions, for how to appease the gods with food offerings.

We don't have to look to the oh-so-distant past to find food magick and rituals though. Modern Paganism has invented, borrowed, reimagined, and created brand-new food magick and rituals. Think about pub moots, living room blots, cakes and ale, feasts for the ancestors, black-eyed peas to ring in the New Year, and even the dreaded potluck after a public ritual.

Food plays a central role in most modern Pagan practice. And why shouldn't it? Food is amazing. Sharing food with other magickal people is incredible. And when you think about it, sharing food with someone is another way of saying that you care about them. The underlying message is that their existence means something important to you. Remember, we celebrate life with food and ritual because we're not dead.

Food and ritual go together like ginger and lemonade because food and life go together. Pick a culture, pick a time in history, and you'll find rituals with food and food for rituals, and rituals about food, and rituals about the chapters of our lives and the foods that go with each phase. Food and life and ritual are practically inseparable. There is a magickal component at work here too, and that's the power of transformation. When we create food together, for almost any occasion, we transform the very mundane and human act of fueling our bodies with plant matter, proteins, minerals, and essential vitamins into something sacred.

For the last five hundred years or so, we have looked to the twin disciplines of alchemy and science to break food down into its component parts so that we can better understand nutrition and flavour. This has worked to varying degrees. In the mid-twentieth century, we made mass food production, with additives and preservatives and ready-to-eat meals, the norm for many folks in the world. There is something truly amazing and advantageous about having food on demand. This is a luxury our recent and distant ancestors never had. However, there's a growing body of evidence that shows mass producing food robs those same foods of their inherent nutritional value and, more importantly, robs us of a real, visceral connection to the food we consume.

Cooking methods and recipes that tell the stories of places or families or cultures are disappearing in favour of quick meals bought online. That's the *reductive* part of science at work there. On the other end of the spectrum we have molecular gastronomy, which is part science, part magick, and part tribute to the essence of the ingredients used.

Preparing and eating food in a way that enhances the experience belongs squarely in the magickal purview. Food connects us to our memories, and memories transport us through space and time and culture. Food embodies, or rather allows *us* to embody, the old magickal axiom of changing consciousness at will. But when it comes down to it, when it really gets down to the core level of what we're doing when we cook and share food, it's beautifully simple. We are reaffirming that we, and the people we are eating with, are alive right now.

How to Use This Book

You can imagine that this book is like a sumptuous feast made up of several courses. It's one big meal, but each course stands complete by itself and contributes to the overall experience of the whole meal.

The first course, "A Brief and Incomplete History of Food and Ritual," delves into history and how ancient cultures blended ritual, magick, food, and their gods into their everyday lives. Much of what we know about food, rituals, and offerings comes to us from clay tablets and manuscripts written thousands of years ago.

Think of this first course as a good sampler plate. There's enough information to whet your appetite about magickal food practices from long ago and maybe introduce you to a flavour or two of history that you've never tasted before. There are bonus courses in each history chapter, featuring rituals, recipes, and exercises you can do yourself.

The second course, "Food, Magick, and Rituals for Today," covers modern-day magickal food practices that you can put to good use for yourself, a coven, or your community. There are reflections, exercises, and recipes all designed to enhance your magickal food practices. Nestled in this section is "Wisdom From The Community Pantry," a collection of anecdotes and reflections about food, magick, and cookery written by chefs, cooks, food witches, and kitchen witches from around the world. Their stories contain the potent magick of understanding what it is to cook, share food, and be in the moment.

"All the Recipes" makes up the third course and is chock-full of tips and tricks to prepare you and your kitchen for all sorts of magick. It's a little like a checklist of tools you'll need to earn your first degree in kitchen witchery.

Lastly, there are the recipes. I've included forty-two of my all-time favourite recipes for you to cook, eat, and share. Hopefully you'll try them all and get inspired to borrow them, change them, adapt them, and let them inspire your own kitchen magick.

Secretly, I have a wish to show up in someone's kitchen and see a well-thumbed-through copy of this book, with dog-eared pages and notes scribbled in the margins, and hear stories of how they created a ritual feast or devotional practice featuring these recipes and many more of their own wonderful additions too.

Section I

A Brief and Incomplete
History of Food and Ritual

Michael Pollan posits in *Cooked: A Natural History of Transformation* that "We are the species who cooks. No other species cooks. And when we learned to cook, we became truly human."[1] If it's true that our ancient ancestors became human as soon as they figured out how to cook, I bet it only took ten more minutes on the timeline of human development to craft the first food rituals. We've been creating them ever since. No one knows for sure just when the first food rituals were observed by our ancient ancestors. My imagination tells me that right after that very first meal was prepared there was a ritual to celebrate a good nosh-up. If my great-great-great (many times great) foremothers and forefathers were anything like my family today, there was the presentation of the meal, a heated discussion about who got to eat the juiciest piece of prehistoric chicken, and then a nice long nap on a full belly.

Early humankind did leave us messages about their time on this planet, indicating just what was important to them. They recorded aspects of their lives by painting murals of animals on cave walls. They traced their hands and then carved images of their hands into walls and created enticing spiral pictographs. They even left food scraps and evidence of their eating habits and food rituals. There's a cave in South Africa called the Wonderwerk Cave.[2] It offers tantalizing evidence that human beings knew how to build controlled fires almost two million years ago. We might deduce that these controlled fires were lit for numerous reasons. Fires provided heat. Fires lit in caves probably made for a cozy respite from the elements. No doubt light from the fires added a measure of protection from predators and, who knows, maybe also encouraged extremely prehistoric versions of campfire chats. One has to wonder if meals were cooked on those fires too.

If food was cooked, it indicates that humankind has been gathering to eat together for basically as long as we can possibly trace. Sites, primarily caves, in disparate places like Kenya and modern-day Israel show signs of controlled fires, rudimentary hearths, tools, and even "cooked" bone fragments dating back nearly eight hundred thousand years.

The people of the Mirrar Clan in northwestern Australia have teamed up with archaeologists from Queensland University to preserve sites that show human activity in the

---

1. Michael Pollan. *Cooked: A Natural History of Transformation.* London: Penguin, 2014.

2. NA "An Ancient Underground Abode: The Wonderwerk Cave, Northern Cape." South Africa Inspiring New Ways. https://legacy.southafrica.net/za/en/articles/entry/article-southafrica.net-the-wonderwerk-cave?gclid=CjwKCAiAk4XUBRB5EiwAHBLUMc0cdurkHdqdq0z3fNkh-p0wv19U1Iyzochtj8Ldz8yIe7Y_rOni2hoCLJkQAvD_BwE.

region dated to forty-five thousand years ago.[3] Among the artefacts found there were cooking utensils. These included grinding stones and small hatchets with food residue identified as berries, yams, and nuts. Cave drawings in Leang Lompoa, Indonesia, painted nearly forty thousand years ago, depict large animals and handprints etched into the rock. Importantly, there's evidence of hearths where food was prepared, and the remains of shellfish the inhabitants consumed there. Arguably the most famous cave paintings, those in Lascaux, France, are believed to show hunting scenes in both ritualized and spiritual ways. The hunt itself is a ritual all about food, and one still practiced today throughout the world. The culmination of the hunt, the kill, is also steeped in tradition and ritual, and although we can't know exactly how ancient human beings marked a successful hunt, we can imagine that they certainly did.

Ancient food rituals can only be guessed at. Hunters returning from an exceptional foray may have been greeted with cheers and smiles. Stories of dangerous and exhilarating hunts might have been shared around a communal fire as the bounty of conquest was passed from person to person. I'd like to think that there was a measure of appreciation given to the food makers and an acknowledgment of the skill involved in preparing aurochs au jus with a nice crisp salad of delicious watercress collected from a nearby stream.

Okay, that last point might be a bit of a stretch, but you can see what I'm driving at; as long as humans have been gathering, we've been eating together. It's one of the main reasons we stayed in small clusters and it's a big part of how we survived. Whatever the communication methods of our very distant cousins, communicate they did. And if they communicated about food and set up any sort of repetitious actions about who ate first, or which members of the group cleaned the food and who participated in the hunt, or then argued over who had to fill the mastodon skull with soapy water and go do the dishes, then they were engaging in some form of food ritual.

---

3. Gundjeihmi Aboriginal Corporation. "Kakadu Site of Australia's Oldest Home." http://www.mirarr.net/stories/kakadu-site-of-australia-s-oldest-home.

Chapter 1
Sumer

Now let's take a huge leap forward on the human timeline from the paleolithic age to the relative near past of about nine thousand years ago. The people archaeologically known as the Ubaidians began to settle the area known today as Iraq. The Ubaidians built small villages. In fact, it's generally acknowledged that they were first village builders in the region. The land they settled was unforgiving. There were few trees, the climate was hot and arid, and the soil was frequently lacking nutrients and not at all good for planting crops. The sun and the wind mocked the temerity of the settlers by alternately baking the land with relentless 100° F days throughout the summer months and then eroding what little topsoil was left by blowing everything away in annual wind storms.

However, this same uncompromising land did have two particularly good features, namely the Tigris and Euphrates rivers, and these two rivers flooded. In fact, they flooded a lot, especially in winter and spring. The floodwaters brought much-needed nutrients to the soil and formed temporary marshlands that teemed with seasonal fish and fowl. The ancient Ubaidians learned that when the often unpredictable and destructive flood waters receded, they could actually grow things. Better yet, they could eat those things or feed those things to their goats, and then eat well-fed and delicious goats.

For a couple thousand years, the Ubaidians flourished. They became accomplished farmers, raising enough food to feed themselves and their livestock, and they developed agricultural technologies that would ultimately come to shape and impact human civilization to this very day. Along with agriculture and village building, the Ubaidians set trade routes. The Ubaidians traded pottery, food, livestock, textiles, and ideas.

It's speculated that in roughly 3300 BCE, settlers from beyond the nearby mountain areas began to arrive on the Ubaidian landscape, perhaps following trade routes back to the source. Over many subsequent generations, these newcomers merged with the Ubaidians and their culture changed, eventually becoming the Sumerian, and later Akkadian, cultures. The new population built on the technologies of the past and created walled cities, with even better irrigation and food growing techniques. Importantly, they also developed food storage. Being able to store food gave a certain measure of security and sustainability for the inhabitants and is often cited as a cornerstone for the development and expansion of human civilization.

Civilization Started as a Drinking Game

It's true. If it wasn't for a young queen, an overconfident uncle, and an all-night competition to see which one of them could drink more beer, we might not be the world we are today. But before we get to that, let's talk about writing in Sumer. I promise we'll get to the drinking game.

One of the many innovations that came from the Sumerians is writing. The history of *cuneiform* (a word meaning wedge-shaped) is fascinating. The very short version is that the Sumerians wanted to count things like sheep and grain and other commerce items. Clay tokens were used to symbolize particular products. Each token was marked with a pictograph representing goats or ducks or sacks of grain. Clay tokens, each with the symbol for "goat" etched on them, gave an accounting of how many goats someone had bought or sold. Initially, these clay tokens were put into containers and sealed. The problem was, if the number of tokens in the container was forgotten or disputed, the seals had to be broken and the process had to start all over again.

Some upstart came up with the idea of simply marking the outside of the containers with symbols and did away with the whole token idea. The next innovation involved flattening out the containers into tablets and "writing" the symbols vertically. The process kept being refined until cuneiform "letters" were written in rows from left to right. Here's why this is important. As the development of writing continued, the Sumerians began documenting other events too, like names and poems and religious rites. They even recorded recipes (more on that exciting development later).

Cuneiform tablets surprisingly survived for a very long time, but were largely inde-cipherable until the mid-nineteenth century. The mysteries of cuneiform were finally unlocked and translated into modern language due to the discovery of the Behistun inscriptions. The inscriptions were carved onto a cliff in the side of Mount Behistun, in Kermanshah, western Iran. The carvings are massive, extending more than one hundred yards in length and fifteen yards in height. They chronicle the life and times of King Darius and, most importantly, are written in three separate, newer cuneiform languages. These inscriptions, in Old Persian, Elamite, and Babylonian, cross-referenced between each language, became the base rubric for translating the oldest forms of cuneiform.[4] For the first time in several thousand years, archaeologists and linguists could quite literally read accounts of the daily life and times of a people long gone.

Apart from commerce and trade, the Sumerians wrote extensively about their reli-gious beliefs. The names of the first goddesses and gods, and a whole cosmology explain-ing how the world, Underworld, and heavens were formed, was painstakingly and lov-ingly put down onto clay tablets. Food, drink, hospitality, and the stories of the gods show up quite a bit in these early texts. It seems that food and drink were as big a deal to the Sumerians as they are to us today. The scribes of the time certainly wrote a lot about food and beer and what to do with it all. And it's these stories and poems for the god-desses and gods that tell us civilization started as an epic drinking game gone bad.

In the stories, Enki, the god of wisdom, learns that the young queen, Inanna, is about to show up on his doorstep. He gives directions to his staff to prepare the household for Inanna's visit:

> *When Inanna enters the holy shrine,*
> *Give her butter cake to eat.*
> *Pour cold water to refresh her heart.*
> *Offer her beer before the statue of the lion.*
> *Treat her like an equal.*
> *Greet Inanna at the holy table, the tabe of heaven.*[5]

---

4. NA. "Behistun Inscription." *New World Encyclopedia.* http://www.newworldencyclopedia.org/entry/Be-histun_Inscription.

5. Diana Wolkstein and Samuel Noah Kramer. *Inanna Queen of Heaven and Earth.* New York: Harper & Row, 1983.

Well that's a nice way to welcome a visitor into your home, isn't it? A little butter cake, some beer, cooling water to shake off the heat of the day, and treatment as an equal. Clearly, hospitality was important to the Sumerian gods.

Enki and Inanna, however, don't stop at butter cakes and a quick, refreshing pint of fine Sumerian IPA. They start drinking, really quaffing it back in fact. And as we'll learn later, Sumerian beer rivalled many modern beers, with an estimated alcohol content of around 3.5 percent.

> *Enki and Inanna drank beer together.*
> *They drank more beer together.*
> *They drank more and more beer together.*
> *With their bronze vessels filled to overflowing,*
> *With the vessels of Urash, Mother of the Earth,*
> *They toasted each other: they challenged each other.* [6]

In my experience, drinking beer, drinking more beer, then drinking more and more beer is going to end badly for someone. And I somehow suspect that someone might be Uncle Enki.

> *Enki, swaying with drink, toasted Inanna:*
> *In the name of my Power! In the name of my holy shrine!*
> *To my daughter Inanna I shall give*
> *The High Priesthood! Godship!*
> *The noble, enduring crown! The throne of kingship!*

See, I told you it was going to end in tears for Enki. Inanna, perhaps slightly less drunk than her favourite uncle Enki, responds, "I take them."

When you think about it, it's an astute thing to say. When drunk uncles, especially drunk uncles who are gods, start handing out power and the foundational tools for building civilizations, it seems like a good idea to take what's on offer.

Enki and Inanna keep drinking, and as they do, Enki continues to give Inanna many wonderful gifts, known as the *Me* (pronounced like the month of May). The Me include

---

6. Diana Wolkstein and Samuel Noah Kramer. *Inanna Queen of Heaven and Earth.* New York: Harper & Row, 1983.

truth, the art of lovemaking, the giving of judgements, and the making of decisions. Also, shepherding, libation priests, the holy tavern, procreation, kindling the fires, the art of feeding pens, leather making, scribing, purification rites, and the heaping up of hot coals. In fact, Enki and Inanna raise their cups fourteen times and, on each occasion, good ol' uncle Enki gives Inanna more and more Me. Each time, she simply replies "I take them," until Inanna is left with all of the Me. Reading a full list of the Me, one can see that they represent all the facets of civilization and show how to organize city-states and the activities that go on in them, including how best to properly worship the goddesses and gods of each city by offering them lots of food and drink.

Enki eventually passes out. Inanna loads her barge full of Me and departs rather quickly. Enki wakes up the next morning a little worse for wear, blearily looks about the palace, and discovers that everything is gone. His staff recounts how he generously gifted Inanna anything that wasn't nailed to the temple floor. Enki dispatches monsters to capture Inanna and bring back the Me, but to no avail. Inanna has made it home to the City of Uruk and has shared the Me with the people, for which they adore her.

Inanna suggests a giant festival be thrown in her honour and, even after a marathon drinking session with her uncle, decides that there should be plenty of food and beer on the menu.

Let all of Uruk be festive.
Let the king slaughter oxen and sheep.
Let him pour beer out of the cup.
Let all the lands proclaim my noble name.
Let my people sing my praises. [7]

And for several thousand years afterward, they did.

We Know the Gods Liked to Eat, but What about the People?

The really good news here is that the Sumerians kept great records. Their cuneiform tablets recorded commercial transactions, like how much barley and grain was bought and sold, but they also recorded recipes. It's believed that most of the recipes recorded came

---

7. Diana Wolkstein and Samuel Noah Kramer. *Inanna Queen of Heaven and Earth*. New York: Harper & Row, 1983.

from dinner parties thrown at the homes of the wealthy elite and from temple records showing offerings given to the gods.

We see recipes that included meats such as lamb, mutton, and gazelle. Temple cakes dripping with date syrup and elaborate sweet and savoury breads were detailed extensively. These foods were considered luxury items and would have been too expensive for the average citizen. The general population wouldn't have as much access to such delicacies on a regular basis, but would have substituted ducks, pigeons, and fish that were plentiful in the seasonal marshlands.[8]

Sumerian records show that the most common food ingredients included grains like barley, semolina, and wheat, which could be made into simple breads, beer, and porridge (like mashes that could be served both sweet or savoury). Vegetables were plenty—there were peas, beans, lentils, leeks, onions, and garlic. It's also believed there were cucumbers and varieties of lettuces available, although linguistically the words used to describe these vegetables don't translate exactly. Fruits played a big role in the Sumerian diet. Chief among them were dates, a beloved favourite of the goddess Inanna. Apples, melons, figs, and grapes are mentioned too.

The Sumerians had a well-stocked spice rack that would make any cook happy. Salt was used as both a flavouring agent and as a preservative. Coriander, cumin, thyme, turmeric, saffron, carob, and cardamom were readily available. From what we can deduce, several cooking methods were commonplace. Meats, breads, and vegetables were roasted on spits or cooked in hot ashes. Although interestingly enough, most meats were only browned or seared over open flames and then added to boiling broths to finish tenderizing and cooking. Examples of cooking procedures recorded on clay tablets show that boiling and braising were the most employed methods. Foods that were fully roasted, or grilled, as we might frame it today, were given as offerings to the gods. Roasted meat does smell delicious, and it was believed that the aromas wafting about tempted the goddesses and gods to stay close by.

Breads and barley-based cakes were cooked in small domed ovens. *Ki.ne*, which translates in Sumerian to "place of fire" or hearth, could be applied to a temporary fire pit, much like today's campfire. Foods were cooked on skewers, and pots were set to boil. Ki.ne also referred to small household ovens. Later in the Akkadian period, the

---

8. Jean Bottero and Teresa Lavender Fagan. *The Oldest Cuisine in the World: Cooking in Mesopotamia.* Chicago: University of Chicago Press, 2004.

word *Ki.ne* evolved into *kinunu*, which meant "oven."⁹ A kinunu was made of clay bricks and had an opening at the bottom where wood and compressed briquettes were added. Above the heat source was the cooking area. Breads were placed on wooden planks or clay plates. Most households had such an oven.

As Sumerian culture flourished, communal ovens and what we might consider local bakeries developed. In Iran, the piping hot *tanur* oven is still used to this very day, much the same way it was used in ancient Sumer. If you've ever seen a brick-fired oven at a pizza restaurant, you'll get the idea of how such ovens worked. Vegetables and smaller proteins, like locusts and crayfish, would also be cooked in the household kinunu.

When you stop to think about it, not much has changed in the several thousand years since the times of the ancient Sumerians. They grilled, boiled, roasted, and braised their foods. We may have fancy gadgets, six-burner gas stoves, microwave ovens, stainless steel smokers, and centuries of culinary techniques at our disposal, but the basic methods remain pretty much unchanged: foodstuffs plus water plus heat plus spice equals a delicious meal. Even with basic cooking utensils and preparation techniques, I can imagine amazing, delicious, and nutritious meals being prepared with these ample Sumerian ingredients.

Let's Talk about Beer and Ninkasi

Now, I'm one of those people that believes there are six major food groups—*meat, dairy, bread, fruits and vegetables, chocolate, and beer.* Chocolate wouldn't be available for many, many centuries, so in the case of the ancient Sumerians we must leave that one out. But oh my, did they know about beer. Barley beer, made from a mash of barley, honey, and fermenting dates, was so popular that it was currency. People were paid in beer![10] Let that sink in for a minute or two. I could get used to the idea of compensation packages being a combination of wages, paid vacation time, and a beer allowance, but I digress.

This delicious Sumerian barley concoction wouldn't have resembled the beer that you can find at your local brew pub today. There were no hops used, and the finished product certainly wasn't a golden amber or unfiltered pilsner. Sumerian beer was something more like alcoholic oatmeal, complete with chunks of fruit and barley mash. Drinking a

---

9. Jean Bottero and Teresa Lavender Fagan. *The Oldest Cuisine in the World: Cooking in Mesopotamia.* Chicago: University of Chicago Press, 2004.

10. Peter Dockrill. "This 5,000-year-old artefact shows ancient workers were paid in beer." *Science Alert.* https://www.sciencealert.com/this-5-000-year-old-clay-tablet-shows-ancient-mesopotamians-were-paid-for-work-in-beer.

vessel full of Sumerian beer would have been tantamount to eating half a loaf of bread. But you know, there's something particularly enticing about half a loaf of alcoholic bread. There is one famous cuneiform tablet that shows two people drinking out of one large cup, using straws. The beer was so thick, clay tubes were used to suck up the liquid and filter out some of the solids. Who knew that the invention of beer was also responsible for the creation of drinking straws?

As you might imagine, with beer being such an important part of early Sumerian culture, there was a goddess connected to the brewing of beer. Her name was Ninkasi. What I find particularly lovely is that the deity who oversaw beer and alcohol production in general was a goddess, not a god. When I think about most brew pubs, brew masters, and advertisements that show beer drinking today, it's a particularly male-centric affair. This wasn't the case in ancient Sumer. Women oversaw brewing beer and other alcoholic beverages. So sacred and exalted was beer making that a poem called *Hymn to Ninkasi* was inscribed in cuneiform. The hymn is not only a praise poem to the goddess but a clever mnemonic device, detailing the recipe and techniques for brewing beer.[11]

This brewing song or poem was translated by Miguel Civil, professor of Sumerology at the University of Chicago, in 1964. Beer enthusiast and founder of the Anchor Brewing Company, Fritz Maytag, recreated the beer, appropriately named Ninkasi beer. In 1991, at the American Association of microbrewers, Professor Civil noted, "The brewers were able to taste 'Ninkasi Beer,' sipping it from large jugs with drinking straws as they did four millennia ago. The beer had an alcohol concentration of 3.5%, very similar to modern beers, and had a 'dry taste lacking in bitterness, similar to hard apple cider.' In Mesopotamia, hops were unknown and beer was produced for immediate consumption, so the 'Sumerian' beer didn't keep very well, but everyone connected with the reconstruction of the process seems to have enjoyed the experience."[12]

If you have a mind to recreate Ninkasi Beer for yourself, you may want to spend some time in devotion to this very popular Sumerian goddess.

A Dinner Party Four Thousand Years in the Making

The Sumerian world began roughly nine thousand years ago. The culture continually changed and adapted. Language and technology evolved as new people moved in, assimilated, or took

11. Joshua J. Mark. "The Hymn to Ninkasi, Goddess of Beer." Ancient History Encyclopedia. https://www.ancient.eu/article/222/the-hymn-to-ninkasi-goddess-of-beer/.

12. Miguel Civil. "Modern Brewers Recreate Ancient Beer." The Oriental Institute no. 132, Autumn 1991.

over by conquest. But one thing always stayed very much the same—the love of a good dinner party. It's important to note that the Sumerians drew a worthy distinction, much like we do today, between "eating" and "dining." Every creature eats. Only humans and the gods dine. There's a profound difference between fueling our bodies to stave off death and the sheer human joy of eating and sharing a meal with others. Now, we know precious little about the day-to-day celebrations and dinner parties the ordinary Sumerian people partook in. But we do know a fair bit about the food practices of the temples and the wealthy folk.

Jean Bottero, a renowned Assyriologist, provides, in *The Oldest Cuisine in the World: Cooking in Mesopotamia,* impressive lists of ingredients for a magnificent ten-day feast thrown by King Ashurnasirpal II to mark the occasion of renovating his capital city. Among the opulent ingredients, we see one thousand barley-fed oxen, fourteen thousand sheep, five hundred gazelles, ten thousand locusts, ten thousand eggs, one hundred roses, one hundred onions, one hundred leeks, one hundred garlics, and the list goes on and on.[13] The feast was for sixty-nine thousand people, so it appears they did have to get a few extras! As you might imagine, there was a veritable army of people employed to cook all of this food, and they were broken into various brigades of cooks, bakers, roasters, beer makers, and servers.

Bottero is responsible for translating three cuneiform tablets containing thirty-five distinct recipes. These records, known as the Yale tablets, show an assortment of broth and stew recipes, as well as roasted fowl dishes, and even a few desserts. Unfortunately, many of the recipes have ingredients that Bottero can't identify, especially some of the spices, and several recipes make assumptions that the reader knows contemporary facts that have been lost to time. Imagine you have a recipe that says "use the typical holiday spices." We might assume that means cloves, cinnamon, and orange peel, but that's because when we hear "holiday spices" we commonly think of holidays celebrated in the West in late December. Of course, that's not what was written. I just said "holiday spices," which could also mean any spices for any holiday, but you knew what I was referring to. Imagine that knowledge now spread out over several thousand years, and you can see where problems might occur.

Here are three interpretations of traditional recipes that were found on the Yale tablets. The ingredients, except for the oatmeal stout, are as true to the original recipes as we understand them. I substituted oatmeal stout in place of Sumerian barley mash beer. A barley beer could be used too, but they tend to have much higher alcohol contents. The cooking techniques are approximated as noted on the Yale tablets too, but modern appliances were used.

---

13. Jean Bottero and Teresa Lavender Fagan. *The Oldest Cuisine in the World: Cooking in Mesopotamia.* Chicago: University of Chicago Press, 2004.

Tuh'u Broth: Lamb and Arugula Stew

You are about to make a meal that is several thousand years old. Think about that for a moment. It boggles my mind imagining all the people that have eaten some version of this meal. I'm not a Sumerian or Assyrian scholar by any stretch of the imagination, but as near as I can piece together, the word Tuh'u basically means "meat broth."

Serves 4	Prep Time: 10 minutes	Cooking Time: 1 hour and 15 mins

2 tablespoons of fat, divided (butter, oil, meat drippings)

1 medium yellow onion

1 leek

2 cloves of garlic

2 handfuls of arugula (plus one handful of garnish)

1 tablespoon of cumin

2 tablespoons of coriander

Salt to taste (about two teaspoons)

1 bottle of oatmeal stout

3 cups of water

1 pound of lamb stew meat

4 tablespoons of semolina

Heat one tablespoon of fat in a large saucepan or pot over medium heat. Peel and roughly chop the yellow onion into large pieces. Clean and chop the leek, including the green parts. Peel and chop the cloves of garlic. Add the onion, leek, and garlic to the pot. Give a quick stir to coat with the fat. Stir occasionally for 8 minutes until softened, but not browned. Add one generous handful of arugula. Stir until the arugula wilts. Add the cumin, coriander, and salt. Stir. Pour one half of the oatmeal stout into the pot. Pour the other half into a glass and enjoy. (You are doing all the cooking, after all.) Add three cups of water to the pot and stir. Bring to a near boil, then turn down the heat and reduce to a gentle simmer. Heat a skillet (cast iron preferred) on high heat for 2 minutes. Add the other tablespoon of fat to the skillet. Let sit for one minute. Add lamb stew meat to the skillet. Brown the meat on all sides. When the meat is nicely browned, add it and any juices to the saucepan with the vegetables and beer. Stir in four tablespoons of semolina.

Let simmer on low heat for an hour or until the meat is tender. Ladle the Tuh'u broth, vegetables, and meat into a large serving bowl. For each serving, ladle into a bowl and garnish with the remaining arugula.

For a more modern version of Tuh'u broth, see page 218 in the recipe section.

Simple Flatbread

Flatbreads have been and continue to be a staple throughout the world. Their recipes and cooking methods remain simple and effective, just like this one.

Serves 4	Prep Time: 15 minutes	Cooking Time: 30 minutes

2 cups of barley flour

½ teaspoon of salt

1 clove of garlic (cumin and/ or coriander could replace the garlic or be added to it. Try ¼ teaspoon of each. For a sweet version, replace the spices with chopped dates or dried figs)

1 cup + 2 tablespoons of room temperature water

Preheat the oven to 350° F. Put the flour into a large mixing bowl. Add the salt. Chop the garlic finely and add to the flour and salt. Pour in the water slowly, approximately ¼ cup at a time, and mix until a dough forms (do this by hand if you can; it's messy but so much better). Knead the dough for about 10 minutes on a lightly floured surface. Make small dough balls, each about the size of a golf ball, then flatten them between your hands until you have flat, thin discs about the size of coffee can lids.

Place the dough circles onto a baking sheet or pizza stone and cook for approximately 30 minutes. Remove to a plate and eat while the bread is hot.

Rolled Date Bites

Fruit, nuts, and honey. This dish is so simple to make. I can see why these were so popular back in the day, and why they continue to be enjoyed now.

Serves 4	Prep Time: 30 minutes

24 dates (pitted dates are easier to work with)

3 tablespoons of honey or date syrup

1 cup of shelled pistachios

Chop the dates into small pieces. You can use kitchen scissors to do this with ease. Place the date pieces into a medium bowl and beat into a chunky paste. Use a large mortar and pestle to do this if you have one. Add the honey. Set aside. Take half of the pistachios and grind them to a powder using a mortar and pestle, food processor, or coffee grinder. Put the pistachio powder into a small bowl. Bash the remaining pistachios with a rolling pin until you have nice little chunks, and place them in a small bowl.

Roll the date and honey mixture into small balls. You should be able to make about eight of them. Roll in the crushed pistachio powder, pressing the chunks into the date and honey balls, so it adheres and coats the balls.

Move to your favourite serving plate and eat. Then lick your fingers. You'll thank me later.

A RITUAL FOR INANNA

Prepare the recipes for Tuh'u broth, simple flatbread, and rolled date bites ahead of time, or incorporate the cooking into your ritual. Alternatively, simply fill bowls with dates, pistachios, figs, apricots, flatbreads, honey, and any other foods that are sacred to Inanna.

Raise a temple to Inanna. You can create an elaborate temple as you choose, then within that temple create a place to gather and eat. Decorate this place, perhaps a dining room or kitchen table, with bowls and plates and fabrics the colour of cinnamon and cumin and coriander. Imagine Inanna, Queen of Heaven, is coming to dine with you. What would you want her to see in this temple you are making for her? Say these words to her:

> *Bring the Tuh'u broth, hot and delicious.*
> *Bring the bread, fresh from the oven.*
> *Bring dates and pistachios and honey.*
> *Bring beer, bring more beer, bring even more beer.*

And as you build your temple for Inanna, call to her. Invite Inanna to share the feast you have created in praise of her. Recite these words:

> *I make the Queen of Heaven a great feast.*
> *I make the goddess of the evening star a great feast.*
> *I make Inanna, Queen of Heaven and goddess*
> *of the evening star, a great feast.*

Call out and ask Inanna to join you. Remind Inanna that there is plenty of food for her.

> *We bring Tuh'u broth to your temple.*
> *We bring bread and beer to your temple.*
> *We bring sweet dates, nuts, and honey to your temple.*

Eat with Inanna. Slurp the broth and dip the bread. Taste the garlic on your fingers. Bite into the tender lamb. Breathe in deeply the scent of spices and onions and good beer. Fill your mouth with dates and pistachios and bread dipped in honey. Remind Inanna what it is to have a belly full of delicious food, prepared in service of her.

Tell Inanna that you remember her story.

We offer you praise, dear Inanna, for drinking with your uncle.
We offer you praise, dear Inanna, for bringing the Me to us.
We offer you praise, dear Inanna, for breadmaking and sharing of food.

Reminisce with Inanna. Laugh and sing and eat food with Inanna. Treat her like an honoured guest, a beloved friend returning home from a long journey. Let the meal and the remembering take a long time.

And when you've eaten so much, and drank even more, and told your stories to Inanna, ask her to stay a while longer as you pick up the dishes, wrap any leftovers, and slowly put her temple away. Just before you put away the last piece of the temple, take a moment in silence and listen. Just listen. Does Inanna have a story to tell you?

Thank Inanna. Thank the goddess evening star. Thank the Queen of Heaven. Put away your temple until it's time for another feast.

Chapter 2

Greece

Much like Sumerian history, the history of Greece spans an incredible amount of time, dating back to a period before agriculture really took root. Archeological evidence suggests that the areas of the Greek islands have been inhabited for roughly nine thousand years. As you might imagine, the earliest inhabitants lived in small enclaves of huts, caves, and rudimentary dwellings. Food consisted of native plants, fish, livestock, berries, and, eventually, cultivated grains. Over the next several thousand years, huts became houses, houses became villages, and villages became cities.

What's important to remember here is that Greece, as we might think of it today, didn't really exist. Greece, at least in antiquity, was rarely ever one unified concept, but rather a collection of city-states, allied island nations, and colonial outposts. That system continued right up through the beginning of the Greco-Roman era in about 150 BCE.

What usually comes to mind when folks talk about ancient Greek culture are the Olympian gods, the Parthenon, the Acropolis, Plato, Socrates, and the formation of "modern" government. All of this belongs to three distinct yet overlapping periods in Greek history. First is the Archaic period, which dates from about the ninth century BCE to the sixth century BCE. Broadly speaking, this is the age of the poets Homer and Hesiod. During the Archaic age, the stories of the gods and goddesses emerged and creation myths evolved. Then the Classical period of Greece, which dates from roughly the fifth century BCE to the third century BCE, is when the buildings we associate with ancient Greece were built—the Parthenon and Acropolis, for example. Plato, Aristotle, and Socrates lived in the Classical age. The Hellenistic period, which followed the Classical period, lasted right through the first century BCE. It could be said that these three epochs are representative of when Greek culture was at its most widespread and influential throughout the Mediterranean region, Britain, Gaul, and even places as far-flung as India, Pakistan, and Afghanistan. These three periods are most closely associated with Greek enlightenment, which birthed poetry, government, literature, medicine, religion, philosophy, and the occult sciences of divination, astrology, and the oracular arts.

Basically speaking, this nine-hundred-year period in a several-thousand-year history makes up a golden age complete with gods, myths, religious practices, wars, and conquests. Oh!—and excellent food. But the Greek food of the Archaic, Classical, and Hellenistic periods also isn't what you think it is.

So Much Food, but Not a Gyro in Sight

Plato was walking down the avenue one sunny afternoon with his sister Potone. They were popping olives and eating cheese curds, as the cool kids did back then. Plato leaned up against the walls of the Acropolis and thought deep thoughts, as young philosophers are prone to do. Potone said, "I think Greece is rad. It's the best country ever. Let's go worship Athena, then get some gyros and ouzo."

Clearly this is a fictional and farcical account. Well, I suppose it's possible that Plato and Potone did hang out together and eat, given that they were brother and sister, but neither gyros or ouzo would make their way to Greece for another two thousand years or so. In fact, much of what you find in Greek restaurants today would be largely unrecognizable to Plato and Potone.

Let's look at a Greek favourite like gyros. My guess is that right now you're picturing bread, meat, cucumbers, onions, tomatoes, and a tangy white sauce. Now pita bread, or flatbreads like it, were certainly around in Plato's time. Lamb too. In fact, lamb and goat were special-occasion meats, but the various by-products they produced, like milk, yogurt, and cheese, were staples of the ancient Grecian diet. Cucumbers were popular in ancient Greece and so were onions, but that's about where the similarities stop. Tomatoes? Tomatoes date back to about the seventh century CE and the Aztec culture of what is now Mexico. They wouldn't appear in Greece until the sixteenth century of the common era. Tzatziki sauce is a bit of a mystery. The word *tzatziki* has its roots in Turkish and dates to the period when the Ottoman Empire ruled Greece. Yogurt and goat cheese sauces certainly existed in Greece before this and were used as side dishes,[14] but there's nothing to suggest yogurt sauce was dolloped on top of pita bread, gyro style. Likewise, ouzo is a relative newcomer, appearing in Greece in the fourteenth century CE. Monks from a monastery on Mount Athos are credited with the discovery. The first ouzo distillery was founded in Lesbos in the nineteenth century CE.[15] The classic gyro sandwich was invented in Berlin in 1971. The story is that a Turkish immigrant stumbled on the idea and started serving doner kebabs as sandwiches to late-night drunken revelers.[16]

So, if the Archaic, Classical, and Hellenistic Greeks didn't eat Greek food, what Greek food *did* the Greeks eat? Believe it or not, there are virtually no surviving cookery books from the golden age of Greece. I find this fascinating and frustrating given the amount of literature, poetry, and myth that does survive from this era. You'd think that a historian or two would have thought it important to write such things down and save recipes for posterity! The truth of the matter is that there were cookbooks. Household chefs from wealthy families wrote down menus and shopping lists, how to stock pantries, and the like. Unfortunately for us, virtually all of these books were lost or destroyed. In the fourth century BCE, a poem called "Pleasant Living" was written by Archestratus. The "Hedypatheia," as the poem was known, gives the reader advice on all manner of food matters, including how to make exquisite appetizers, wine selections, and even where to find the best foods in town. Essentially, it was the Michelin Guide of its time. We only know about this poem because six hundred years or so later, in the third century CE, a man by the name of Athenaeus wrote a series of volumes called the *Deipnosophists*,[17] translated as "the Learned Banqueters." The volumes depict a series of fictional dinner discussions, and in doing so the author preserves important dining, cooking, and entertaining practices from ancient Greek culture. Athenaeus quoted "Pleasant Living" extensively and referenced some twenty other food authors in the process, but virtually none of the recipes survived.

---

14. "Philip Chrysopoulos." *News from Greece.* July 15, 2018. https://greece.greekreporter.com/2018/07/15/the-ancient-roots-of-greek-souvlaki-the-first-fast-food/.

15. "Stella Tsolakidou." *News from Greece.* August 18, 2013. https://greece.greekreporter.com/2013/08/18/ouzo-the-greek-drinks-history-health-benefits/.

16. "The Man Who Invented the Doner Kebab Has Died." *The Telegraph.* January 20, 2009. https://www.telegraph.co.uk/foodanddrink/4295701/The-man-who-invented-the-doner-kebab-has-died.html.

17. Naucratita, Athenaeus, and S. Douglas Olson. *The Learned Banqueters*. Cambridge: Harvard University Press, 2006.

Most other references to food, cooking, and eating that do survive come to us from the tales of the time. In Homer's *Odyssey* and *Iliad*, for instance, countless meals are described. Characters discuss food, offerings, and hospitality with some frequency. As is often the case, the characters in the tales believed that anyone else who didn't eat *what* they ate and *how* they ate were barbarians. Food, especially feasting, played quite the role in the *Odyssey*. The austere Greeks of the Archaic age viewed feasting as synonymous with gluttony and laziness. Odysseus, the fabled king of Ithaca, had to constantly rescue his shipmates from excessive feasting and the wallowing about with full bellies and wine-induced sleep that followed. Apparently the average hero of the time did just fine fighting monsters and mythic beasts, but throw together a platter of figs, honey, and roasted lamb and they became useless. The peoples from the island of the Lotus Eaters, the Cyclops, and even Circe herself all "tricked" unsuspecting would-be heroes because they were tempted to feast on plentiful and exotic foods.

Three Meals a Day

Alright then, so if you were an ordinary Athenian going about your day, making pottery, dusting the Temple of Zeus, or arranging the Olympic games and not a marauding hero being tempted with huge feasts by witches and giants, what did you eat?

The ordinary, everyday person ate three meals a day. In fact, the whole notion of eating three meals a day—breakfast, lunch and dinner, with dinner being the main meal—comes to us from ancient Greece. A typical *akratismos*, or breakfast, was barley bread dipped in wine. Barley bread is dense, chewy, and hard, so softening it up by dipping it in wine would make perfect sense. Think of how similar this is to our modern practices of starting the day by drinking a cup of coffee and eating a piece of toast. Pancakes were popular breakfast items too, although they would have been topped with honey and cheese curds, rather than being drowned in maple syrup. You can make a version of these pancakes, called *tiganites*, yourself. They're quite simple (and delicious).

Modern-Day Tiganites

These pancakes, known as tiganites, were cooked in a copper frying pan in a small amount of olive oil. The tagēnon, the copper frying pan, was heated over a simple home hearth.

Serves 2	Prep Time: 10 minutes	Cooking Time: 10 minutes

1 cup whole wheat flour or barley flour

¼ teaspoon salt

1 cup water

3 tablespoons honey, plus a bit more for topping the pancakes

1 tablespoon olive oil

In a mixing bowl, combine the flour and salt. Pour in the water and the honey and stir until the batter is mostly smooth. Really, what you're looking for here is for the flour to be incorporated. I actually like my batter a little lumpy. Heat the olive oil in a small frying pan and let it get hot, but not smoky. Pour ¼ cup of batter at a time into the frying pan. Cook for 3 minutes, then flip the pancake over using a spatula, and let it cook for one additional minute. Repeat this until all the batter is used. You might need to add a bit more oil to the frying pan between pancakes.

Top your tiganites with honey or cheese curds and enjoy. If you're feeling daring and don't have to drive anywhere or be responsible too soon, pour ⅓ cup of red wine into a goblet. Pour ⅔ cup of water into the same goblet and mix. Pancakes, cheese, honey, and red wine. Now that's what I call breakfast!

The next meal of the day was lunch, or *ariston*. Lunch consisted of bread, honey, figs, olives, cheese, and maybe salted anchovies or sprats, which were pretty common and inexpensive. All of this was washed down with a tasty cup of red wine cut with water. Lunch was eaten in the early afternoon as a midday snack to keep folks going until dinner. Again, pretty much the same as how we do lunch today.

Lastly was *deipnon*, or dinner, which was the main meal of the day. Like most other meals, bread, cheese, wine, fruits, and vegetables were the staples. You'll notice that outside of fish, there's not much talk of meat. That has as much to do with geography as dietary preferences. Most of Greece and the Greek islands are mountainous and rocky. There's not an abundance of pasture land for grazing, which made raising cattle virtually impossible. Pigs could be penned and sheep and goats could be raised in small herds. Still, the scarcity of land made eating meat an expensive proposition.

Religious practices also played a part in the lack of meat in the Greek diet. For meat to be consumed it had to ritually slaughtered and a portion offered to the gods first. The ordinary Greek person mostly ate barley bread, lentils, wine, cheese, fruits, vegetables, nuts, eggs, fish, and fowl. Rabbits, birds, and fish, although clearly meat-based proteins, were not subject to religious practices and could be eaten by anyone at any time. Considering Greece was (and is) a nation of islands, seafood was plentiful both fresh and preserved and made up the majority of animal protein at mealtime.

Vegetarians and Demeter

The Greek philosophers of the Archaic and Classical ages debated vegetarianism. A few noted schools of philosophy and religious cults practiced and even required one to be a vegetarian to participate in their academies. The Orphic cult and the followers of Pythagoras were vegetarian or, at the very least, promoted the ideals of vegetarianism. There are three primary reasons for this. The first is a belief in a golden age, when humankind lived in an abundant world, where figs, dates, breads, wine, and vegetables and fruits of all sorts grew on trees. Humankind lived in harmony with its animal neighbours, and there was no need to consume animals for food. The second reason had to do with the soul, or, more properly, the idea of transmigration of the soul. Transmigration of the soul, later a main tenet in Druidry, came to the Greeks through their interactions with early Aryans and the practices written in the Rigveda. Basically, the idea of transmigration suggests that the soul moves from one body to another after death. In other words, if your friend died and their soul moved into the sheep across the street, and then you ate that sheep for dinner … yikes!

I like the idea of vegetarianism. In fact, I practiced it for nearly five years. However, for me it never quite sat right with my body. Sally Fallon Morell, in her book *Nourishing Diets: How Paleo, Ancestral, and Traditional Peoples Really Ate,* notes "All traditional diets contained animal products,"[18] and goes on to cite that there's absolutely no isolated culture in the whole of humanity that relied entirely on a plant-based diet. The idea of a perfect world of abundance, with a lush garden filled with baskets of fruits and vegetables, just never existed. That's not to say that there aren't benefits in being a vegetarian, including not accidentally eating your friend after their soul has transmigrated to the nearest sheep, of course.

The third reason had to do with the goddess Demeter. One of Demeter's wondrous gifts to humankind was grain and the storage of grain. Much like Inanna, in bestowing grain, Demeter reduced the reliance on hunting and the need to consume vast quantities of animal flesh. Demeter is the goddess of the harvest, of grain, of cultivation, of agriculture, and of breadmaking. Her gifts were those of plant-based foods, which were completely sufficient for sustaining life.

The story of Demeter, her daughter Persephone, and the attendant rites of the Eleusinian Mysteries played a huge part in the religious lives of the ancient Greeks for centuries, reaching their height in the Hellenistic age and the Orphic cults. Thought to be a continuation or an evolution of much older practices from the Mycenaean age, some nine hundred years before the time of Homer, the Mysteries are still mostly that—mysteries.

In the recipe section of this book, I've included one of my favourite vegetarian meals, which I've titled "Demeter's Vegetarian Feast" (found on page 222). It relies on ingredients that were abundant in Greece during the Classical and Hellenistic periods. It's a meal fit for the goddess Demeter and I enjoy it frequently, offering the first plate to her as an act of gratitude for her gifts of grain and food and plentiful harvests.

If your devotional practice includes working with Demeter, you might be interested in a recipe for kykeon. Kykeon was a popular drink in Greece and featured prominently in the rites of the Eleusinian Mysteries. Now, my version uses all traditional ingredients, except one. The missing ingredient is a psychoactive fungus called ergot, which forms on

18. Sally Fallon Morell. *Nourishing Diets: How Paleo, Ancestral, and Traditional Peoples Really Ate.* New York: Grand Central Life & Style, 2018.

barley and rye. The ergot wouldn't have been used all the time by the entire population. If the ergot was even present—and that fact is highly debatable in and of itself—it would have been only for the priestesses being initiated, rather than everyone in the Grecian world. It is said that the fungus caused a very, very altered state of mind for the initiates of the Mysteries. Speaking from my own experience of mysterious and profound initiation rites, if a priestess said "drink this before you enter into the mysteries," I'd get as high as kite even if I was just drinking water. The power of suggestion plus ritual is potent.

Here's a recipe for kykeon, minus the mind-altering fungus.

Kykeon

Kykeon is the ancient Greek version of horchata or similar "milk" drinks. It was the Coca-Cola of its time.

Serves 2	Prep Time: 5 minutes	Cooking Time: 30 minutes (plus an hour if you want your kykeon chilled)

2 cups barley

12 cups water

1 handful mint leaves, minus
   the stems

1 tablespoon lemon juice

2 tablespoons honey

Grab yourself a nice big pot. Add the barley and the 12 cups of water and bring it to a simmer over medium heat. Cook the barley for 30 minutes. Using a sieve, strain the barley into a large bowl. Use the back of a large wooden spoon or a potato masher to get all of the water out of the barley. Discard the mashed barley, saving the water. Roughly tear the mint leaves and add them to the barley water. Stir in the lemon juice and the honey. Refrigerate until cool or enjoy the kykeon as a warm drink. It's totally up to you. I prefer my kykeon chilled.

If you're working with Demeter, you may choose to pour a small glass of Kykeon for her and recite the following lines, created by me, but inspired by the Orphic Hymns:

> *Great Mother, Demeter, source of all abundance*
> *May your name be remembered forever*
> *Great Mother, Demeter, goddess of seed and sweet fruit*
> *May your name be remembered forever*
> *Come bright goddess, come to us*
> *Come bright goddess, come and drink with us*

Athena's Gift Most Useful

As the legend goes, in the reign of Cecrops the king, two deities grappled to see who would become the patron of the city. They devised a contest, each providing the citizens with an invaluable gift. The god whose gift was most cherished would win the contest and be worshipped forevermore. Poseidon, god of the sea and other waters, plunged his trident into the ground, and from there sprung a saltwater well. The well signified free access to the sea, the ability to build a strong navy, and the development of merchant trade routes, thus guaranteeing the city-dwellers commercial and military success at sea. Then Athena touched her spear to the ground, and from that spot grew an olive tree. The citizens mulled it over and decided that success at sea was quite nice, thank you very much, but the olive tree was a superior bounty. Olives and olive oil became an integral part of the city's economy and way of life. The city was named Athens in honour of Athena, and temples were built in her name.

The most famous and recognizable temple dedicated to Athena, Parthenos (literally "Athena the virgin"), was built in 447 BCE. You probably know this as the Parthenon, standing atop the Acropolis high above Athens. Imagine for a moment walking into this temple of white marble columns. The center of the temple featured a nearly forty-foot-tall statue of Athena made of gold and carved ivory. A flame burned constantly in front of Athena's likeness. A second temple, the Erechtheion, constructed in 421 BCE, housed a depiction of Athena Polias (Athena of the City), carved entirely from an olive tree. An annual festival celebrating Athena's birthday saw her statues draped in robes while sacrificial animals were brought to her temples, blessed, roasted, offered to her, and shared with the people. Games were held in her honour, and the winning athletes received vases (amphorae) containing precious olive oil.

The Arrephoroi, young priestesses dedicated to Athena, were "selected from aristocratic families by the Archon Basileus (king archon/ magistrate) to live on the Akropolis in a house in, or rather in the neighbourhood of, the Erechtheion temple, and to serve Athena for a year. They got their name, 'bearers,' or 'maidens who carried the symbols of Athena Polias in procession,' from the fact that they carried closed baskets (kistai) with secret objects."[19] They washed the goddess Athena and anointed her with olive oil.

---

19. Evy Johanne Håland. "The Ritual Year of Athena: The Agricultural Cycle of the Olive, Girls Rites of Passage, and Official Ideology." *Journal of Religious History* 36, no. 2 (2012): 256–84. doi:10.1111/j.1467-9809.2011.01169.x.

I don't know about you, but I wish, I truly wish, that I could have witnessed this rite. It sounds so stunningly beautiful. We can't come close to replicating those rites. But here's a simple ritual to Athena you can do instead.

A DEVOTIONAL FOR ATHENA

Gather three bowls, preferably wooden. Collect olive leaves or bay laurel leaves and tie them in a bundle with string. Procure Greek olives or any green olives you can find. Buy (or make) the best olive oil you can—a small amount is perfect. Make or buy pita bread. Find a white, unscented tealight candle or a small, white, unscented glass-encased votive candle. Find golden fabric (yellow will do, but gold is best). Get a statue of Athena (wood is best, resin will do just fine). If you can't get a statue of Athena, print off a picture. Better yet, find a piece of wood, perhaps a foot tall. Carve it with her name or some symbol that represents Athena for you.

Prepare yourself for ritual. This could mean taking a bath, changing clothes, or breathing deeply and intentionally for a few moments. Begin your ritual by lighting your olive leaf or bay leaf bundle. Let the smoke fill the room. If burning leaves is problematic for you because of your space or health, dip the bundle of leaves into fresh, clean water and sprinkle the water about the ritual space.

Clearing a central place, put out the items you've gathered. First lay out the golden fabric. Next fill three bowls, one with olives, another with olive oil, and the third with bread. Place the bowls on the golden fabric. Next, carefully drip olive oil onto the candle, taking care not to drown the wick. A few drops will do. Put the candle on the golden fabric, by the three bowls. Complete your temple to Athena by adding her image to the temple. Give it a central place. Perhaps you'll find a way to have Athena raised above the olives, olive oil, bread, and candle.

Light the candle and say:

> *Athena Polias, Athena of the people. We come to*
> *honour you and make offerings in your name.*

Reach for the bowl of olives. Pass the olives quickly and carefully through the flame of the lit candle and place the bowl at the feet of Athena. Repeat with bowls of bread and olive oil. As you do, exclaim:

Athena, we make these offerings of bread, and olives,
and oil in your name. We remember your sacred gifts
from long ago. We honour you with them again today.

Dip your fingers in the olive oil, anoint the goddess Athena, and say:

Athena, we anoint you with olive oil as an act of devotion.
We ask nothing in return. Athena, accept our gift.

Then sit with her. In the words of Doreen Valiente, author of *The Charge of the Goddess,* "assemble in some secret place and adore the spirit of me." In this case the *"me"* is Athena herself. Continue to sit with her. If you know her stories, tell them. Find a book of mythology or any resource you have and find some tale of Athena. Read it aloud as a devotional prayer. Anoint Athena again and again.

When the time feels right, when just enough time has passed, eat an olive. Dip the bread in the olive oil. Savour every drop of oil, taste every morsel of bread, imagine picking the olive from an olive tree on the Acropolis.

Stay with Athena as long as it serves her today. Return to her temple throughout the day until it's time to thank her for her presence and end the rite. To close the ritual, thank Athena. Snuff out the candle. Deconstruct your temple until it's all put away. Say "this temple is now closed." Enjoy any remaining bread, olives, and oil.

Dionysus, the Wildest of Gods

Dionysus was the son of Semele, a mortal woman, and the god Zeus. He was also the child of Zeus and Demeter. In a rather odd twist that might have started an awkward conversation with Demeter and her daughter Persephone, Dionysus was also born of Persephone and Zeus.

In a rather tragic series of events, Semele was unable to bring Dionysus to term, because she asked to see Zeus as his true self. He begrudgingly agreed, and Semele was instantly turned to ash. Fortunately for the embryonic Dionysus, Zeus immediately sewed him into his thigh, and several months later a happy and healthy baby Dionysus made his entrance into the world.

If you think his birth story is confusing, you should read up on the rest of his life. Depending on the storyteller, he was also raised as a girl, was drop-dead gorgeous, incredibly athletic, soft, masculine, feminine, androgynous, clean-shaven, bearded, eternally young, and handsomely matured. It's said that Dionysus is a god of paradox and duality. He is revered and reviled, sacred and profane, a god of cultivated vines and wild abandon.

Dionysus is also a traveling god. It's said that he is a wanderer, never really settling in one place for very long. He had many names and qualities attributed to him. For instance, he was known as "the twice born," as well as "the liberator," "the goat killer," "the warlike," "the wild god," "the god of the tree," "the raw flesh eater," "the god of wine," and "the drunken god." And that's not to mention all of the epithets attributed to the places he lived, traveled to, was born in, or died in. Dionysus got about a bit, which might have something to do with the fact that he was associated with the vine and the wines that derived from them. Two chief exports of Greek culture were wine and the knowledge of planting and cultivating vineyards. Everywhere Dionysus went, vines popped up. Or perhaps, everywhere wine went, the worship of Dionysus popped up.

Wine was a big part of the diet. The Greeks drank wine with breakfast, lunch, and dinner. We know they also drank wine at festivals and religious rites. Wine was used for offerings. I suspect that wine was consumed for all sorts of occasions, including rainy Tuesday afternoons when there wasn't a marathon being run or a good tragedy playing at the local theatre.

Now the Greeks were, by and large, a conservative bunch. Although they consumed a lot of wine, it was generally cut with water. In other words, if you want to enjoy your wine the way the Greeks did, you put one part wine to three parts water in your glass. Anything stronger than that was considered barbarous and dangerous. If one did drink wine in its undiluted form, they could surely expect drunkenness, ecstasy, madness, and even death to follow. Wait a minute, what was that about ecstasy? You see, Dionysus and his followers were big fans of ecstasy (and drunkenness and madness). It is said that a rite or a life devoted to Dionysus brings the knowledge that "the more alive this life becomes, the nearer death draws, until the supreme moment—the enchanted moment when something new is created—when death and life meet in an embrace of mad ecstasy. The rapture and terror of life are so profound because they are intoxicated with death."[20] To participate with Dionysus, in drinking his creation in its unadulterated form, is to affirm life and wrestle life back from death, which is surely waiting for us all.

The recognition that life is fleeting is tragic, and no one knows tragedy like the Greek poets and playwrights. It's no coincidence that a principal festival honouring Dionysus, called Dionysia, was both a jolly good excuse to drink lots of wine, eat goat, and cavort around a bit, as well as a time when poets revealed their new plays, often tragedies.

I've created and participated in devotional rituals or revels for Dionysus. Depending on the setting, they've been wild, orgiastic, wine-soaked, fingers-glistening-with-the-fat-of-roasted-goat-meat affairs that left me satiated and thirsty for more all at the same time. Other devotionals have been less raucous, but no less meaningful. Moderate amounts of food and wine, the kind Dionysus might enjoy, were served. Poetry was read aloud and lounging about was the order of the day, while conversation about the beautiful and tragic state of the world ensued.

A FEAST FOR DIONYSUS

Here's a feast I'd serve for Dionysus and his followers. This one comes with a warning or an invitation, depending on how you like your revels. Your mileage may vary with Dionysus but he's one of those gods that shows up when called or when he hears the pop of a cork, and divine madness often follows. This feast calls for wine, but if wine isn't something you shouldn't imbibe for your own health reasons, substitute grape juice or non-alcoholic wine.

As with other rituals and devotionals, let's start by building our temple to Dionysus. Imagine you're on the island of Naxos. It's 80° F. There's a salty breeze blowing in from the sea. The rugged island is covered with juniper bushes, plane trees, grasses, and annual flowers. Natural springs create riparian groves perfect for a devotional feast. You move along a hidden trail, picking your way through undergrowth, when suddenly you stumble across a columned temple.

Keep this vision in mind as you build your temple to Dionysus. Is there a landscape like this where you live? Can you transform your living room

---

20. Walter Friedrich Otto. *Dionysus: Myth and Cult*. Bloomington: Indiana University Press, 1995.

or dining room table into a temple by adorning it with flowers and altar cloths? Once you've discovered and adorned your temple, fill as many pitchers as you need with three parts water and one part red wine. If you're more daring, fill half the pitchers with diluted wine and the rest with undiluted wine. Earthenware pitchers formed by an artisan's hand are best, but glass carafes will work well too. Add bowls filled with any or all of the following: olives, olive oil, lemon juice, feta cheese, sheep's milk cheese, goat milk cheese, pistachios, dried apricots, honey, anchovies, octopus, mussels, cucumbers, and hard-boiled eggs.

Find poems by ridiculously angst-filled and romantic poets. Discover bawdy or erotic poems or stories. Place these on the altar or around your temple. Wear as little as you can and invite any guests to do the same. I suggest setting good boundaries here so that everyone can participate comfortably. Begin reciting this poem when you're ready to call Dionysus:

> *Welcome, Dionysus.*
> *I have filled your cup.*
> *As always, there's far too much wine for us,*
> *but we know it's never enough.*
> *Welcome, Dionysus.*
> *I have set your table.*
> *As always, there's a surfeit of food to*
> *fill our ever-hungry mouths.*
> *Welcome, Dionysus.*
> *I have built your temple.*
> *As always, there are poems, and*
> *conversations, and pleasures awaiting.*
> *Welcome, Dionysus.*
> *Welcome, the Liberator.*
> *Welcome, the Wild God.*

What happens next is between you, your guests, and Dionysus. Just remember to take the temple down, piece by piece, when you're finished and thank Dionysus for his presence.

Chapter 3
Rome

A she-wolf was out enjoying her solitary Thursday morning stroll. It was about 9:37 a.m. She stopped at a stream for a quick drink of water. To her surprise, she found a basket bobbing about in the reeds. Being a curious sort of she-wolf, she retrieved the basket and found twin boys inside. She did not eat them, as other wolves would do, but decided to foster them as her own. Romulus and Remus, the twin boys, grew up, took revenge on the king that had so callously left them to drown in a basket, and founded an empire that would last a thousand years. Well, Romulus founded an empire. Remus was killed by Romulus because they couldn't agree upon which hill their city should be built.

Roman history, much like Sumerian and Greek histories, can be viewed as one long story or as separate epochs. Rome started as a monarchy in about 753 BCE, became a Republic in 509 BCE, became a dictatorship with the ascent of Julius Caesar in 49 BCE, then spectacularly imploded and became the seat of Christendom under Constantine in 325 CE. Along the way to their eventual decline, the Romans conquered Greece, Turkey, and most of Europe, including Spain, France, Britain, and Belgium. Libya, Tunisia, Morocco, and Egypt were all under Roman rule. Syria, Iraq, Israel, and Jordan were Roman territories as well. The Roman empire was fanatically interested in land because land meant more farms, more cattle, more fish, more wine, more spices, more tin, more copper, more gold, more riches, more gods, and more people. In return for ever so generously invading

41

sovereign land, the Romans brought peace (albeit at the end of a sword), prosperity (to those willing to sell out their own countrypeople), industry (wall-building was especially popular near Scotland), culture, sophistication, aqueducts, and roads. Well, of course the roads. That goes without saying. Oh!—and they gave us cookbooks too.

Apicius: The First Rockstar Chef

A chap from the first century CE by the name of Marcus Gavius Apicius lived an extraordinary life and had a rather anticlimactic death. In between birth and death, Apicius became a cook. Maybe more accurately, he became *the* cook of his era. Apicius's very name became synonymous with the word *gourmet*. He was the ultimate Roman foodie.

He ate everything in excess. He's famously known to have sailed to Libya on a whim in search of jumbo prawns. Upon docking, several vendors brought him samples of the prawns. He disliked them so much that he pulled up his anchor and left without ever so much as getting off the ship to pick up a postcard and a souvenir shot glass to remember the trip by.

His cookbook, *De Re Coquinaria,* which means "the art of cooking," contained nearly five hundred recipes. It was broken into sections, just like most modern cookbooks, with categories for vegetables, sauces, stocks, meats, and desserts. The cookbook, like the cuneiform tablets from ancient Sumer, assumed that the reader knew how to cook already and had an army of free labor to make the recipes. Now, his book was written three hundred years after his death, which is an incredible feat on his part, when you come to think of it. The published work was based on existing recipes written by Apicius. More accurately, it's estimated that most of the recipes in the book were created by Apicius, but roughly a third of them were written by other cooks also known as Apicius. You see, he was so popular among the cooking elite that some appended their names with his name. Imagine if I called myself Gwion Escoffier Ramsay Bourdain, or something like that. The use of Apicius's name conferred a certain level of skill and knowledge, so lots of cooks bolstered their appeal by adding his name to their own.

Well before his death, Apicius was a gazillionaire in Roman terms. But at some point he lost most of his fortune, having spent it on rare foods and the odd trip to Libya for a prawn cocktail. Apicius was reduced to a not-so-humble millionaire, which upset him greatly. Faced with a future of frugality and boring food choices and only being able to afford a lavish nosh-up every other day, he decided he just couldn't live as a peasant and took his own life.

Super-Quick Bonus Recipe for Apicius's Libyan Shrimp

Apicius went all the way to Libya for his giant shrimp. You only need go to the grocery store, and you also don't have to be a billionaire. I use frozen, cooked shrimp for this recipe. I prepare this as an appetizer, but you could easily pair it with jeweled rice or couscous and make a whole meal of it.

Serves 4	Prep Time: 20 minutes	Cooking Time: 15 minutes

1 teaspoon red pepper flakes

1 teaspoon ground cumin

2 teaspoons ground coriander

½ teaspoon ground turmeric

½ teaspoon salt

1 ½ tablespoons olive oil

1 teaspoon red wine vinegar

1 pound frozen, precooked
    shrimp, thawed

Combine the first five ingredients in a small bowl. Drizzle in the olive oil and vinegar, then mix until it forms a paste. Place the thawed shrimp in a large bowl. Pat them dry with a paper towel to remove any excess moisture. Coat them with the spice, oil, and vinegar mixture and let the shrimp marinate for 10 minutes. Grab a large skillet and place it over medium heat for 2 minutes. Add a tablespoon of cooking oil and leave it for a minute. Let it get hot, but not smoky. Add the shrimp in equal batches and cook them until they are hot, about 6 minutes per batch. You'll want to flip the shrimp over just once, so they cook on each side for about 3 minutes. Remember, the shrimp are already cooked, so you are basically just getting them warmed through and activating the spices here.

When finished, place the shrimp on your favourite serving platter. Pour a glass of crisp pinot grigio and thank Apicius. Maybe just for this afternoon, refer to yourself as Nora Apicius. Or just use your own name and append it with Apicius.

Street Food

Apicius couldn't bear the thought of eating like an ordinary Roman. So how did the ordinary Roman eat? Well, first we should probably define who the ordinary Romans were. Really, we're talking about two very different groups of people. First of all, there were the patricians. They were the rich and famous. The patricians were the lauded gentry of their time—the senators, politicians, wealthy landowners, and the like. They ate well, as you might imagine. We'll spend more time with them later. The second group of people were the plebeians, which just included everyone else—farmers, tradespeople, freed slaves, tavern owners, jugglers, actors, the unemployed, and cooks.

Now the plebeians, or common folk, that lived in Rome were crammed into small homes called *insulae*. These were the ancient forerunners of apartment buildings. They were often several stories high, single-roomed, and without a proper bathroom or kitchen. This made cooking at home virtually impossible. Can you imagine a modern-day apartment complex with hundreds of people cooking over small open fires without chimneys or proper ventilation? So, what's an honest plebeian supposed to do for dinner? That's right! Pop out for a cheap meal at the local restaurant, bar, or street vendor.

Street vendors and *tabernae*, taverns that served food, were everywhere. In the excavated city of Pompeii, which had a population of only fifteen thousand people, there were one hundred eighteen restaurants and twenty hotels.[21] That works out to be nearly one restaurant for every one hundred people. Now the term *restaurant* is a bit misleading, but funnily enough, if you've ever visited your local dive bar, you'll have a pretty good idea of what the average taberna was like. The buildings were as simple as the food they served. They were quite literally holes in the wall, usually nothing more than an alcove with a brick oven that heated huge clay pots of food. Patrons sat at a horseshoe-shaped bar (see, just like every dive bar you've been to).

The food served at these restaurants was usually simple, cheap, and plentiful. A thick porridge was common almost everywhere, made from boiled grains. Herbs and vegetables were added for flavour, resulting in a rudimentary risotto-like dish. Lentils and beans were staples of the Roman underclasses and often provided by way of subsidies from the Roman government. Most restaurants only served food, but the *oenopodium* also served wine. Meat was a rarity, mostly because of the expense, but also because restaurants were forbidden by decree of the emperor to serve meat. The little meat that

---

21. Patrick Faas. *Around the Roman Table*. Chicago: University of Chicago Press, 2005.

would have been served was probably pork fat, and that would have been cooked by street vendors, which got around the whole decree nonsense. You see, the Romans had a belief that animals like sheep, goats, and cattle were useful because they produced wool, milk, cheese, and hides. Pigs didn't do anything for humankind, which was rather unfortunate for the pig. Pork became the most popular meat in Rome, and pork fat was cheap and divvied out to the poor.

If boiled porridge and pork fat isn't your ideal meal, then maybe we should look at what the wealthy Romans ate. Remember the patricians?

Pop Round to My Place Later for a Convivium

If the Greeks were responsible for standardizing three meals a day, then the Romans must be credited with segmenting *cena*, dinner, into three courses. Of course, the ever-opulent upper classes of Rome then divided each course of the cena into several smaller courses, especially when they were entertaining, perfecting the seven-course meal. The three-course meal was typical for family dinners, but the seven-course meal was reserved for the convivium. The convivium, which translates roughly to an obscenely huge, great big banquet, was a social gathering like no other.

A convivium wasn't just a meal of food though, it was a veritable feast for the senses. Along with the food, there were entertainers, musicians, orators, poets, and parasites. That last group might need a little explaining. Don't worry, parasites weren't microbial beings infecting the food. It's much worse than that. Parasites were fully formed human beings infecting dinner parties. A parasite was a class of entertainer also known as a professional flatterer. They would attach themselves to a wealthy patrician in hopes of being invited to a convivium and getting a free meal. In return for a good nosh-up, they were expected to be good conversationalists, speaking about current events of the day with ease, avoiding the vulgar subjects of gossip, politics, and sex, and of course, saying very complimentary things about the host. If they didn't procure an invite, you'd find them with the plebeians at the taberna, eating porridge.

The convivium took place in the host's dining room. The dining room was bedecked with wall paintings, textiles, sculptures, and portable furniture. The seating was arranged in a horseshoe design with a low, flat table in the middle. This is the classic picture you have of a Roman dinner party: wealthy Romans reclining on sofas, being fed. There were strict rules about who got to recline where. Portable tables would be brought in with each course. Food was eaten on plates with spoons or with fingers (forks wouldn't be invented until the fourth century CE).[22] The meal would last for hours and end with a carousal, which entailed much drinking until the wee hours of the morning.

The Lares and Penates

The Romans were Pagan. Well, the Romans wouldn't have called themselves that, but to our way of thinking they were Pagan. *Polytheists* is really a better term, because the Romans had more than a few gods to choose from. There were gods and goddesses for absolutely everything and each one had their own holy day, usually accompanied by a feast. At one point there were no fewer than one hundred sixty different festivals celebrating the gods throughout the year. That's nearly one every other day! No wonder Julius Caesar added three months to the calendar in 45 BCE. Romans needed some time off.

Officially, until Theodosius came along in 383 CE and named Christianity as the religion of the land, there really wasn't an official Roman state religion as such. At various times in the lifespan of the Roman empire, allegiance to Caesar, a living deity, needed to be publicly sworn. Generally speaking though, Romans were free to worship and venerate pretty much any deities they wanted to. Public festivals, offerings, devotions, and sacrifices were made to the gods and goddesses for the health of the empire or republic, or to celebrate an abundant harvest, or for continued peace or victory. Roman state religious practices had more to do with propitiating and appeasing the gods rather than, say, forming a personal spiritual relationship with Mercury or Minerva.

While public religion and religious rites were largely ceremonial, even governmental, in their scope and application, the average Roman did have what we might refer to today as a personal practice. Each household, each family had their own familiar deities, known as the Lares and the Penates. The Lares might be compared to the spirits of place, those beings that inhabit an area and watch over all that happens there. You might consider them to be the tutelary gods of a particular place or the spirits of the ancestors that once walked here.

Think about where you live for a moment. If you live by a large body of water or a forest or even a bustling metropolis, there's an energy, a flavour, a particular feel that imbues the landscape because of the physical features present. That feeling you get that you're not alone in those places is the call of the Lares of that place. You might have your own Lares of the backyard or the Lares of the workshop where your great uncle Jack would sit for hours winding copper armatures.

---

22. Peter James and Nick Thorpe. *Ancient Inventions.* New York: Ballentine Books, 1995.

The Lares held a special place in the lives of average Romans. In upper class villas, special alcoves were created in the main family area, or atrium. Statues, often two statues, of the household Lares were placed there. Offerings were made to the Lares at each meal. Important rites of passage—weddings, births, big family announcements—were made in the presence of the Lares. The Lares were, after all, the protectors and watchers and advocates for the family in the unseen world. Even poorer Romans had a place in their homes for the Lares. Something as simple as a tile molded into the wall to form a small shelf was perfectly acceptable. A rustic statue, a memento connected to the local spirits of place or ancestors was placed on the tile.

The Penates were similar to the Lares, but more specific to an idea than an actual ancestor or spirit. For instance, one might have a Penates of the pantry or a Penates of the hearth. Imagine that your home has its own heart, its own soul—that's what the Penates were. Although they were the heart and soul of the house, they were sort of portable. If a Roman businessperson was off trading far from home and became homesick, they could bring the Penates of their house along with them on the journey, set up a temporary shrine, and make offerings to them. The blessings of the Penates were greatly appreciated; they offered comfort and could keep an eye on the homefront to make sure the family was safe.

Now you might be asking yourself, "What does this have to do with food?" The offerings given to the Lares and Penates were most often food. Food that accidentally ended up on the floor was considered an offering to the Lares. The goddess Vesta, the Romanized version of Hestia, was the goddess of the hearth, and the Penates were closely associated with her as protectors of the hearth. A first bite of bread might be thrown into the fire or hearth as a sign of respect for the Penates. The hearth, the kitchen, the open flame, or the street vendor's pot full of Carthaginian porridge, was the domain of Hestia and the Penates. In short, they were everywhere, pervasive, and frequently called upon.

INVITING THE LARES AND PENATES TO YOUR HOME

As the primary cook for my family, the kitchen and the tools in my kitchen are sacred. The food that comes out of my kitchen nourishes my friends and family. The spice cabinet, the pantry, the fridge, the freezer, the potato barrel, the bread box, and the salt cellar are sacred spaces, and I'd like to think that there I have my own Lares and Penates looking out for the health and well-being of my household. If your home, current residence, apartment, yurt, or tent is sacred to you, perhaps honouring your local deities and spirits of place appeals to you. Here's a simple ritual that you can do over and over again in devotion to those unseen ones that are there with you.

Choose a place where you'd like to welcome and honour your Lares and Penates. If you have a fireplace and consider it your home's hearth, sweep it out. Clean it up in a way that is meaningful for you. If the stovetop, oven, or entire kitchen feels like your hearth, spend time cleaning it. And I do mean *cleaning* it, like with soap and water and a broom and paper towels. Next, find or make two figures to represent your house spirits. The figures could be statues you already have. You might elect to carve them from sticks or branches from the land you live on. If there's a stream nearby, perhaps you'll find a couple of nice big stones that you can draw on. Get creative.

Set your Lares and Penates figures on the mantelpiece, the windowsill, or on your dining room table as a centerpiece. You could even hide them in the back of your food cabinets if circumstances dictate that they're not visible to just anyone. Gather a small bowl filled with salt, a vessel for liquid, and another container to put food offerings in. Set these in front of, next to, or around your two hearth deities and say:

Lares and Penates.
Spirits of this place.
Deities of this house and hearth.
Accept these offerings.
Here is salt, a gift from the earth that sustains life.
Here is water [or whiskey, or wine, or whatever liquid you
deem important], a gift that quenches your thirst.
Here is food, a gift to nourish and delight you.
Stay here with us. Watch over this house. Protect all that dwell here.

Best-case scenario, every time you eat or cook, but at least every time you remember to, place more food in the offering bowl, replenish the liquid, add to the salt, clean the space, and talk with the Lares and Penates. Conspire with them when you're having a dinner party. Invite them to attend the special meal you're cooking for loved ones. Mark a date on the calendar that signifies a festival day for your Lares and Penates. On that day, make a big deal about cleaning their space and create devotions to them. By the time the anniversary rolls around, you may have discovered they have favourite meals and offerings they want you to prepare. For years there's been a tiny glass pot on my kitchen windowsill that's filled with honey, for just this purpose.

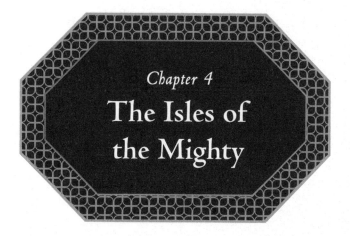

Chapter 4
The Isles of the Mighty

It was an especially dreary Thursday morning. The fog was clinging to the valley floor, making everything damp. Gathering grey clouds overhead signaled that the damp would soon give way to actual wet. Alan woke up, rubbed his eyes, surveyed the landscape, noticed the weather, and muttered something under his breath about it not being as nice here as it used to be. Alan stood up, took in a deep breath, and promptly died.

John lay next to the dwindling fire. The logs from last night, now reduced to embers and ash, gave off virtually no heat. If the rains did come soon, any hope of resurrecting the fire to cook breakfast would be dashed. John was very much asleep, his arm draped over Maureen. Maureen was nestled tightly, small spoon–style, blanketed in the warmth of John's embrace.

John and Maureen, who would later discover that they had both been dreaming about aurochs, bolted upright as they heard Alan's body hitting the ground, and immediately realized that something had gone terribly wrong. Springing into action, they shook Alan's lifeless body, called out his name, and then, when it was clear Alan wasn't going to answer, sat back down and had a good cry. They covered Alan's body in his favourite hide, put his hunting spear in his left hand, arranged a small display of flint spearheads by his right hand in case he broke his spearhead during his hunt, and left a sizeable chunk of meat for him, wrapped tightly in leaves, in case he got hungry.

Seven hundred thousand years later, give or take a couple thousand years, Alan's story would be retold, albeit with a few more facts and words like "carbon dating" and "Lower Paleolithic period" being thrown about very liberally, by a particularly learned doctoral candidate, coincidentally also named Maureen.

While the exact details of Alan's story are a bit exaggerated—okay, completely a work of fiction—this is near enough to how the history of the British Isles began. The earliest remains of humankind in Britain were excavated in Suffolk, and their tools do date to seven hundred thousand years ago. One hundred thirty thousand years ago found Britain home to bands of Neanderthal. Twenty-seven thousand years ago it got extremely cold in Britain, as the Ice Age started and then lasted as a bit of a cold snap for the next thirteen thousand years. Roughly eight thousand years ago, Britain officially became an island, and six thousand years ago people began farming, raising pigs, planting crops, and domesticating cattle, sheep, and goats. It's possible that those were indigenous Britons who had managed to survive the Ice Age, but it's more than likely that they were travelers from Europe who decided to settle. It would be another two thousand years before someone had the bright idea to build Stonehenge and confuse us all for millennia to come. The Celts arrived about twenty-five hundred years ago, and the Romans stopped by for a nice spot of Pax Romana just about two thousand years ago. Four hundred years or so after arriving, the Romans up and left, and the Dark Ages began.

A Dark Age for Cuisine

Virginia Woolf said, "What passes for cookery in England is an abomination. It is putting cabbages in water. It is roasting meat till it is like leather."[23] This is not an uncommon opinion of British food, but is it deserved? Well, yes and no. There has always been a lot of boiling going on in Britain, and the Dark Ages were no exception.

The Dark Ages weren't any darker than any other time in the history of the British Isles. Typically, the period right after the Romans left (400 CE) until the beginning of the Italian Renaissance (1500 CE) is called the Dark Ages, or more politely, the Middle Ages. For our purposes, we're going to focus on the times of the Anglo-Saxons, which lasted from about 400 CE to roughly 750 CE.

There was one big fight going on in Britain at the time, namely, consolidating all the tribes into one unified Britain. Two opposing forces were vying for supremacy over Brit-

---

23. Virginia Woolf. *To the Lighthouse*. Middlesex: Penguin Books, 1964.

ain: the native Pagan tribal leaders and the priests from the new religion that was sweeping all over Europe. And while chieftains and kings and missionaries fought for the souls of the inhabitants (oh, and their land), the ordinary people still had to eat. And eat they did. Mostly boiled things, like cabbages, no thanks to Virginia Woolf.

The typical diet consisted of breads, porridges of barley and oats, beer, vegetables, fruits, rabbit, birds, shellfish, and fish. On a rare occasion there would be pork; rarer still would be mutton or beef. The types of fruits, vegetables, and greens found in Britain at the time were crabapples, plums, gooseberries, raspberries, blackberries, turnips, peas, beans, onions, leeks, cabbages, parsnips, ramps, dandelions, and various wheats and grains. What meat there was to eat was either grilled immediately over open fires or preserved for later use. Smoking and drying meat was a common way to extend the usefulness of meat, as was salt preserving. Breads were simple, made from whole wheat or rye, flavoured with herbs, and tasting a lot like today's sourdough breads. Larger villages would have had a bakery, a small dwelling with a big brick oven that served the entire village.

The two most common cooking tools were the griddle and the cauldron. The griddle was a flat piece of iron or clay that was placed over a heat source. The heat could be provided by an outdoor fire, much the same way we might cook over a campfire today. For inside cooking, a small fire would be built in the middle of the home and a clay pot would be turned upside down and placed over the fire. There was a cut-out to let oxygen in and where more fuel could be added, and the flat, circular bottom of the pot was used as the cooking surface. The cauldron was, by far, the most important kitchen implement. Cauldrons of all sizes were used. They were typically made of copper and iron, but ceramic cauldrons have been found too. Handles were later added, allowing the cauldron to be suspended over a fire with hooks and chains. Freestanding cauldrons with three feet have been found, but were far less common. Often, what was brewed in these cauldrons was pottage, or stew.

Pottage from the Dark Ages

Pottage is thick. The oats were a substitute for meat and give the stew body. I could imagine foraging along hedgerows and using whatever I had on hand to make pottage.

Serves 8	Prep Time: 30 minutes	Cooking Time: 45 minutes–all day

8 cups water or vegetable stock

1 cup cabbage, shredded

1 leek, sliced (white parts only)

1 turnip, cubed

1 large carrot, sliced into coins

1 parsnip

1 teaspoon dried thyme

1 teaspoon dried sage

1 teaspoon dried savoury

3 tablespoons lovage, chopped (celery leaves or parsley will do too)

Salt to taste

1 cup rolled oats

If you have a cauldron and a tripod and want to cook this over an open flame, I highly recommend it. To turn the heat up or down, you can either raise the cauldron or manage the fire accordingly. A stock pot and an oven work perfectly well too. The instructions are easy. Fill the cauldron with the water (or stock) and bring to a simmer. Add all the other ingredients, except the oats. Crank up the heat and boil for 15 minutes or until the vegetables are soft. Reduce the heat and add the oats, then simmer for another 30 minutes. You can leave this over a low heat for as long as you want at this point.

Serve in rustic bowls right from the cauldron or ladle from the stock pot. This is particularly good with a nice crusty piece of sourdough bread. Pepper wasn't available to the average fifth-century peasant, but salt was. If you want to try this recipe as a noble person might have enjoyed it, add 1 tablespoon of turmeric and 2 teaspoons of fresh ground pepper when you add the other ingredients. If you're an omnivore, add a cup of chicken or rabbit. If there are leftovers, you can keep the pottage in the fridge for up to three days and just reheat. I doubt there will be leftovers though.

The Importance of Feasting

Being an Anglo-Saxon chieftain came with perks. There was access to hunting lands, which included wild boar, venison, elk, partridges, pheasants, quail, and pigeons. Locals farmed the chieftain's lands, which in turn the chieftain gave out as tributes to their favourite warriors. The warriors were grateful to have a nice bit of land to farm and hunt on and would, at the drop of a hat, come running to the chieftain's aid when the trumpet of war sounded.

The local chieftains measured their wealth in land and the resources their lands could produce. The best way to show how much wealth was available in the kingdom was to throw a gigantic feast. This achieved a few important goals. First, it showed everyone in the area—friends and potential enemies—that there was plenty of food available. Well-fed soldiers and villagers can wage war with more voracity and withstand sieges for longer periods of time. A generous chief with happy villagers was a lot less worried about their subjects running off to fight for a rival faction. Secondly, banquets and feasts served as community gatherings, celebrating victories, the turn of the seasons, funerals, marriages, and religious holy days. After all, it was a combination of the chief's skills as a strategist, community backing, and the will of the gods that kept the community thriving. Lastly, much like the proverbial lunch meeting on the golf course, feasts were a place to do business, cement alliances, and discuss the vital matters of the day.

Can you imagine coming into the hall of your chieftain? Furs and hides line the walls. A fire burns steadily in a long pit in the center of the hall. Outside, people are preparing venison and boar, roasting them on spits. Cauldrons of pottage flavoured with exotic spices like pepper and cinnamon are bubbling away. There are more loaves of bread than you can count, and not just the brown rye bread you're used to, but the good, soft white bread too. There are barrels of beer and mead, and if the trading has gone well, maybe even a jug or two of wine. All the best warriors are home. The Saxon gods, Woden and Frigg, have shown great favour to your chieftain and your village. Thunor, the god of thunder, has scared your enemies away. Craftspeople have forged raven brooches, swords are etched with runes, there are decorative cauldrons with the faces of the gods hammered inside and out. Everywhere there is food. So very much food.

A Table for the Gods

You know, it's not that different today. Think about the feasts you have with your family and/or friends. There are feasts to celebrate abundance and to mourn the loss of loved ones. There are community gatherings to mark the turn of the seasons and to root on your favourite warriors (okay, sports teams).

Tables are filled with roasted birds and grilled vegetables and heaping bowls of mashed potatoes and huge salads and piles of bread. The best plates are used. Family relics, like Grandma Lillian's favourite lace tablecloth, are pulled out of the cedar chest. If you're lucky there will be much talk and laughter and singing and Uncle Fred won't start banging on about the state of politics today and how the young kids don't know how good they've got it. Back in his day, he only had one cauldron and had to make his own pottage without pepper!

In my house, and perhaps your house too, these big family feasts include an acknowledgment of the gods or ancestors we hold dear. The cook, the matriarch, and the provider of the feast are all honoured, and there's usually some family business that gets handled. A common trope in the US during election season talks about "dinner table" issues, meaning political questions that impact real people all the time, wherever they live and eat. Dinner table issues are the everyday concerns we all have. The Anglo-Saxons of Britain had these same conversations; they just invited all of their neighbours to one big dinner to air everything out. And of course, they invited the gods along to listen as well.

A FEAST FOR THE GODS

I'm proposing you gather with your beloved ones, those you provide for, those that provide for you, your ancestors, and your gods in the style of an Anglo-Saxon feast. If it's just you, invite your gods and ancestors or the spirits of the place you live. No matter what your budget is (or isn't), create a feast (two Twinkies and a Gatorade constitutes a feast if it's all you have, so go for it).

Set the most lavish table you can. Cook outside if your space allows for it. While the meal is cooking and you're chopping food and sautéing vegetables and prepping a mountain of delectables, give thanks for your abundance. I find making food to be a wonderful way to bring myself to center and feel grounded. Connecting with life, ancestors, the gods, and the very planet we walk on every day is pretty easy with a big bunch of carrots in your hand.

Light candles in every room (I do use a couple of the LED ones in certain rooms, you know, just for safety). Bring light into areas where there are shadows. Give thanks for the light and the shadow. And at some point during the meal, say what and whom you are grateful for in this moment, even if you're enduring hard and uncertain times. Each guest should share something that they are grateful for. Taking note of a full table and the faces that are present and not present, remind yourself of what you are thankful for. Remember those that have paved the way, sometimes by their suffering, for you to be here. There's no rush or time limit to this part of the ritual. Perhaps as your meal draws to a close you can recite these phrases:

> *May we never hunger.*
> *May we never thirst.*
> *Let us always remember those who*
> *went before and honour them.*
> *Let us always offer thanks.*

What's That Witch Cooking?

I have some bad news for you. From the times of the Roman occupation of Britain through the coming of the Anglo-Saxons, Jutes, Danes, Vikings, and Normans, right up through the mid-twentieth century, the word *witch* wasn't ever said in a nice way to anyone. The Old English word for witch, *wicce*, was a common enough term, and it's where the word *Wiccan* derives from. The Old English term for a magickal action was *scinn-lac*. One who practiced *scinn-lac* was said to have *scinn-craeft*, or magickal skill. A person who could enchant another person was known to practice *galdor-craeft*, which quite literally means "enchanting skills." The term *wiccecraeft* meant the skill of witchery and was usually applied to the notion that one was working for themselves or their client, rather than the for the good of the community. There were specific names for diviners, plant-based magick workers, sorcerers and evildoers, and astrologers.[24]

---

24. Bill Griffiths. *Aspects of Anglo-Saxon Magic.* UK: Anglo-Saxon Books, 2012.

Much of what we know about the practices of witchcraft, or any of the crafts listed, we know not because there are secret grimoires detailing all the lost spells, but because the new religion of the Christ and the church associated with those practices wrote laws and edicts forbidding Pagan practices. The early church and its missionaries, like Augustine, were responsible for converting the kings and chieftains of Britain, and by about 750 CE, the last Pagan rulers of Britain were gone. There were rumours of Pagan revivals for the next thousand years, but it wasn't until the repeal of the witchcraft act in 1951 that a substantial revival began. But the church had a bit of a public relations problem. You see, the folk practices, celebrations, and feast days were so popular and hard to dislodge that the church just overlaid Christian feast days right on top of the Pagan ones. So, the Pagan practices kept going.

Crops and livestock made up a good part of the diet and fortunes of the landowners. If something went wrong with the crops or the land, the church would go looking for a reason. The specter of "the old ways" was always looming, because the new religion hadn't been around for very long and people were suspicious of it. Church officials met up and said, "Look, those folk ways that involve taking waters from wells and doing things under a full moon and mentioning Wotan every five minutes aren't Christian. If the crops do well, the villagers will think their old ways are still working and their gods are still listening. We can't have that. So, let's outlaw those things, or better yet, let our priests do the same exact things but in the name of our god." And with that, the old ways began to disappear. Sort of.

You see, the new church edicts didn't say that people couldn't eat herbs to heal themselves, or bless new babies, or cure the sick. What they said was you couldn't gather herbs from crossroads or sacred groves or wells that were once associated with the old gods. If you were caught doing those things, then of course you were in league with the demons (which equated to false gods) and that was something you could get in trouble for. The most common punishments were atonement fasts and prayers.

What does this all have to do with food? Witches were supposed to be able to turn good milk sour, and stop goats and cows from giving milk, and blight crops, and make poisons. Essentially, witches were really good at understanding how foods, herbs, spices, vegetables, and meats impacted the health and well-being of their fellow villagers and they traded on that knowledge. That doesn't mean they understood molecular biology or how germs worked, but it did mean they saw a connection between the land, the gods, and the power of a good ritual, especially one done in the privacy of one's own kitchen.

Section II

Food, Magick, and
Rituals for Today

Over the next few chapters of this book, we'll examine modern-day practices combining ritual, magick, and food. One way of engaging with the magickal world is through devotional practice. Making food for one's self, for others, or for one's gods is certainly an act of devotion. It's my belief that we can re-enchant our lives by reframing the so-called "mundane" as sacred and divine. By imbuing the familiar with a sense of wonder and infusing daily life with acts of magick, we choose to consciously make all of life devotion.

I do not find it necessary to place my hopes in an otherworldly paradise to find ecstasy. There is a place of pure and unadulterated ecstasy right here for us to experience. All we must do is fully engage with the sumptuous feast set before us, enjoyed with beloved company or unabashedly, unapologetically, lustfully eaten all by yourself. Our daily food rituals—chopping, slicing, cooking, and eating—can draw us back into harmony with the world and each other.

This re-enchantment, this re-engagement with our own sensuous self, is the best part of magick. The work and the play of magick is so much deeper and more impactful when we are in touch with our senses and our surroundings. We can enter a sacred conversation with the land we live on, the people we live with, and the foods that sustain us. This dialogue is what leads to devotion, understanding, and even healing. Devotion might be to ourselves, the places we inhabit, the communities we are part of, the gods we are aligned with, or the activism we participate in.

Chapter 5

Food and Magick

It is not hard to see where magick and food intersect. Most modern Pagan traditions hold that the planet we live on deserves reverence. "Earth-based spirituality" or "Nature religion" are common euphemisms for various forms of Paganism. Almost all magickal systems honour the elements as sacred participants and invited guests. Air, Fire, Water, and Earth are frequently invoked at Pagan rituals. Everything we eat comes from the earth. Yes! That includes organic vegetables, ethically raised meats, and manufactured foods with additives and chemicals with a list of unpronounceable ingredients as long as your arm. We live here on the earth. The food we eat lives, grows, or is made here too.

Food is transformed by the elements. Fire in all its myriad forms heats our food. Water washes clean our vegetables, boils stew, and turns leaves into tea. Convection ovens employ Air and help foods cook faster. And Earth, well, that's everywhere. Clay dishes, metal pans, the soil our foods grow in. There's no part of what we eat that isn't impacted by the elements.

A basic understanding of the magickal arts reveals that we aim to work in accord with the natural world, stepping into the flow of the landscapes we find ourselves in. The phrase "changing consciousness at will" is frequently applied to all sorts of magickal practices. One of the best ways to change your consciousness and be in touch with the natural world is to be aware of the food you eat. Food has the incredible power to change our mood, impact our energy levels (both physically and metaphysically), and bring us in alignment with the natural forces present in our environment.

Working with food as a magickal practice doesn't require much more than you already have right now. It's possible your refrigerator, freezer, pantry, and spice cabinet are completely stocked to bursting with every imaginable protein, meat, and vegetable you might need, or you might be in possession of one lone mushroom, a box of leftover rice from lunch at Panda Express, and an egg. What you have, what you can afford to buy, and where you are able to buy or grow the foods you eat has little to do with the magick you can create with the food you have.

Each magickal system has its guidelines, rules, and methods. It's no different with food magick. I've concluded that there are five basic principles to understand. Every time you shop for ingredients or sit in your car in a drive-through line or eat popcorn at a movie, you can remember these guidelines and put magickal intentions to work for you.

1. All food is sacred.

2. Eat what you need.

3. Share what you can.

4. Express gratitude.

5. Pass the knowledge along.

All food is sacred. It is. Sit with that for a minute and let that fact settle in. Notice I didn't say "All food is healthy" or "All food should be organic" or "All food is sacred only when it comes from a farmer's market, is locally produced, is cruelty free, and is lovingly prepared by a personal chef named Jacques in sacred space." A McDonald's cheeseburger is sacred. So are potato chips and skinny vanilla lattes. Microwaveable pizza is a gift from the gods, and bags of plain white rice and red beans purchased at the discount grocery store are quite possibly more sacred than the Great Pyramid of Cheops, Stonehenge, and the Charge of the Goddess all combined.

Don't get me wrong—eat well, eat healthy foods, do whatever you can to support local farmers and food artisans, and do grow your own food if you have the resources to. But having access to "clean" and "sustainable" foodstuffs doesn't make them any more sacred than prepackaged foods from the megastore. What it does mean is that you are fortunate enough to be able to make choices about what you buy, grow, and eat, and that's a truly amazing state of affairs. Absolutely revel in and appreciate your good fortune.

For many people, regular access to fresh fruits and vegetables, free-range meat, and organic spices just isn't a reality. There are areas in the United States known as food deserts, whole neighbourhoods, hundreds of square blocks without grocery stores. You couldn't find a bunch of basil if you searched for a month, but you could find every candy bar and fast food restaurant you can name. People must eat. I would love for there to be food equity and justice and access for every single person in the world, and I'll never judge anyone for their food choices when I have more choices than they.

Let me give you an example from my own childhood. Milk sop. I thought milk sop was the best breakfast treat in the world. My mother would make milk sop a couple of times a month and I thought I was the luckiest kid around when I woke up to find a steaming bowl of it waiting for me. Milk sop is bread, sugar and hot milk. Mmm … right?

What I didn't know was that I got milk sop when there was nothing else to eat. The bread was the hard heels of a leftover loaf, ripped up into cubes. The milk was the last inch or two in the container and sugar was to sprinkle liberally over the top so it was sweet and I'd eat it. Milk sop is one of the most sacred and dear meals I can ever eat because it's the meal I ate when we had absolutely nothing else in the house. Eating milk sop meant my mother probably didn't eat that day. Milk and bread and sugar remind me what it is to feed another person the very last morsel you have and that the most meagre ingredients, lovingly prepared, can sustain life and bring joy. And if sustaining life isn't potent magick, then I don't know what is.

Eating what you need speaks to paying attention to internal conversations and the wisdom of our own bodies. These are big questions being raised here. "What do I need to eat?" and "Why do I need to eat it?" The answers are incredibly complex, as they have to do with hormone levels, chemical processes in the brain, mineral deficiencies and excesses, emotions associated with lack and surplus, our childhood, outside stimulation (like advertisements), societal expectations, and taboos. This list could go on and on.

Let's look at this from the perspective of magick. It's a well-held magickal belief that there are forces at work beyond our human understanding. Perhaps that means goddesses and the Good Folk to you. Maybe those forces have to do with the alignment of the planets and stars, or the way that the mycelial network communicates over vast distances. No matter how you define those forces, part of being a magick worker is to pay attention and act accordingly to the messages you receive or interpret from those forces. The highly complex system that is your body is like one of those forces. It sends you messages, even if they are highly encrypted, almost indecipherable, and practically alien in their origins, even though those origins might be right there in your liver, your taste buds, or your hypothalamus gland. The key is that it's not always going to be clear why you are being called to act a certain way, but rather you should try to hear the message, imagine what it might mean to you in this moment, and then act with awareness and purpose.

And that's why it's perfectly magickal to exclaim to the universe, "I need to eat a pretzel right now!" Maybe you just really want a pretzel because the people that own the pretzel stand are nefariously pumping out delicious pretzel smells in hopes of enticing you to buy a pretzel. Maybe your body needs salt right this minute and says, "Hey! Isn't there a pretzel stand around here somewhere?" Align with the magick and act consciously. Buy the pretzel. Eat it. Enjoy it. Or note that you really want something salty right in this moment and decide that a pretzel isn't the optimal choice for you and go get a bowl of miso soup instead.

The forces you are reacting to have a message. You might interpret that message as the need for a specific kind of food or to get certain ingredients, minerals, or vitamins into your system. Beyond that, maybe pretzels remind you of where you grew up or a person you love and adore that's no longer part of your life. The forces at work might want you to eat a pretzel because somewhere in the recesses of your mind you know that it's nearly the anniversary of your favourite aunt Elsie's passing, even though you haven't thought about her in years. Go with the magick. Eat the foods that you are attracted to, that are calling you for some unknown reason, and see if you can find the reason.

Human beings have been sharing food with each other for hundreds of thousands of years, millions even. Perhaps you shared the milk from your own body with another person or you were fed by mother's milk. You would not be reading this book today if someone hadn't shared food with you. A study of college-aged students published in the journal *Appetite* showed that people that shared their food with others were also more likely to give up their seat on public transport, help a friend move, act with more consideration to others, listen better, and exhibit "prosocial" tendencies.[25]

Interestingly enough, there's an echo of wisdom from our ancient Sumerian friends in that the students noted a marked difference between simply "eating together" and "sharing a meal." I define "eating together" as dining with another person. We do that all the

---

25. Charlotte J. S. De Backer, Maryanne L. Fisher, Karolien Poels, Koen Ponnet. "'Our' food versus 'my' food. Investigating the relation between childhood shared food practices and adult prosocial behavior in Belgium." *Appetite* volume 84, January 2015.

time. We find ourselves at a restaurant with someone. We typically order separate meals, and likely we pay for "our" meal. What's on my plate is mine and what's on your plate is yours. Sharing a meal, however, means that we share food with each other. We eat from one pot, we pick foods from a communal platter that we've all contributed to, even eat from one another's plates. There's a real difference in how we conduct ourselves when we're consciously sharing with another person or group.

Again, let's look at this magickally for a moment. One of the main benefits of practicing in a coven or any form of magickal group that works together regularly is the sense of a common bond and common purpose. Feelings of sympathy, empathy, genuine concern, even love are present when the group gathers. There's an egregore, a shared consciousness, that begins to impact the group on subtle, magickal levels. These feelings don't happen in a vacuum though; they need to be cultivated. Preparing and sharing meals together is one way to stimulate the process of bonding. Sharing food together requires trust, restraint, paying attention to who has eaten and who has not, so you know when it's okay to fill your plate again. If you learn that a new coven member doesn't eat tomatoes, you might consider bringing a wider variety of fruits and vegetables to your next meeting. That shows care and attention and that a person's food needs are important. Egregore grows.

What if you are a solitary practitioner? Share your meals anyway, as often as you can, with the non-magickal people in your life. Let me tell you a short story of a birthday dinner I once had at a local restaurant as an example. My partner and I were seated next to a married couple. We could hear them discussing their menu choices. We settled on our choices. All the appetizers showed up about the same time. I looked over and commented on "his" dish. I'd considered it but opted for something else. Turns out, he was mulling over what to get and was stuck between ordering what he did and what I'd ordered. I asked if he wanted a bite or two of my meal. His wife was initially appalled at the suggestion, but he was totally game. He offered me a forkful of his appetizer. We exchanged names. We discussed food. Talked about where we lived. We discovered that we shared the same birthday and that our partners were treating us to a special meal. We pulled our tables together and ended up eating our meals "family style," sharing everything that came up. We even split the bill when we were done. It is one of the best birthday meals I've ever had, and it was with two total strangers.

Maybe eating a meal with someone you don't know is a little too far for you to go just now. Maybe you could organize a potluck at work. Bake a cake and share it with your neighbour. Share your gummy bears with a stranger you meet on the bus. What does this have to do with your magickal practices? Sharing food means you must interact with others in real life, even if that's awkward. It means navigating personal food preferences, letting go of having all the control, and learning from and about others. Lastly, and most importantly, sharing what you can with others connects you with folks on a very human level. I can share my food with you and know that at the present moment in time, you are not hungry or thirsty. You may hold wildly different beliefs than I do, or not be the kind of person I would choose to hang out with in the future, but we can share food together and celebrate the fact that we both have something to eat. Magick is often cited as being about power. I can think of no greater use of magickal power than ensuring the health and happiness of one other human being, albeit temporarily, by making sure they are fed.

A simple "thank you" goes a long way. There's a spell called "the Thermos of Gratitude" included in the recipe section of this book. It speaks in detail about the practice of gratitude. Expressing thanks, being grateful for what others have provided for us, is a profoundly satisfying practice, but what does it have to do with magick? Well, a lot actually.

Very few magicks left in the world are done entirely alone. Even if we practice by ourselves, we're probably reading books written about the magick other people have done and repeating those spells, incantations, and rituals. If you work within a particular magickal tradition, unless you started that tradition yourself, there's a good chance there are elders and founders and folk that have shown you the magickal ropes. It's a fair bet that almost every part of your magickal practice owes something to someone else. If the magick you do means a great deal to you, your family, your coven, and the tradition you practice in, recognizing that fact and saying "thank you" once in a while is a simple and elegant way to remember those that have contributed to your life and impacted your well-being in a positive way. One of the easiest ways to express gratitude is to say "thank you" at every meal. Maybe you're thanking the person that cooked your meal, or served your meal, or perhaps you're saying the "big thank you" to the goddess in your chosen pantheon, your ancestors, or the planet you live on.

There's a phrase I heard at a large gathering of witches. As the spell work was drawing to an end for the evening, the cry of "the magick must move" began echoing around the stone circle where the ritual was happening. I understood that chant to mean that we must move our magick out of the cauldron, so to speak, and take it out into the world. We do that when we pass our magick along, sharing our skills and knowledge with others, writing down spells and recipes and the best cooking techniques. There is a power in freeing the magick and letting the intention of a spell go where it must to do its best work.

It's the same with food magick. The collecting of ingredients and the alchemy of cooking a meal, coupled with the magickal workings embedded into each herb and vegetable, are temporary vehicles for the magick being created. There is no ever-filling cauldron where ingredients replenish themselves whenever there's a need for more food. As much as I wish it were true, the magick of a full harvest table only lasts in that form for a few brief hours until the food is eaten and transformed into calories.

The magick must move, and move it does. The food moves through our physical bodies and, at some point, we literally pass it on. But there's a magickal way in which we're passing it along too. Food replenishes us; it nourishes us and those we share our food with. If eating together or providing food for others is a regular part of your magick, you are passing your magick along through the actions and thoughts of everyone that eats your food. If there's spell work kneaded into every loaf you bake, if each spice and herb is chosen for its magickal properties as well as its flavour profile, if gratitude is expressed for the life of the animal that died to be reborn in another form on your dining room table, then when your oven has cooled and the dishes are done and folks leave to go about their business, the magick will move with them. It must. The ones you feed carry the spells out with them into everything they do. That's powerful magick indeed.

THE BEST MEAL YOU EVER HAD

Food has the magickal ability to anchor specific moments in our minds and in our bodies, perhaps like no other magickal tool can.

Try this magickal exercise right now. Get comfortable. Close your eyes. Exchange a few deep breaths with the world around you. Feel your lungs expanding with each inhale. Imagine the air traveling down into your belly. As you breathe, cast your mind back to a favourite meal. Maybe the best meal you ever had. Was it a family gathering or an after-ritual feast with your coven? Perhaps your best meal happened in an exotic location or a world-class restaurant. Picture yourself back there. What do you remember about the food? Is there one particular dish that comes to mind? Is it served hot or cold? Are you imagining a specific bowl? Is the meal resting on a table or spread out on a blanket? Picture yourself putting the food in your mouth. What are those first tastes like? As you recall this delicious meal, look around you. Where are you? Who is there with you? What time of day or year is it? How many details can you recall? Spend some time here reconnecting with that moment, the food, and the people you shared this meal with. Notice if your body has relaxed. Is your mouth filling with saliva? Are you smiling, just thinking about this special time?

What would it be like if every meal, or at least a greater number of the meals you eat, were as memorable as this meal? What made this meal so very different? One magickal ingredient might be time.

A Little Bit of Time Magick

Thomas Moore, the former monk turned author and lecturer, published a book in the late 1990s titled *The Re-Enchantment of Everyday Life*. A substantial part of my magickal practice has been directly influenced by this excellent book. A well-thumbed and dog-eared copy occupies a prime spot on my bookshelves and I often find that I'm leafing through it to reacquaint myself with a particular passage on this or that. The major premise of the book is that far too many people have become disenchanted with their own lives. Moore goes on to say that living a life devoid of wonder and connection slowly robs us of our humanity, fosters a sense of "aloneness," and leaves the soul desperately searching for more of an ineffable *something* that seems impossible to define, let alone attain.

Now, re-enchanting a whole life seems like a lot of work. Worthwhile work, to be sure, but a daunting task nonetheless. I like to take on my enchantments in bite-sized pieces. Let's start by examining our relationship to time in relation to food. Because no matter what we might choose to do with our time or what choices are made for us about how we should spend our time, time is the only thing we really have.

REVERSE MENU

Try this ten-minute magickal exercise. Arrange your world so that you can be undisturbed for ten minutes. Grab a piece of paper and something to write with. Get comfortable. Rewind your life to yesterday, whenever your day started. What was the first thing you ate or drank? What were the next things? Recall everything you ate and drank yesterday. Write down each meal. Then go back to the first entry and detail where you were. Were you sitting in a vehicle? On a sunlit veranda? At your kitchen table? Repeat this as you move along yesterday's timeline. Go back to your list a third time and note what you were thinking about when you were cooking or buying the food you ate. Can you remember any details about each meal? Was it sunny or cold? What tastes stand out to you? Who were you with and what were you talking about or doing?

If it hasn't been ten minutes yet, just stay there with yesterday and the food and the memories. Take the full ten minutes.

To be clear, it doesn't really matter what you ate. If it was organic beets harvested from your own garden, potato chips purchased from a local convenience store, or half a gallon of coffee hurriedly polished off before the rest of your household woke up, that's just fine and dandy. This is not about judging yourself for the food choices you made. It's about time. How did you spend time with food and yourself?

There's a particular enchantment in slowing down time and eating purposely. One of the first lessons many magick workers discover is the art of being present. You may know this as grounding, centering, mindfulness, the ability to draw in one's breath and be here now. Almost every magickal system, in fact virtually every spiritual tradition, has a practice of intentionally paying attention and participating, being acutely aware of what's happening in this specific moment. The practice of becoming present, aware of the moment, is often ritualized at the beginning of spell work, public magickal events, or coven gatherings. Maybe you've been asked to take a breath, turn off your electronic devices, shower, wear certain clothes, disrobe, or hold hands in a circle and acknowledge the presence of the other human beings you are convening with. All of these methods are designed to bring you, or you and the group, or you and the magick you are creating, into accord with one another, thereby making the connection to the magick that much more potent, powerful, and personal. Apply the practice of becoming present when you next eat or cook. You may find that an interesting thing happens when you slow down and become mindful of your interactions with food. You'll appreciate what you're eating and, maybe more importantly, the food will taste better.

AN ENCHANTED CUP OF TEA

Do you have a favourite beverage, something that you can drink pretty often, maybe even on a regular basis? That simple glass or cup of liquid is going to make you a better witch and spell worker. I enjoy a cup of tea, so I'll use my love of tea as an example. I like tea in the morning and in the afternoon. English tea, Irish tea, tea from Ceylon, green tea, jasmine tea … pretty much any collection of leaves and water and I'm good to go. My cousin, who still lives in England, asked me once how I made my tea. "Do you just put a tea bag in a cup or do you still make it properly?"

I told her I still made it properly. She went on, "Properly, like with loose leaves in a teapot or with tea bags?" Now, if the truth is to be told, I do sometimes pop a PG Tips tea bag into a cup, pour water over it, and call that a cuppa. But more often than not, I prefer to use my trusty old brown Betty teapot. There's something magickal that happens when I do.

The first step is to grab the teapot. I wipe it down if it's dusty and look inside to make sure it's clean. I swish hot water around the inside of the teapot to warm it, just like my grandmothers taught me to do. Water gets boiled and a couple of heaping teaspoons of tea are added to the teapot. There's that magick moment when water and tea leaves meet and swirl together as the tea begins to steep. While the tea is brewing, I find a cup or mug that draws my attention. There are probably forty cups in my house. Some were gifted to me by friends or family members as mementos of a trip they'd been on. Others have been collected at thrift stores because I thought they were neat, or cool, or odd, or pretty, or attention grabbing in some way. My cups reflect my mood, and I'm convinced they affect the taste of the tea. There are dainty, flowery cups, pretty as a Victorian garden, and hefty, handcrafted mugs that beg to be held close to my heart, warming my insides and my outsides at the same time.

Once I've selected the perfect vessel, I take the teapot and cup over to the kitchen table and I pour the tea. Frequently someone will join me. It might be a person. It might be the cat or one of the dogs, but I don't tend to drink the tea alone. And it tastes better the longer I savour it. And conversation happens. (Yes, I talk to the dogs. The cat mostly ignores me.) And that conversation usually turns into a second cup of tea. The second cup of tea has even been known to turn into a second pot of tea. These few minutes of letting loose leaves and ideas brew becomes a spell of re-enchantment. Making an afternoon cuppa becomes a magickal moment of connection, a gift to myself.

Your version of this ritual might feature sipping tea in a tall glass while sitting in your backyard or milking your goat and enjoying fresh milk every morning. Heck! A beer on a Friday night, drunk straight from the bottle as you take time to reflect on the week you had works just fine too. The idea is to create space and contemplate your life. What's your life's work? Have you seen the vision of the magick you want to manifest? Let inspiration well up from those hidden recesses of your being that rarely get listened to because they're drowned out with louder thoughts. This simple ritual may let worries and stresses fall away and open your magickal practices up to something wonderful. Creating time for a simple drinking ritual adds a splash of re-enchantment to the mundane.

THE MAGICK OF DINING OUT

The following is a process for creating magick with any restaurant experience. Some of these suggestions might be difficult, but I promise with these magickal workings, eating in restaurants will never be the same.

Decide where and when you are going to eat. Go to the restaurant alone and then step into the process. In order for the magick to work, you have to give up three things and then do three things during the meal. First, give these up:

1. **Judgement.** Easy-peasy, right? Arrive at the restaurant and begin letting go of your judgements. This might be your own inner conversations about your food choice, about spoiling yourself by spending money on a meal, or any number of other things. Let that go. You deserve this meal, wherever you find yourself. Imagine leaving your judgements in a paper bag right outside the front door. If you want my advice, right after you drop your concerns and interior conversations into your judgement bag, purposely forget to pick that sack of judgements back up again when you leave.

2. **Expectations.** Try it, you'll like it! You might order the big bowl of clam chowder every time you go to Jes's Chowder Shack. Maybe sitting in the booth near the back is what you always do. That diner on Trinity Street could be a place you only go with certain friends or for a special occasion. Let that all go. Give it up. You are not there with friends today, it's not your wedding anniversary, and ordering what you order every other time is not a menu option today. In fact, you're not going to order the food at all.

3. **Decision making.** This is a doozy. It's a challenge for sure, and it's just possible that you'll read the next guidelines and exclaim "Forget that nonsense!" You are going to intentionally and consciously hand over the decision-making process to someone else. The person at the counter, your waitstaff, or the cook is in charge of your entire dining experience. Choosing what we want to eat is a big deal and giving up that choice is likely to dredge up all sorts of fears about scarcity, not liking particular foods, and giving your power away. This magickal working, to be successful, requires you to sacrifice a little. Here's how it works. Look over the menu. Be sure to note if there are foods you cannot eat for health reasons, like if you have an allergy to shellfish, for instance. Look over the menu and discount only the foods you cannot eat, as opposed to the dishes you wouldn't ordinarily eat. Now the menu is wide open and you're about to let someone else order your food.

Now here are the three things you must do:

1. **Engage in personal contact.** You must make eye contact with the waitperson when they are at your table, and you must refer to them by name. Most chain restaurants give their staff name tags, so this is simple enough. In other restaurants you might have to pluck up the courage and ask them for their name. It's okay. This could bring up some awkwardness for you, but I promise you'll survive if you do this. I'll explain why this step is so important later, but for now, just trust that this is an important piece of the magick.

2. **Ask for recommendations.** I find this part the most exciting and I know a fair few people who are mortified by the prospect of what I'm about to propose. This is a big step; are you ready? Ask your server what their favourite dishes are on the menu. I usually start the conversation with something like this: "Hey Andy, what do you love to eat here?" If they say, "I love the French onion soup. It's the best in town," you respond with, "Great! I'll have that. What would you suggest after that?" To make it easier on them, I might let them know that I have a total of $50 to spend on this meal (or $20 or $100, or whatever your budget is). To help them hone in on the perfect meal for me, I might comment that I'm super excited to try anything on the menu, as long as it doesn't contain peanuts. Other than that, they get to completely surprise me by bringing me only what they love to eat. I take the extra step of assuring them that they can't make a bad choice and won't screw this up no matter what they bring me. I'll often note that I've perused the menu and everything looks good, so no matter what bowl, plate, or glass appears before me, I'll be good. This takes any fears they may have about giving you the wrong dish or making a poor choice and having it impact their tip or worse yet, causing you to make a complaint to their manager.

3. **Tip.** Tip the waitstaff well. They worked hard for you. They selected your dishes, thought about how one course would build on another, highlighting their favourite combinations of food. They deserve to be rewarded for this, no matter how much you enjoyed the meal (or not). If the establishment you're dining at builds the tip into the bill or you're frequenting a place where tipping isn't a customary practice, there's an additional step you get to do. Call over the manager, maître d', or even the host that greeted you. Praise the waitperson. "I asked Andy to bring me a selection of courses that were their top choices and the meal was just delicious. Please let them know how much I appreciated their care and attention and for playing along with me today."

There's solid magickal reasoning behind the three things you've been asked to give up and the three things you've been asked to do. As magick workers we often call on the gods or elements or mystery to intervene in our rituals and rites, but we script the results so tightly that we don't leave a lot of room for anything wondrous or surprising to happen. We know when the magick will begin, what words will be said, and who does what. Even in ecstatic, non-book-centric traditions, there's often a common format or expectation that a ritual or spell will look and sound a certain way and be completed in a specific time frame. While there is tremendous value in repeating magickal structures that work, there's an inherent danger that our magickal practices can stagnate, become comfortable and predictable, and then be less effective. There's an old saying, "magick happens where your comfort zone ends," and I believe that to be true. Human beings are extremely habitual. We like what we like and, unless we're forced to, most people rarely move beyond their comfort zone and try anything new. Our food choices display our habituation blatantly and absolutely.

Step one, dropping your judgement, challenges your own motives and moves you beyond questioning what you want to do versus what you think you should do. Look, if your feet take you to "Charlie's Cheesecake Emporium," go with it. Right now, something in you wants whatever magick cheesecake holds and you don't need to spend seven hours pacing backwards and forwards from your car to the front door of the restaurant, chastising yourself for wanting a huge slice of New York–style cheesecake topped with the most decadent blueberry sauce in the world. You want what you want, so go get it and enjoy every sumptuous mouthful. The magick here is all about honouring what is calling you in the moment, fulfilling your heart's desire. On another level, the magick here deals with listening deeply to your body and turning off the chattering in your head that tells you the thirty-seven reasons why you shouldn't eat a perfectly seasoned center-cut pork chop, red bliss potatoes, and garlicky green beans for lunch by yourself just because you want to. You know what? You totally can.

Letting go of your expectations is crucial for the magick to work. One of my dear mentors has drummed it into my head that the magickal intention set for any spell work or ritual needs to be specific enough to be clear, but open enough to leave room for mystery. If you show up at a different restaurant than you expected, that's a great start, but if you go ahead and order the vegetable curry like you do every time you find yourself in a southeast Asian restaurant, you're going to have expectations about what a navratan korma is supposed to taste like. It's not that expectation in and of itself is a bad thing, but magickally speaking, expectation can limit how you view the results of your spell work, because you could dismiss or outright miss a result that didn't fit what you believed would happen. When you eat something new or unexpected, you may discover tastes and nuances in the dish that enliven your taste buds, or warm your belly, or inspire you to explore similar flavour combinations. Those curiosities might open a whole world of culinary and cultural adventures and, quite literally, flavour your magick for the rest of your life.

Giving your decision-making power over to the waitstaff really can push your buttons, but it is totally worth it. The magick here is an invitation to mystery, to chance, to calling in the unexpected and reveling in it rather than fearing it. For the past several years on my birthday, I get whisked off to a different restaurant. I never know where I'm going or what kind of food is going to be served. I've found myself pampered in three Michelin-star restaurants and standing in line on a cold winter's night waiting for tacos from a truck. There have been birthday lunches at a converted brothel and high tea with scones and jams and petit fours, made with all-vegan ingredients.

One memorable birthday meal was at a small, family-run, newly-opened Ethiopian eatery. Our party was greeted at the door by the thirty-year-old owner, who had recently immigrated to the area. I looked over the menu, realised I knew nothing about Ethiopian food and asked for his recommendations. His face absolutely lit up as he went through each dish on the menu. For sure he listed ingredients, but it was the tales of where he learned to cook *wat*, an Ethiopian stew, that really captured my attention. Describing how his mother's recipe for *kinche*, an oatmeal-like breakfast dish, reminded him so much of his childhood and how he was cared for and nourished by his family. I wanted to eat kinche right then and there.

He excused himself for a few minutes and emerged from the kitchen with an elderly woman in tow. Turns out this short, round, beaming person was his mother and he wanted to introduce her to us. Still a bit bemused by the sheer number of dishes on the menu, I asked if she would just bring us what she loved to cook. Nothing that came out of the kitchen that day was on the menu. We learned how to pile our food onto injera bread, and quaffed tej, a honey wine similar to mead.

Each person present for the meal thoroughly enjoyed exchanging stories about the "food where I come from." The whole meal cost less than $30 per person and we were there for hours. It was one of the best food experiences of my life, but imagine if I'd gotten to the front door of the restaurant and said, "I don't know anything about this kind of food, let's go to the local burger joint because I know what I can order there." Opening to the mystery and magick of the unexpected led to a new appreciation and passion for the incredibly rich, savoury, and complex flavours of Ethiopian cuisine. Engaging with your magickal practices with the same sense of mystery and earnest exploration, and seeking out new and different information will change how you approach magick, how you make magick, and the way you measure how effective your magick is.

In many magickal traditions, offering thanks to the gods is part of, maybe even the reason for, engaging in ritual. For non-deity or non-religion-based craft practices, appreciating the wonders and incalculable permutations, mutations, and variations of nature can be fulfilling components of regular practice. It's common to thank the gods and notice the beauty of our planet; it's not always so easy to notice and appreciate the person bringing you pancakes, scrambled eggs, hash browns, bacon, and orange juice at seven-thirty in the morning in the hotel restaurant, while you're reading work emails on your phone or checking your secret social media group to catch up what your coven mates are doing. But appreciating your waitstaff, calling them by name, and saying please and thank you is just as important, maybe even more necessary, than your devotional practice to the goddess Bridgit or your daily ablutions to Thor.

Think back on the last time you ate at a sit-down restaurant. Did someone greet you at the door and take you to your table? Another person may have dropped off water or brought you coffee. Yet another person came by and asked if you were ready to order, told you all the options (hash browns or country fries, sourdough or whole wheat toast). Do you remember their name, the colour of their hair, or what the tattoo on their wrist said? Did you ask them how their day was going? If their shift had just started or if they were getting ready to head out for the day? Many witches spend hours, weeks even, planning spells, researching herbal combinations, the phases of the moon, the best time to do money-drawing work. Ask a hundred witches to rattle off the ingredients for a love brew and you'll get a veritable Book of Shadows' worth of detailed information about their most successful spells. Ask those same magick workers the name of the person that just brought them eggs benedict and a steaming cup of Earl Grey tea and you'll likely get blank stares.

Witch work is all about connections and correspondences. Spells will work faster, stronger, longer if we get the correct combination of components gathered in just the right configuration. No herb, no drop of essential oil, no word in our incantation is unimportant, right? Apply that same idea to a dining experience. The waitstaff, the bus person, the host at the front of the restaurant, the dishwashers, and the cooks all contribute to your experience of the meal. No contribution is unimportant and, in this case specifically, no person is unimportant to the process. Just as you would thank the gods or your ancestors or the planets or the herbs or your teachers for the wisdom they bring to your magick, also thank the person that brings you a knife, fork, spoon, and a timely hotter-upper when your coffee cup is almost empty.

THE BUFFER ZONE

Tell me if this sounds familiar. You finally match up your schedule with your best friend's schedule and you plan to meet for lunch at Bistro XYZ. On the way to your lunch date, you go to the post office, swing by the office supply store to get printer ink, drive around looking for parking, and arrive just in time to sit down and order your meal. A few minutes into hearing about your friend's day, which consists of them telling you how busy they've been, you realise that you've got to pick the kids up in an hour or need to get to the next thing on your list and before you know it, you are talking about that instead of talking with your friend.

Try employing a buffer zone. Agree that the meal is going to start at 12:30 p.m. Also agree to arrive by 12:00 p.m. That extra half hour is dedicated to putting away coats, ordering the first drink, or finding the right table. In other words, set aside a specific period of time to get all of the busyness out of the way, so that when it's time to sit down, eat, and chat, everyone can be fully present for that purpose and that alone.

If circumstances are such that you don't dine out all that often, employ the buffer zone at home as well. You may have a busy household with housemates, kids, partners, or four-legged companions. Meal times can be hectic and not at all fulfilling. Again, the Sumerians had it right when they noted the differences between simply shoveling food into our mouths and actually dining. If your household mealtimes are frantic, rushed, anything but calming and restorative, consider employing the buffer zone. And to be super transparent, one doesn't need a house full of other people to have a less than wonderful meal or to have need of a buffer zone. I've had more than my share of meals when I rush home from my day, throw my car keys on the counter, hurriedly grab something from the fridge, dance around the stove clanging pots and lids together, and throw a meal together quickly, all before the next thing I'm supposed to be doing begins.

What often occurs when you apply a buffer zone is this delicious moment when each person connects, makes eye contact, and takes a big breath together. It happens pretty organically, and it happens virtually every time. We begin settling into the time we have rather than being engaged with the time we don't have because it's filled with all sorts of other things to do. And that breath, that pause, is like a mini devotion honouring everybody present. Time slows down and shared food can then become the vehicle for connection and magick.

A Collection of Old Bowls

If time is the vehicle by which we appreciate the exquisite tastes of life, then what we fill our life with must be the spices. I choose to fill my life with a collection of old bowls. Oddly shaped and old bowls made of ceramic or wood fascinate me. I wonder what lives they've led before making their way to my cupboards. I have a wooden salad bowl that I bought at a thrift store I don't know how many years ago. It is rough-hewn on the outside, but perfectly smooth on the inside. When I run my fingers around the outer edges, I feel indentations that remind me that someone else's hands made this and cherished it. Over the years I've served rustic salads of wildcrafted greens, homemade sourdough rolls, and who knows what else out of this bowl. It's been placed on more magickal altars that I could ever recount. Serving food in this simple handmade bowl that I love so much makes a meal special in a way I find hard to define, but I believe it has to do with three distinct facets: I've formed a connection with this bowl. It's handmade. The bowl is made of natural materials. Each of these facets add a certain magick to the bowl and, ultimately, serves the magick I'm creating.

The materials that bowls or plates or serving platters are made of are important. Beyond the practical and mundane features of what makes them durable or easy to wash, for instance, is the connection to nature and our fellow human beings. Most of my most cherished serving bowls and cooking pans were gifted to me. None of them were overly expensive or top of the line, but they are all special to me. As I look at them, I'm struck by how many of them are handmade or, at the very least, had a human's hands on them to finish the making process. Because of that they are always just a little unique. One edge is a little thicker than another, there's a flaw in the glaze. I'm not sure just why, but salads are always tastier when they are served up in a large wooden bowl. Perhaps it has to do with the fact that the components of the salad were once living, growing plants and so were the components of the bowl. It could be that the variegated colour tones of brown and taupe and the swirl of the grain compliment the fresh green shades found in the food. There's a vague memory that container and contained are from the same source, and something in that adds an extra, invisible, ingredient that perfectly completes the flavour of the dish.

The memory of the thing transforms an ordinary cup into a magickal chalice. Plates that are hand painted carry a piece of the person that decorated them. A silver serving dish purchased at an antique store brings back memories of your romantic getaway with a beloved partner all those years ago. There's an egg cup for serving soft-boiled eggs, in my cupboard. It's plastic and has two outstretched feet with faded baby blue Mary Jane shoes. My grandmother bought it somewhere when I was three or four years old. Once upon a time there was a matching egg cup with pink shoes. One was hers, the other mine. There were probably a million of those egg cups mass produced, but the one in my cupboard is a one-of-a-kind treasure because her hands touched it. She taught me how to make "dippy eggs" and when to pull the bread out from under the grill and cut the warm toast into "soldiers" to dip into the yolk.

TAKING STOCK OF YOUR KITCHEN

Look around your kitchen, your dining room, the box you keep childhood mementos in. What cooking items do you have that instantly transport you elsewhere, to another time, another version of you? What memories are contained in the cracks and chips and worn paint? If you haven't done this already, share the stories of your beloved pots, pans, bowls, plates, and mixing spoons with other people in your life. Is there a chalice your coven uses during ritual? Where did you get it? Did you order it from an online retailer or find it in a thrift store at the bottom of a plastic tub full of odd cups and glasses? Why did you pick that particular plate to serve your magickal offerings on? Is it a family heirloom, a gift from another person in your magickal tradition, found at booth at a Pagan conference where you got to meet with the artist and learn what inspired them to create the horned-god motif baked into the clay? Every item you cook or serve with came from somewhere and has a story.

Stand in your kitchen. Find one bowl, plate, cup, whatever. Hold it in your hands, or if it's too big and heavy, place it on the counter or a table and feel all around it; top, bottom, inside, outside. How have you used this item? What meals has this item been part of? Who has eaten from this? Whom have you fed? If this item had a voice, what stories would it tell about the magick it's been involved with? And lastly, what stories have you told about this magickal piece of earthenware?

You might be asking, "Why am I standing in the kitchen talking to the mixing bowl"? It's a fair question. If your magickal belief system encompasses the theory that every rock, stone, tree, wand, athame, and statue has its own life and experiences, then by that same magickal logic it follows that so does every teaspoon, baking dish, beer mug, and little round bowl you always make your famous guacamole in. If your kitchen gadgets and implements have been used to make magickal meals, then it's quite likely that they carry a piece of that magick with them (it's a proven fact in my household that no amount of dish soap can clean off magick…or burnt lasagna!).

The word *soul* comes to mind here. You needn't necessarily believe in a soul, or that inanimate objects are somehow alive, but by using a thing over and over again for a specific purpose it does become imbued with a certain ineffable *something*. Maybe your word is different than mine. Your connection to your special cooking tool might be characterized as memory, or quirkiness, or personality, but there's a definite *something* that happens when you mix your bread dough with *that* spoon, or serve your grandfather's paella in *that* bowl. That's the soul coming through. Another way to think of it is residual magick. Have you ever had the experience when cooking that the oven or mixer or bowl knows what it's doing even when you don't? It's like it's saying, "Oh! I'm filled with enchiladas again. I remember this recipe; it was handed down by their *abuelita*. They like it best when I let the edges get just a little too crispy. I'll get to work on those edges right now!"

Just as doing the unexpected can bring new insights to your magick, working with familiar tools, proven recipes, and beloved cooking artefacts adds a certain known quality to the magick you're making. Another word for familiarity might be *tradition*. Family and magickal traditions ensure that the knowledge and wisdom and practices that served those that have gone before us live on and thrive. When you next pull out your favourite dish or magickal tool, reflect on all the magick, laughter, sorrow, and community you've shared with this bowl or spoon.

Sing to Your Food

Yes! You read that correctly and it means exactly what you think it means. Sing to your food. It's simple and great magick. I'd also recommend expanding the idea to singing for your food, singing about your food, and singing with your food. After all, singing to your food is a terrific way to remember simple recipes. For example, I don't know anyone that puts the coconut in the lime and stirs it. We all know to put the lime in the coconut, and then, shake it all up. If you're familiar with this recipe, there's a good chance that right now you have a song in your head that will be there for the rest of the day. You're welcome.

But why would you sing to your food? Well, it has a lot to do with joy and connection. I cannot tell you how many times I've cooked chicken, potatoes, and broccoli. Ask my children and they'll tell you they've eaten it about a gazillion times. Cooking, especially cooking every day for other people, can get monotonous. Don't get me wrong, I love cooking for friends and family, but negotiating the foods that everyone *can* eat versus what they *will* eat, versus what they *want* to eat, plus what's in the budget to provide said foods can render food preparation an act of total drudgery. Throw in the shopping and the chopping and washing the dishes and you have a recipe for kitchen burnout. And that's where joy comes in.

Singing releases endorphins. Endorphins are frequently referred to as the body's "'feel good" chemicals. Singing, even if you do it under your breath so no one can hear you, increases the flow of oxygen to your brain. Oxygen feeds the brain and improves your overall mental alertness. When most people sing, they experience joy. Even if you're listening to other people sing, your "joy" levels increase. As you sing, or hear others sing and your body releases endorphins, you stave off those feelings of "Sweet Brigid's ghost, am I really baking skinless chicken and making mashed potatoes *again*?" Quite literally, you're singing away any feelings of drudgery and replacing them with more joyful sensations. Singing to your food lowers your stress levels, curtails cortisol production, increases your joy levels, potentially enhances the experiences of those in your proximity because they also derive pleasure from hearing you sing, and makes the food taste better because you are more mentally alert and less likely to confuse the salt for the sugar.

The science and psychology of singing to your food is clear, but what about the magick? That's pretty clear too, and it has everything to do with connection. Part of being a magick worker is to see and act upon the connections we feel with the totality of what's around us. The artichokes in your garden are alive, and so is the basil growing in your kitchen window. When you sing to them, you are connecting with them. You might sing to your vegetables about how beautiful their leaves look today or the cleverness of knowing how to face the sun so that the ears of corn they are working on just this minute will be ever so sweet in a couple of months. Maybe you'll feel silly singing to runner beans or acorn squash. I say go ahead and feel silly. Part of being a witch is to be wonderfully eccentric anyway, isn't it?

Let's stay with this idea of magickal connection though. Do you believe in nature spirits, or garden fairies, or ladybugs that eat aphids? You see, singing is a well-attested-to pastime of the fairy folk. In William Shakespeare's *A Midsummer Night's Dream,* Titania, the queen of the fairies, exclaims:

> *First, rehearse your song by rote.*
> *To each word a warbling note:*
> *Hand in hand, with fairy grace,*
> *Will we sing, and bless this place.*

Singing and blessing the places where our food comes from seems like a very good use of magickal energy. How do the nature beings, seen and unseen, contribute to your food? When you sing to your food, you invite the Good Folk or the spirits of place or the Devas of the vegetable patch to do their best work. Singing encourages connection with the unseen forces of nature that work with us to transform these incredible materials of flesh, seed, and fruit into wonderful meals that sustain the human folk that then, in turn, plant more, sing more, and connect more to the world around them. Again, when you connect with the food growing in your garden or window boxes, or the foods you buy from the grocery store, or even the fast food you pick up because you're running late and you connect with it in some way, you're doing magick.

Chapter 6
Food and Sex

Let's talk about making out. Now, I realise that some people might find it odd to mix recipes with a discussion about magick and doing the deed, but they really do go hand in hand. Speaking of hands, think about all of the wondrous things you might do with your hands when being intimate with another person, or persons, or by yourself. Have you ever had the experience of ever so lightly brushing the back of your hand against the hand of a lover, or soon-to-be lover? That slightest of touches sends a million sensations rushing up and down your nervous system. Hands and fingers play a significant role in how we experience intimate physical contact. When we touch another person, especially someone we're close to, our bodies release oxytocin. When we release oxytocin, our nervous system is flooded with this "feel good" hormone. We relax, we feel love, our capacity for trust increases, and we remember other times in our lives when we felt comforted, safe, and happy.

Part of what makes really good sex and great touch so enjoyable is that it involves all of our senses, our imaginations, and our bodies. Guess what else involves all of our senses and our hands, feels great, brings comfort, and increases happiness? That's right! Cooking and eating food.

Why Aphrodisiacs Work

A good meal, even just one perfect bite, does it for me. Maybe you're the same way. Our friends the ancient Greeks certainly believed that the appetite for food and the appetite for the pleasures of the flesh were inextricably intertwined. They even invented the term for foods that stimulate the libido. The name comes from one of the most famous love goddesses ever, Aphrodite. As the story goes, the god Cronos had issues with his father, Uranus. Cronos grabbed a scythe and hacked off his father's genitals, which he then tossed into the sea, as angry scythe-wielding Titans are prone to doing. As the severed naughty bits hit the water, a white foam formed around them, and from this unlikely source, the goddess Aphrodite rose from the roiling waters on a clam shell.

Aphrodite was beloved. Aphrodite was beautiful and voluptuous and went on to become the goddess of love and fertility and all things having to do with the attainment of physical pleasure. Not bad work. I can imagine Aphrodite as the muse for the line in Doreen Valiente's *The Charge of the Goddess:* "ye shall dance, sing, feast, make music and love, all in my praise." Festivals, called *aphrodisiacs*, were held in honour of the goddess, and by some accounts, purportedly were an excuse for debauchery and a money-making scheme for the temples. Today the term *aphrodisiac* quite literally means foods, drinks, and potions that make us more likely to be amorous. But how do aphrodisiacs actually work? Oh, let me count the ways!

Spend two minutes doing basic research about aphrodisiacs and you'll find one of three basic answers: (1) Yes! Science says some common aphrodisiacs have an impact on your sex drive; (2) No! The science says most common aphrodisiacs don't have much of an impact on your sex drive; and (3) You guessed it, maybe some foods do have actual aphrodisiacal properties, but more studies need to be done.

Let's delve into the science for a quick minute. Certain foods commonly associated with being aphrodisiacs, like chocolate and oysters, do have chemical compounds in them that, in theory, could increase your sex drive or level of arousal. In the case of oysters, it has to do with zinc levels. Zinc plays a role in the production of testosterone, and testosterone has an impact on sex drive.[26] The science is pretty clear. A diet with sufficient zinc levels can aid in the production of testosterone. Now, while eating oysters and other foods high in zinc might be good for your overall health, it's super unlikely that gulping down a dozen oysters is going to do anything for your sex life tonight. There are no

---

26. Elizabeth Brown. "Zinc for Appetite Control." *Healthfully.* https://healthfully.com/421465-zinc-testos terone.html.

results that show a direct "eat this and experience that" correlation out there that have ever been proven. But the nutrients in food is only a small portion of the story.

Human beings and our bodies are paradoxically incredibly complicated and maddeningly simple all at the same time. In a very broad and general sense, two of humankind's strongest desires are hunger and sex. Biologically speaking, one ensures that we survive as an individual, the other makes sure that we continue on as a species. When we eat food, our bodies produce something called leptin. Leptin is released when food is being broken down and stored as fat. Interestingly enough, leptin is a key ingredient in the process of arousal too because of what it tells the body. Leptin says, "Hey body! You've eaten enough food for now. We aren't going to starve today. Well done you for eating." The body responds with "Oh! Excellent news. Thanks for the message, leptin, much appreciated. I'm going to concentrate on that other basic need now." Basically, leptin shuts off certain processes that regulate the need for food, paving the way for other hormones, like dopamine, to ramp up their activity.

But what does this have to do with magick? I'm glad you asked, but first let's talk about colour and taste.

Colour and Taste

There's a basic principle in magick that says "like attracts like." Plato said it in about 390 BCE in his *First Law of Affinity*. The core practice is that similar things are attracted to each other and tend to go well with each other. This is where the whole idea of magickal correspondences comes from. Working with certain herbs, tools, and magickal items that have some form of mystical connection on particular days or nights will increase the likelihood of the magickal spell being effective, because similar things will produce similar results. It's much the same with sex and food and aphrodisiacs.

Contemplate warmed figs as an example of like attracts like. Have you ever eaten warmed figs? Flick your tongue into the soft, pink flesh of a ripened fig, hot from the oven, and inhale the juicy, aromatic stickiness as it fills your mouth. The shape and colour of figs are suggestive enough, but add heat and hold on! The way a cooked fig feels in your hands and mouth is tantalizing and evocative. Heat a fig and you've got something highly charged with aphrodisiac properties. I like my figs drizzled with honey and topped with feta cheese, to add more sweetness, saltiness, and let's be honest, sheer sexiness.

Super-Quick Bonus Recipe for Warmed Figs

There are amino acids and nutrients in fresh figs that are good for your health, but it's the way they look and feel and taste that makes them such good aphrodisiacs. The shape, colour, and taste are truly suggestive of something else. What works on our brains is the fact that figs are like something else we want and, on occasion, when served in just the right way, can bring about or approximate what we desire.

Serves 2 (or more, depending on how voracious you are)	Prep Time: 10 minutes	Cooking Time: 8 minutes

12 fresh figs, destemmed, cut in half, and arranged on a baking tray

3 tablespoons honey

1 tablespoon olive oil

Crumbled feta cheese (maybe ¼ teaspoon to ½ teaspoon per fig)

Preheat your oven to 400° F. Cut the figs in half and place on a baking sheet. Combine the honey and olive oil in a small bowl and slather each fig with the honey and olive oil mixture. Top the figs with crumbled feta cheese. Bake in the oven for approximately 8 minutes. The cheese should be melted and gooey. Serve on a nest of blankets and pillows, with the lights turned low.

Staying with colour and taste for a moment, imagine going to a restaurant and being served a plate of greyish mush. How do you think you might feel about that food? Is it likely to wow you and scintillate your senses? Probably not. Before food ever gets into our mouths and activates our taste buds, our eyes start sending messages to our brain about what deliciousness is coming our way. Foods that excite our eyes are likely to stimulate all sorts of other areas in our brains too. When we find food visually stimulating, our curiosity neurons start firing. What does this food taste like? How is the texture going to feel in my mouth? Is that red morsel hanging out on the edge of the plate spicy or sweet?

Remember leptin and dopamine? As our curiosity grows and we get excited about the meal we are about to eat, leptin chimes in and says, "This is gonna be great. We aren't going to starve. Cue the dopamine." And just like that, dopamine levels spike. Now, dopamine is connected to the pleasure and reward center in our brain. Our brains are hardwired to reward curiosity because being curious is one of the ways humans learn things. "What is that fascinating fruit over there hanging on yonder tree? Perhaps I'll take a bite and see what I might learn" says the brain. We taste the apple and love it and dopamine kicks in and cries, "It was worth the risk. Look! That ripe, red apple was delicious; I knew it would be and now you know it too."

At the same time, other fascinating things are going on in our bodies as the dopamine moves about. We get more social. We talk a little more. We engage with the person or people we're eating with just a bit more freely. We get curious about what's on their plate (here comes more dopamine), and reach across the table to snag that tender piece of braised short rib or succulent chocolate-covered strawberry. I bet you can guess where all of this is leading. Colourful, intriguing, tasty, spicy, sweet, "oh hello taste buds, this is going to be exciting" foods packed with unexpected flavours and textures and unique combinations get us chemically all hot and bothered. As we explore the dishes set before us and ask more questions (more dopamine on table four, please), we associate the good feelings with the people we're with. The food is exciting. They are exciting. The food is spicy and so is the conversation. The food tastes great, and … well you can finish that thought by yourself, I'm sure.

Super-Quick Bonus Recipe for Chocolate Fondue and Strawberries

Juicy, red, chilled strawberries. Dark, hot, lush, silky chocolate. Combine the two and the result is pure decadence. And now that you're right there imagining this dish, here's the recipe. It's quick and sure to please your new friend, dopamine.

Serves 2 (or more)	Prep Time: 10 minutes	Cooking Time: 15 minutes

12 ounces chocolate (semi-sweet, dark, milk, your choice)

1 cup heavy whipping cream

2 tablespoons brandy (mix up the flavour by using Grand Marnier or flavoured brandy to match the fruit of your choice)

1 pint whole strawberries (substitute strawberries for sliced peaches, bananas, or forego the fruit altogether and just lick the bowl)

Grab a medium saucepan and fill it halfway with water. Set it on high heat.

Place a bowl (glass preferably, but stainless steel will work fine too) in the saucepan as the water begins to heat up. Add all of the chocolate to the bowl and let it begin to melt down. Stir a lot to help it melt. Pour in the cream and brandy when half of the chocolate is melted. Keep stirring until the mixture is smooth. Remove the chocolate from the heat, place in a serving bowl, and dip your fruit in it.

Serving suggestion: Put way too much chocolate on your strawberry so it spills onto your chin, chest, or belly and use your fingers to scoop up the chocolate. Smile as you do this.

Making the Magick Just Right

Depending on your view of magick, leptin and dopamine might not be the first components you think of when creating an amorous food spell. So, let's focus on the magick for a bit.

Imagine you're cooking a magickal meal for yourself, an intimate partner, or beloved ones. What's your intention for this meal? Are you looking to pamper them with their favourite foods or ignite their passions? Is this magick about creating a lavish, sumptuous meal that will cause love to deepen, or do you need just a few delicious bites to excite the brain and stimulate a more immediate reaction?

One good rule about making magick is to have an idea of what the outcome could be and leave enough room to make changes along the way as the magick develops. When you combine magick and cookery, the need for precision *and* flexibility is even more prevalent. Things go sideways in magick and cooking pretty quickly, so having a plan and sticking to it until you need to throw it out the window and move to Plan B is always advised. Plus, sometimes magick and cookery work so well that you forget what you did and don't care. Do you really think that someone intended to make coffee such a good marinade for tri-tip? No! They went on a camping trip with the intention to marinate some beef and impress their date, forgot to pack what they needed, and used coffee and sugar, and said "let's see if it works." Then they got married. True story.

But let's return to the piece of magick we're working here. In this case we're talking specifically about foods that will stimulate sexuality or desire or passion. Our spell starts long before the food ever hits the plate and any clothes hit the floor. This magick begins at the supermarket, the farmer's market, the quickie mart around the corner, your backyard garden vegetable patch, or wherever you get your food from. If you are fortunate to live in an area with plenty of fresh foods, try this.

SHOPPING WITH YOUR SENSES

Walk around the produce section (without a cart or basket). Just wander a bit. Notice what colours draw your attention first. Is it the bright red of a fresh tomato? Are you attracted to the deep, glossy purple of an eggplant? Maybe it's the greens that call out to you—deep green kale, containers of mixed, verdant lettuces, beet greens, collard greens. Just saying the word *green* over and over again starts my imagination firing. Now pick up a melon, or mushrooms, or a bunch of broccoli. Hold them to your nose and bury your whole face in them; fully inhale the scents. Can you smell soil or sunshine or sweetness? Touch the food. Simply handle the produce, noticing firmness and softness, weight and texture, size and shape. What calls to you in this moment? Which colours excite you? Which aromas can you not live without right now? Grab a handful, a bunch, and find a basket.

Your sensual, magickal, potent spell just started. Keep it going. What would complement whatever you selected? Move through the marketplace, touching and smelling and tasting as you go. Only pick up items that you have a reaction to, even if you're not sure why, and forget about what *should* go with whatever you have in your basket. Ask the butcher which meat or fish they are excited about right now, not what's on sale. Check in with the person restocking bottles in the beer and wine section. Ask them which beer they would want to quench their thirst. Taste the free cheese samples and discover something you've never had before! For the love of Aphrodite, taste the free samples!

Let your senses dictate what you choose. I'm going to say that again. *Let your senses dictate what you choose.* Most of the time, we pick out our foods like we're on autopilot. Check in with yourself and think about the last time you went grocery shopping. Did you buy lettuce because the lettuces said "Eat me! I'm delicious" or did you shove a pre-cut bag of romaine in the cart because you figured you might have a salad for lunch at some point that week?

Remember, you are creating a sumptuous, sexy, provocative meal designed to excite passion and evoke the true meaning of the word aphrodisiac. You are combining magick and cucumbers, science and sesame oil, desire and ice cream, spell craft and sex. Build this food spell the same way you might create other spells, layering one thing upon another, using all of your senses and memories and imagination and intuition.

You have two parts of this magickal working completed: the intention and the ingredients. Preparing the food comes next, followed by setting the space for the magick to happen.

A FEAST FOR THE SENSES

Food and sex and magick are full-contact activities. I know you can do little magicks, but let's be real here, when you have the chance to pull out the robes, light the candles, run naked in the woods, dance around a raging bonfire, or whatever you consider to be your best magick, don't you want to go at it fully and completely? It's the same with sex and food. Recalling what our wise Sumerian friends said about the differences between merely *eating* as compulsory fueling and *dining* as necessary for a good life, I'll choose dining every time.

So, you've made it home from the grocery store. You've let your intuition guide you and there's a wild collection of meats, spices, vegetables, and whatever else you've purchased spread out on the kitchen counter. How do we turn these ingredients into a feast for the senses? It's easier than you think. We've talked about the science of aphrodisiacs and how creating unique combinations of foods can stimulate the reactions in the brain. That's the place to start.

Take a look at the ingredients you have. Imagine serving each item by itself, on its own plate, letting that one food item take up all of the space and all of the glory. Try it! Let's say one of the ingredients you've selected is a potato. Cook one potato, just the way you like it—roast it, boil it, whatever makes you happy. Arrange the cooked potato in the middle of a wooden cutting board and make a pile of salt off to one side. Maybe add one single pat of butter elsewhere on the cutting board. And then comes the good part. Smell the rich and earthy aromas making their way up from the potato to your olfactory senses. Taste the potato just as it is, unadulterated and unadorned. Now sprinkle another forkful of potato with a little salt and taste it. Repeat with the butter, savouring each mouthful and appreciating how the addition of one new flavour at a time changes the potato. And then, of course, mash everything together and hungrily fill your mouth with buttery, salty, potato goodness. You get extra points if butter and salt dribble out of your mouth and you have to lick your fingers.

Speaking of fingers, eat as many foods as you can with your hands. When we think of food and our senses, we mostly think of smell, taste, and sight, but touch plays a huge role in the way food tastes to us. Touch tells us how soft and warm fresh bread is and starts the process of salivation before the bread even touches our lips. A roasted head of garlic is sweet, pungent, and delicious, and is rendered utterly irresistible when placed in your hands. The garlic is hot and there's something wholly primal about breaking it apart, pulling out the soft cloves, and getting oily, garlicky goodness all over your fingers.

Don't forget sound either. Music plays a key role in the way food tastes. Studies commissioned by restaurant groups have shown that light piano music causes patrons to rate desserts as sweeter than they actually are. Whereas those same patrons, eating the same dessert, noted that the food tasted less appealing, less sweet, and even had notes of sour if they were listening to music featuring brass instruments. Noisy restaurants promote an entirely different atmosphere than quiet restaurants.[27]

Picture a perfect meal, with the right person or people present. Smells are wafting out of the kitchen, tantalizing everyone's tastes buds. There's a burst of thunder in the distance or pouring rain tapping out its song on the patio awning. The songs of cicadas in the trees mix with the gentle breezes of a hot summer evening. Sound elevates a meal and adds to its flavour just as much as salt and pepper. Of course, you might have favourite songs, or artists, or genres of music that add that special something to your meal plan. Create a "while we're cooking" playlist and then a "while we're eating" playlist and even a "Yes! We're leaving the dishes in the sink until the morning" playlist.

Take all of the senses into consideration when you are preparing your sensual feast.[28] The plates, dishes, cutlery, music, and feel of the food are as essential as the way you prepare the meal. In preparing a sensual feast to enrapture a lover, what you eat is only a small portion of the fun. The experience of the food is practically equal to the taste of the food.

27. Charles Spence. "Noise and Its Impact on the Perception of Food and Drink." *Flavour.* November 20, 2014. https://flavourjournal.biomedcentral.com/articles/10.1186/2044-7248-3-9.

28. "The Tasting Experience: Our five senses and some of the ways they influence each other." http://www.scanews.coffee/2012/07/06/the-tasting-experience-our-five-senses-and-some-of-the-ways-they-influence-each-other/.

The feast of the senses has to happen somewhere. The food might be prepared in the kitchen or delivered from a favourite restaurant, but there's a physical place that the meal will be eaten and enjoyed. You can amplify the impact of the spell by paying attention to your surroundings and bringing them in alignment with your magickal working. A summer tryst may be made all the more exciting by serving syrupy, succulent peaches on blood red plates, placed on a sun-coloured chenille throw blanket, surrounded by luxurious scarlet pillows. The meal oozes unbridled sexuality, and the placement of the plates near the floor sends a signal that those in attendance should relax, get comfortable, and prepare for a veritable orgy … of the senses.

In a previous section, we talked about old bowls and favourite spoons, and the treasured items that we might cook and eat with. This is the perfect time to bring them out and use them as an integral part of your spell. The magick is rendered so much more deep and satisfying because the plates or goblets or lined tablecloths are so beloved to you or the people connected with this spell. The magickal properties and power contained within boosts associations, and corresponding past magick becomes manifested and palpable and will absolutely add to the overall flavour of the meal. And in case you're thinking that everything has to be perfect and you need to be a gourmet chef, home styling expert, and powerful magick worker all at once, let me assure you that nothing could be further from the truth. Creating the perfect sensual spell for yourself and/or others is about finding the correspondences that mean something to you. An inexpensive bottle of sweet prosecco, a two-pack of frozen French bread pepperoni pizzas, the soundtrack to *Drumline*, and a musty old sleeping bag sends a profound and immediate message to all of the pleasure centers in my body, and it's directly connected to one of the best dates I ever went on.

It's all well and good to combine magick, sex, and food. In the right setting they go perfectly well together. Up to this point, we've largely been focusing on the "how to" portion of the food, sex, magick dynamic. It's also important to look at the "why." When we engage with magick, combining food and sex, we have all the ingredients for something extremely potent. Potency is a condition usually favoured by spell workers, as it points to how efficacious a magickal working has been. The more potent the magick, the more likely we are to get the desired result.

For the majority of people, food and sex are prime motivating forces. Even if those forces are instinctual rather than particularly conscious, they are there nonetheless. Using two such primary and primal ingredients makes for spectacularly powerful magick. After all, sex is often equated with the very act of creation itself. I'm not talking biological creation here, although that's a fine aim for an afternoon of food and sex and magick if everyone is onboard with that plan. I'm referring to tapping into the manifesting, life-enhancing, creative forces that make the universe possible. If sexual energy is the creative force we're working with, then the food we eat during this spell is the matter that fuels and sustains the growth of the magick we're manifesting.

Unless you have a developed practice of food, sex, and magick, I recommend starting your explorations by yourself. Think of it as perfecting a recipe by cooking it over and over again alone, adding a little more salt here and an extra dash of dried mint there, before serving the dish to someone else.

A PERFECT DATE FOR ONE

Look at your calendar, your schedule, your next couple of weeks, and find a day that you can devote entirely to a date. The more time you can carve out, the better. Think in terms of eight hours at a minimum and add more if you can. Arrange for a dog sitter or a babysitter, take a personal day off of work, inform the significant people in your life that they will have to fend for themselves on Saturday as you won't be around. Encourage them to go somewhere else for long stretches of time so that you have plenty of space to be alone. The date you're planning is just for you.

Prior to your date, begin forming an intention for a spell. Something like this might fit the bill for you:

With this magick, I create _____ for myself.
Each moment of my special day, set aside for only me,
will feed and nurture what I am bringing into being.

Write your intention down in a diary or on a yellow sticky note. Keep the magickal intention somewhere you can access it, but not somewhere anyone else is likely to see it. Of course, if you have private space, display your intention as prominently as you like. The key is to look at it frequently as your spell date develops and takes shape. Then make a second version to keep handy so you can refer to it often throughout the entirety of your date.

Before your solo date begins, plan ahead and go shopping for your favourite foods the day or two before. Walk through the market and only purchase what you *want* to eat and drink, not what you think you *should* eat and drink. Put aside your judgements and get two maple-glazed donuts just because you can. Plan for mimosas or after-dinner cocktails, and don't forget dessert. Remember to get red foods, silky foods, decadent foods, juicy foods, foods that excite your senses and leave you craving more. *Caveat here: If you have any taboos, medical restrictions, or agreements about not drinking alcohol or eating certain foods, stick to those agreements. Remember, your health and well-being must come first.* If your time is a little more limited or you just love shopping for food, make the grocery trip part of the magick of the day.

The next step happens when you first wake up on the day of your date or shortly after the roommates or kids or significant others have vacated the premises. Mark your day as sacred, in any way that is important to you, by ritualizing the day. Perhaps that means casting a circle, lighting candles, or calling on a deity you work with. Continue making your day sacred by opening the windows or closing the curtains. Rearrange the furniture so you have plenty of room to make yourself comfortable if your perfect date involves spending time in your home. Drag out your favourite ritual clothes or wear nothing at all. Blast music, dance in the kitchen, or revel in the silence and stillness of having a place all to yourself for once. Get out your fancy bowls and plates and set the table (or floor, bed, or table tray) with flowers or photos, anything that supports the magickal intention you've set for yourself. If part of your perfect date for one is happening elsewhere and then you'll be returning to your home, make the setting beautiful before you leave, so that you'll return and be able to slip into the moment easily.

How the next part of your date happens is all up to you. Here's a suggested list of ways to spend your day. The aim here is to indulge yourself by going on your perfect date. Make it a feast for your senses by trying foods you're unfamiliar with, or make foods you absolutely adore but rarely get a chance to spoil yourself with. Remember you can order your day any way you want, selecting from this list or making up your own perfect date for one.

- Make breakfast for yourself and eat it in bed or sitting by the window—anywhere that is special for you.
- Take a long, luxurious bath. Sprinkle the tub with rose petals and herb mixes, or essential oils that transport you somewhere you'd love to be. Eat chocolate or sip mimosas while you bathe.
- Visit a favourite cafe, order something you've never had before, then people watch (Starbucks totally counts as a cafe).
- Make a picnic and head to a local park, the beach, the lakeside, or the forest and eat outside.
- Get on the bus and finally see that art exhibition that you promised yourself you'd visit. Eat lunch nearby and splurge by getting dessert and eating it first.
- Eat Ethiopian food, asking the waitperson to bring you only their favourite menu items. If you happen to be Ethiopian, find a Cuban restaurant and ask their waitstaff. If you're Cuban... alright, you get the idea. Try a cuisine you've always wanted to and let the servers pick your meal.
- Sit in a rose garden and quite literally take time to smell the roses. Enjoy soup from a thermos.
- Stroll through a farmer's market, asking the farmers to share their favourite recipes.
- Binge-watch TV for hours, eating the good ice cream or cheese or pate, wearing only your pjs or nothing at all.
- Plan a romantic, candlelight dinner with wine, music, and the most decadent food you can imagine. Remember, only invite yourself!

The last step, which can happen at any time during the date and can be repeated if you're up for it, is to get lucky! Enjoy the pleasures of your own flesh in whatever ways you desire. Let the excellent food, scenery, artwork, sights, sounds, smells, and tastes of your day energize you in your magick. Whenever you get around to this part of the day and the temperature is starting to heat up in the bedroom (bathtub, dining room table, all the above), recite your intention aloud. Hold the magick of what you are bringing into being, merge it with the memories of your perfect day filled with luscious foods and divine self-pampering and "made just for you" adventures. Repeat your intention over and over and over again, the same way you might call out to a lover. Keep your desire and your will focused on the magick you most want until your senses reel and you collapse, breathless, spent, and wrapped fully in the magick of food, sex, and creation. This spell is over for now. Was there any dessert left? Now might be a good time to check.

As often as possible, return to this spell. Combining magick with food, memory, all of your senses, and sex is potent and life changing. You deserve this kind of magick in your life, the magick of pleasure and time with yourself and foods that make your spirit sing. When you're good and ready, share this magick with someone and notice the differences in intensity and power and pleasure. Bring this spell to friends or coven mates by agreeing to work with food, sexual tension, creative energy, and sensual feasting, but omit the actual sex—or don't, depending on the nature of your friendships, your clear personal boundaries, and enthusiastic consent from everyone involved.

Food is the first medicine. Broadly speaking, if food is available, plentiful, and has nutritional value, a person can survive quite well. Eating delivers essential calories, minerals, and vitamins that feed our bones and nourish and support our cognitive development. The act of eating food at mostly regular intervals is, in and of itself, a healing practice. If you are very fortunate you can choose the foods you wish to eat. Being a vegan, vegetarian, subscriber to a grain-free diet (outside of medical necessity), or an omnivore by choice says a great deal about a person's privilege and access to resources. One of the benefits of knowing where your next meal is coming from is less stress. Lowered stress levels go a long way for staving off such diseases as high blood pressure, depression, heart disease, and stroke.

Unfortunately, the opposite is also true. When people experience "food insecurity," the very real experience of not knowing if there's going to be enough food for the current meal or the very next meal, stress levels go up, anxiety increases, depression is more likely, and surprisingly, obesity rates increase. The obesity rates increase because folks that experience food insecurity are more regularly relying on food pantries and charity organizations to supplement their "food income" and most donations tend to be prepackaged, nonperishable foods filled with corn syrup and other sugars. Fresh fruits and vegetables perish quickly and are often discouraged as donations. These discouraged food types are the exact foods with the most nutritional and health benefits.

Fresh fruits and vegetables are also conspicuously absent in food deserts. A food desert is an area where a large percentage of the population lives without a car or reliable public transport, and must travel at least a mile to get to a supermarket.[29] In the United States, one of the wealthiest countries on the planet, hundreds of thousands of people live in urban environments, disconnected from fresh foods. What takes the place of a grocery store or fruit stand or affordable farmer's market are convenience stores, corner shops, liquor stores, and fast food restaurants. These establishments are chock-full of high calorie, high sugar, high fat foods with low nutritional value. A startling economic fact shows that the prices of fruits and vegetables have increased 24 percent since the early 1980s, while sugary foods like sodas and highly processed packaged food prices have dropped by nearly 27 percent.[30] The modern medical establishment heaps all sorts of health woes on the consumption of low nutrition, high sugar foods combined with a lack of fresh foods.

As a stark example, it's likely you know the expression "an apple a day keeps the doctor away." The original version of this saying comes to us from mid-nineteenth-century Wales and went, "eat an apple on going to bed, and you'll keep the doctor from earning his bread."[31] There's real, honest-to-goodness science that supports this common anecdote too. Apples are filled with phytochemicals, which are strong allies in the fight against cancer. Apples are well known as a substitute for toothpaste. Gum diseases and tooth health are huge indicators of your long-term health. The healthier your gums and teeth are, the less prone you are to certain chronic diseases. Fruits and vegetables in general, especially colourful fruits and vegetables like apples, blueberries, pomegranates, bananas, tomatoes, avocados, peaches, and peppers provide a bevy of antioxidants, lycopene, and other health-promoting and disease-preventing nutrients.

What do food pantries and food insecurity have to do with being a kitchen witch? Quite a bit, actually. If you hold the belief that witches are a force of change and good in the world, then it's important that your witchcraft practices include cooking often, eating

---

29. Michele Ver Ploeg, David Nulph, and Ryan Williams. "Mapping Food Deserts in the United States." US Department of Agriculture. https://www.ers.usda.gov/amber-waves/2011/december/data-feature-mapping-food-deserts-in-the-us/.

30. "The New Face of Hunger." *National Geographic*. https://www.nationalgeographic.com/foodfeatures/hunger/.

31. Caroline Taggert. *An Apple a Day: Old-Fashioned Proverbs and Why They Still Work.*

as well as you possibly can, and sharing nutritious meals with those people in your life you are responsible for, circle with, or care about.

You see, modern food production methods, prepackaged foods, and food deserts not only rob people of decent food, but they destroy culture. If your food always comes from a fast food restaurant, you'll have a tough time learning how to cook or properly meal plan. The magick of opening a refrigerator or cupboard and being able to throw a meal together will become a lost art.

Many, maybe even most, witchcraft practices look back in time to the "old ways." Now, many of those old ways aren't very old at all, but there are some real nuggets of wisdom in the ideas of "old ways." The tradition of passing along local and occult knowledge is pretty popular in modern witchery. Family recipes, food preservation techniques, hunting practices, making tinctures, creating herbal remedies, finding foods to aid and support healing, wildcrafting, and foraging are fairly common subjects in magickal circles. If you need any evidence of that, just ask any metaphysical shop owner or book reseller to name one of the bestselling Pagan books of all time and Scott Cunningham's *Encyclopedia of Magical Herbs* will no doubt be near the top of their list. Before there were pharmacies, the best places to find medicines were hedgerows and forests and farms.

The Pagan world, both modern and ancient, is filled with stories and lore of gods, goddesses, and Mysterious Ones associated with herbs, food, and healing. Airmed, Brigid, and Cerridwen are three deities from Britain and Ireland closely connected with herbs and healing. The Greek gods Apollo and Asclepius were healers and doctors, well versed in herb lore. A Yoruban Orisha, Aja, is said to call her devotees to the wild places and forests so she can teach them the medicinal properties of the plants and herbs found there.

Gods and goddesses were not the only ones that recorded the healing ways of food and herbs. One of my all-time favourite books is an English translation of the Welsh book *The Physicians of Myddfai*.[32] The actual physicians lived in the twelfth century and were what we might today call homeopathic doctors or herbalists. There's a long recounting of proverbs and precepts contained in the book that speak directly to food and health practices. Even today, the wisdom here is pretty clear.

- *"A supper of apples, a breakfast of nuts"*: Sounds suspiciously like a recipe for clean, fresh breath at bedtime and granola for breakfast. I like it!

---

32. John Pughe and John Williams. *The Physicians of Myddvai = Meddygon Myddfai*. Cribyn, Lampeter: Llanerch Press, 2008.

- *"Cold water and warm bread will make an unhealthy stomach"*: Hot bread is harder to digest and cold water does slow digestion even more. So, this phrase is completely accurate.

- *"To eat eggs without salt will bring on sickness"*: Okay, this might not hold as true today as it did in the twelfth century. I mean, you can eat eggs without salt and not get sick, but the idea of the saying still holds true. Salt is a necessary essential mineral for overall good health. It regulates fluid balance and provides electrolytes. Salt also prevents or discourages bacterial growth.

- *"The three feasts of health, milk, bread, and salt"*: Fresh sheep, cow, or goat milk can be drunk, turned into cheese, or churned into butter. Bread is filling and warm and seemingly magick because it appears practically out of nowhere and doubles in size. From humble flours come steaming, massive loaves. Salt, we've already talked about, but it bears repeating that salt makes virtually everything taste better.

- *"He who sees fennel and gathers it not, is not a man, but a devil"*: This doesn't need much explanation at all. If you've got wild fennel growing nearby or on the shelves of your local supermarket, do indeed gather it.

Super-Quick Bonus Recipe for Wine-Soaked Fennel

Fennel is not only delicious, but filled to the brim with everything from protein to estrogen to vitamin K and lutein. It's a wonder food. Also, making this dish will prove you are not the devil, at least in the minds of twelfth-century homeopaths.

Serves 2	Prep Time: 10 minutes	Cooking Time: 30 minutes

1 bulb fresh fennel

3 tablespoons butter, divided

1 clove garlic, diced

Salt and pepper

⅓ cup white wine

Water (enough to cover fennel in skillet)

First clean the fennel bulb, then cut the stalks off, right down to the top of the bulb. Cut the fennel bulb into quarters. Set the fennel aside.

Heat a large cast iron or non-stick skillet over medium heat until it's almost smoking (but not quite). Melt 1 tablespoon of butter and toss in the diced garlic clove. Add the quartered fennel to the skillet in a single layer. Season the fennel with salt and pepper and gently toss around in the pan to coat the fennel in the butter. Now pour in the white wine and give everything a light stir. Pour in enough water just to cover the fennel. Bring the fennel, butter, water, wine mixture to a boil and then reduce the heat to medium. At this point, cover the skillet with a lid. Leave the fennel and braising liquid to do its magick for about 15 to 20 minutes or until the fennel bulbs are very tender. There shouldn't be much braising liquid left after this time. This is when I melt another tablespoon of butter in the pan to give an extra burst of buttery goodness. Stir the fennel and second helping of butter for 3 minutes.

Remove to a plate, add a little more salt and pepper if you like, and eat. I like them by themselves, but they pair really well with pork and heavily-flavoured fish. Oh! And that third tablespoon of butter? If you're serving the fennel in a bowl, spoon that last tablespoon over the top. Extra style and taste points if you chop a teaspoon of the fronds (little green feathery bits at the end of the stalks) and sprinkle them on the braised fennel bulbs.

Spice Is the Variety of Life

In 1783, William Cowper was asked by Lady Austen to write a poem about a sofa. Up for the task, Cowper put pen to paper (or quill to parchment) and began crafting an epic, sprawling, dizzyingly long paean to the humble sofa. By 1784, the blank verse poem was published, with the less than creative title "The Sofa." Buried in one of the myriad verses was this phrase: "variety's the very spice of life, that gives it all flavours." The brilliant but long-winded ode to a settee has been largely forgotten, but that one line about spice and variety has stuck around. And it couldn't be truer. Of course, as this is a book about food and magick, I've magickally moved the words around a bit, and what do you know—spice becomes the variety of life!

Spices and herbs both derive from plants, but what differentiates an herb from a spice is which part of the plant is used. Spices come from the bark, root, or seed, whereas herbs are collected from the stems, leaves, and flowers of a plant. Both spices and herbs are used for flavouring a dish. Spices also tend to colour foods—think of the golden yellow of saffron or the brown and red of cinnamon.

Spices originated in south Asia and throughout the region known today as the Middle East, and were traded throughout the region, and most of Europe and Africa for thousands of years. Spices have been used for everything from food flavourings to components in prescriptions and as preservatives. Spices show up in the earliest medical records, one of the oldest of which is the Ebers Papyrus[33] hailing from Egypt some thirty-five hundred years ago. The papyrus contains more than seven hundred magickal formulas, complete with incantations, spells, and remedies. The ancient Egyptians clearly understood the connection between food, medicine, magick, and health and developed robust systems and disciplines for diagnosis and pain management.

As is often the case, modern science and ancient wisdom dance around the actual beneficial properties of using spices. There's clear evidence that adding spice, especially to meat, really does help with food preservation. Spices like cinnamon and cloves slow the growth of bacteria and add flavour, but only if you're using actual cinnamon. A lot of cinnamon you find these days isn't cinnamon at all, but a similar spice known as cassia. Turmeric absolutely has a whole host of *mostly* verifiable health benefits. What makes turmeric so special is a compound within the spice called *curcumin*, which acts as an

---

33. New World Encyclopedia contributors. "Ebers Papyrus." *New World Encyclopedia*, http://www.new worldencyclopedia.org/p/index.php?title=Ebers_Papyrus&oldid=950819.

anti-inflammatory agent,[34] but claims about it curing some forms of cancer are over-stated. What is undeniably true about adding spices to your food is that your meals will taste more exciting. Eating a diet full of fruits, vegetables, proteins, carbohydrates, and fats liberally sprinkled with spices is better for you than, say, a bag of magickal dough-nuts. Mmmm … spicy magickal doughnuts though.

So, what can modern food witches do with spices? Well, the obvious thing is to use them as flavouring for meals, beverages, and spicing up spells. Here are my top five spices and a few of my favourite magickal uses for them.

Cinnamon

The heat of cinnamon is said to activate spells and make them work faster, which is why it's a common ingredient in spells you need to work right now.

CALM HOME SPELL

Add cinnamon sticks, two cups of red wine, a cup of water, and a sliced orange to a saucepan. Heat slowly until the steam perfumes your space.

LOVE SPELL

Add cinnamon to pancakes, toast, muffins, horchata, cocktails, homemade chilis, and Moroccan stews. In magickal quarters, cinnamon is a well-known aphrodisiac.

GET OUTTA HERE SPELL

Mix a quarter teaspoon each of cinnamon, black pepper, and chili powder together. Sprinkle it in the shoes of someone you don't want around or have them walk through it. This is commonly known in American Hoodoo as a hotfoot spell.

---

34. Oregon State University, Linus Pauling Institute. https://lpi.oregonstate.edu/mic/dietary-factors/phyto-chemicals.

Turmeric

Turmeric is well known for its medicinal and anti-inflammatory properties and can be added to virtually any healing spell.

VITALITY SPELL

Add 2 tablespoons of lemon juice and a ½ teaspoon of turmeric to 8 ounces of room temperature water. If you like your turmeric water a little sweeter, you can add a teaspoon of honey (or your favourite natural sweetener). Drink this daily, first thing in the morning. It's a great alternative to caffeinated morning drinks and is said to aid in digestion too.

HEALING SPELL

To aid in fast healing of sprains and joints swollen from too much activity, add this dressing to salads. Mix together 2 tablespoons of honey or agave syrup, 1 tablespoon of apple cider vinegar, 2 teaspoons of ground turmeric, ¼ teaspoon of ground ginger, and 3 tablespoons of olive oil.

Black Pepper

Black pepper is a must if you're doing protection magick. I've heard old-school kitchen witches say that placing necklaces and rings in a bowl of pepper adds to their protective properties.

HOUSE PROTECTION SPELL

Mix three tablespoons of black pepper with three tablespoons of coarse white salt and three teaspoons of minced garlic. Put the mixture in a jar and spread it around your property—in a circle if you want to be super official, but it's not always easy to walk in a circle around an entire apartment complex. At the very least, hit up the corners and the entryways.

NO TRESPASSERS SPELL

This is another take on a protection spell. Mostly I love this spell because it involves using a cauldron, and who doesn't like that, right? In your cauldron mix 6 tablespoons of course salt, 1 tablespoon of black pepper, 1 tablespoon of ash from a recent fire, and 1 tablespoon of iron filings. Stir the mixture with a ritual knife or consecrated spoon and then spread the concoction all over your property. For an extra touch, substitute the iron filings with scrapings from your cauldron. If you can't have a fire and therefore don't have ashes to add to the mix, grind up a charcoal briquette.

Nutmeg

Nutmeg has long been associated with prosperity, so I like to add nutmeg to my food spells in surprising and unexpected ways, just like I want money to show up in surprising and unexpected ways

PROSPERITY SPELL

Add nutmeg to scalloped potato dishes or mix a teaspoon into mashed potatoes. Sprinkle a tray of veggies like cauliflower, turnips, carrots, onions, and potatoes with salt, pepper, and nutmeg, then roast them.

PROSPERITY SPELL II

Candle magick is one of my all-time favourite and go-to spell methods. If you're looking to increase your prosperity, grab a six-inch green or golden candle, colours associated with money and wealth. Dress the candle by rolling it in one teaspoon of almond oil (or jojoba oil) and then sprinkling one teaspoon of ground nutmeg all over the candle. Depending on your situation, you can use a larger or smaller candle and burn it for several days. Of course, use good fire safety practices here. Never leave an unattended candle burning. If the candle is going to burn for multiple days, snuff it out rather than blowing it out.

Cumin

Demanding work schedules, being constantly plugged in online, and getting bombarded with information from myriad places seemingly all at once is a recipe for exhaustion. Cumin may just be what you need to fix that. Cumin contains lots of iron, and iron helps generate healthy, strong red blood cells that transport oxygen around the body. Cumin works well in love spells too, revitalizing parts of your relationships that might be worn and tired.

AVOIDING EXHAUSTION SPELL

In a bowl, combine 9 tablespoons of ground cumin, 3 tablespoons of salt, 3 tablespoons of coriander, 2 tablespoons of chili powder, 2 tablespoons of paprika, 2 teaspoons of allspice, and 2 teaspoons of black pepper. Store in an airtight jar. Rub onto your favourite protein dishes, sprinkle onto vegetables, or mix into soups and stews.

ANOTHER LOVE SPELL

This is so very simple and incredibly effective. Mix one teaspoon of ground cumin with one teaspoon of cinnamon. Place ½ tablespoon of the mixture into an incense burner or mini cauldron and light it. Just let the incense waft about the room. You can add a charcoal briquette if you have trouble lighting the cumin and cinnamon, but I rarely need to. Simply place the charcoal in the cauldron, light it, and then heap the cumin and cinnamon on top.

Pickle Everything

Fermentation has been around since our long-departed and ever-so-smart ancestors left some food in a jar in the sun and let it rot. Some brave soul said, "Okay, I'm game. Let me eat that cabbage. It looks terrible. It smells terrible. But I think with a little salt it will be delicious." And it was. If you've ever eaten kimchi, kefir, wine, sourdough bread, kombucha, sour cream, or pickles, you've eaten fermented food. Which is odd when you think about it, because if I offered you a meal of carefully rotted foods you'd normally say, "Um … no thanks. I'll stick with a sandwich, please."

Pickling, fermenting, and salt curing are related processes. Their main function is to extend the life and usefulness of fresh foods like vegetables, fruits, and meats. Pickling basically makes the environment deadly for most bacteria because of the highly acidic vinegar solutions used. Salt curing slows the onset of rot caused by bacteria, by drawing out any moisture molecules in food and replacing them with salt molecules. Fermentation works by carefully cultivating certain bacteria, yeasts, and microorganisms that thrive by dining on the bacteria that can't survive the fermentation process. And by "carefully cultivating" I mean basically leaving nature to do what it does best, at barely perceptible levels, which we humans accidentally stumbled upon when we did not die the first time we ate fermented bread or wine or cabbage.

For most of human history the ability to preserve food meant nothing short of survival. The folks from Sumer pickled and fermented foods. They had gods and goddesses of fermentation. The Greeks, Romans, Japanese, Koreans, Chinese, Pacific Islanders, North Africans, West Africans, Norse, Celtic, and Slavic peoples all learned to pickle, salt cure, and ferment their foodstuffs. Virtually all cultures mastered "let it rot" techniques. Most of those same peoples had deities that oversaw the preserving process.

Wisdom from the Community Pantry
OFFERINGS TO PRESERVATION
By Stephen Pocock, salumiere at large

The fire burns high. Men and women are gathered around. The priest/ess enters the circle and offers a supplication. Animals are brought forward and slain—the blood is caught in bowls, the beasts butchered. Some of the flesh is placed on the fire as an offering, some of the blood is poured. The ritual ends.

This is a smallish community, not some large temple with many priests, wealthy patrons, and flocks of supplicants. The animals they sacrifice have great communal value, not just to the Godds (a non-gendered term that encompasses gods, goddesses, mysterious ones, queer gods, and non-binary deities). They work hard to raise them and have few animals to spare, so they only offer up parts of the animals slaughtered—perhaps a few choice cuts, some of the offal (some perhaps used in augury). The rest will feed the people, but not all at once, that would be profligate! There is no refrigeration, of course, no quick-seal vacuum packaging. There is salt, there are spices and herbs. There is, for some, saltpeter. There is the sun and there is smoke. There is preservation. It is a kind of magick.

There are examples of food preservation, both recorded and passed down, that span millennia. The earliest could have been simple drying. The Mesopotamians were drying (and salting) in the third millennium BCE, Native Americans dried fish and game in the sun or by using smoke pits, and the ancient Chinese pickled vegetables in earthen jars and eventually fermented fish and soy to create the sauce we know and love today. The Celts, Greeks, Romans, Sumerians, Africans, Egyptians, Incans, and so on all through history have all found ways of taking elements supplied by nature and using them to transform the food they relied on to exist. With a few exceptions, salt has been the basis of all preservation. Salt production was key in establishing settlements, in building roads, and as currency and payment (the word *soldier* comes from salt, as does *salary*).

Salt. Salt preserves. Salt has been mined or harvested since before recorded history.

The Aztecs, Navajo, and Hopi all had female salt deities. Salt has power. The early Italian Streghe knew that and used it in spells and wards. The medieval and Renaissance alchemists revered salt as the one of the three primary alchemical elements along with mercury and sulphur. This was, to all of them, inherited knowledge. The alchemical process, *solve et coagula*, the breaking down and reforming of elements, is at the heart of not just the metaphorical lead-to-gold transformation, not just the process of passing through stages of spiritual growth, but also what happens in the process of transforming raw food (animal or vegetable) to preserved food.

I'll use the example of salting meat. When salt is applied to meat—and this was done in a number of ways, from sprinkling to packing in drums or crocks, even burying or mixing with chopped or ground meat—it instantly goes to work. What science now tells us is that on a cellular level there is a constant striving for balance; in magickal terms "as above, so below." There is more salt on the outer wall of the meat's cells than inside, so the cells give off water to dissolve the salt and bring it through the cell wall to create that balance. This process continues toward the center of the mass of meat. In this process a number of other things happen. One is that not all the water comes back with the salt, so the salt is then aiding in the faster-than-normal drying, which helps make it safe to eat. Water is necessary for bacterial growth. Secondly, the salt begins to denature the protein, changing its metabolic structure so that the strands break down and combine again, essentially cooking it. Solve et coagula. Usually what happens next is that the salted meat is put somewhere to give off more moisture—it can be hung or put on racks either indoors or outside. It could also be smoked, which adds flavour and also increases the drying time. The result is that the meat becomes completely safe to eat. It's storable. It's transportable. For the traveler/soldier/sailor, a little dried meat is light and nutritious. Who knows, perhaps also a suitable offering at a roadside shrine?

If one adds other ingredients to the salt, then those elements are also broken down and drawn into the meat. This is not just great for adding flavour. Many cultures with herb wisdom discovered their properties and used to add things like thyme and juniper to foods for their medicinal and antibacterial properties. Juniper is widely used in curative recipes today.

If we can fast-forward through time to the current day and step away from the large producers of preserved meats and pickles, if we go out into the smaller communities of Spain or France or Italy or anywhere food and community are still linked, we can find something like the ritual fire I imagined earlier. The families congregate and bring out the animals. I'll use pigs as my example; cows give milk on one hand and make a lot of money on the other, so they are often not kept for communal eating.

It's a big, festive day—the pigs are killed and bled, the blood is kept for making puddings and sausage. The hair is torched off (pew!). The pigs are butchered down, the offal preserved. The intestines are emptied and cleaned for sausages (fresh and dried). The legs are carefully salted—they will be prosciutti or jamons in two years. The shoulders are ground and salted right away—they'll be stuffed into the intestine casings in a day or two. The bladder could be used to house a curing cut, or it could be blown up and tied to be used as a soccer ball by the kids while a huge stew is made from the leftover bits. The bones are used for stock. The feet will be pickled perhaps. Every iota of the pigs is used for something and will feed everyone in that community for a good while. It's a lot of work, but it's generally all done in a day. Generations have done this, using the same houses, the same tools—it's ritual.

The old-school ways (aka "artisanal") are still in practice today, whether in smaller communities like the one I generalized here or in larger "first world" places by food enthusiasts and quality producers. The magick abides in all places—meat alchemy born of ritual and necessity.

Modern science can determine just how pickling, fermenting, and salt curing work, and, as you might expect, are concluding that what is created in jars, underground, and without much help from us has significant advantages to our health and well-being. Well done, science. The short version is that fermentation specifically, and pickling and salt curing generally, break down the nutrients in foods, making them easier to digest and absorb into our system. Also, fermented and pickled foods contain live bacteria and microorganisms that have been shown to aid in digestion, reduce the conditions that promote diseases, and even help with the removal of pesticides and other human-made food additives.

When you think of magickal numbers, three, seven, nine, and forty-two might quickly come to mind. Here are a couple more you can add to your list: 1,000 and 100 trillion. There are about one thousand different species of bacteria making their home in you and on you right now. One hundred trillion bacterial cells make up your body, skin, organs, bones … basically everything you are. Don't panic. No need to get the Lysol, antibacterial soap, or mouthwash out—those microbes are much needed and mostly harmless. In fact, you couldn't function without them, and that's what brings us back to cookery and witchery. Pickling and fermenting foods promotes good gut health, and almost all of your immune system gets its start in your gut.

Pickling and fermenting your foods attracts certain microorganisms into your home (that's how sourdough bread works). Put those delicious pickled and fermented foods in your mouth and you'll invite, promote, stimulate, and otherwise encourage a veritable bacterial Bacchanalia in the microbiome that is your belly. This is the theory behind probiotics. A healthy gut, full of partying bacteria and microorganisms, just might make you live healthier, sidestep common ailments, hang about the planet longer, and generally contribute to your overall well-being. And I'm a fan of witches hanging about the planet for as long as we can, because by and large we do good things.

In my kitchen, I tend to quick-pickle foods. Quick pickling doesn't require as much time or rigorous sterilization as other picking methods do. Plus, although I appreciate time as an ally when it comes to making and eating food, I do like a wee bit of instant gratification. Quick pickles can be made in under an hour and can last in the fridge for up to two weeks. If you're going to experiment with quick pickling, you'll need the following items:

- Vinegar (white wine, rice, or apple vinegar are the best). Avoid balsamic, red wine, or malt vinegars for pickling.

- Mason jars or similar. I reuse all manner of jars. Just make sure they are cleaned and dry before putting anything in them.

- Fresh herbs like dill or rosemary

- Ground herbs like oregano or marjoram

- Salt (I just use regular kosher salt)

- Garlic, peeled and halved

- Black peppercorns or ground pepper if you must

- Sugar (regular white sugar)

- Water

- And of course, whatever vegetables or fruits you are going to pickle. Usually about one pound. Onions, cucumbers, squash, carrots, radishes, and green beans are my personal favourites.

Super-Quick Bonus Recipe for Gwion's Red Onion Pickle Bliss

Red onion pickle bliss adds a crisp, acidic burst and goes with practically everything.

Fills one pint-sized jar	Prep Time: 10 minutes	Cooking Time: 20 minutes, plus 30 minutes to cool in the fridge

1 medium red onion

½ cup water

⅔ cup white wine vinegar, rice vinegar, or apple cider vinegar

3 tablespoons sugar

1 clove garlic, peeled and halved

10 black peppercorns

¼ teaspoon red pepper flakes

1 sprig rosemary

Slice the onion very thinly and place it in your clean, dry jar. Set it aside. Add the rest of the ingredients to a medium saucepan and bring to a boil until the sugar has fully dissolved. Stir carefully so you don't break the rosemary. The sprig is in there to add flavour, and you'll discard it before the next step.

Let the pickling mixture (the water, vinegar, and spices) cool down for about 10 minutes. Discard the sprig of rosemary and pour the remaining ingredients into the jar of onions. Make sure all of the onions are submerged in the picking liquid. If you have to, use a spoon to push the onions down in the jar. Seal the jar and put it in the fridge to cool. The onions are ready to eat once they are cool, about 30 minutes.

Serve them on avocado toast, burgers, salads, or just with a fork straight out of the jar. Remember to kiss your partner or partners before eating the onions out of the jar, unless they're into pungent kisses.

The Magick of Chicken Soup

Once upon a time when I was quite young, I got sick with the flu. My mother heated a bowl of chicken soup and poured it over mashed potatoes. Within a few hours I was bouncing off the walls, right as rain and feeling fine. Was it the chicken soup? Was it the care and attention? Was it the kiss on my forehead and the admonition to "eat it all so you'll feel better"? Yes. The answer is yes, it was all of those things.

Homemade chicken soup is filled with magick, attention, and intention. Think about it. As a cook and a magick worker, you know there are vitamins and herbs and ingredients in chicken soup that are nutritious and tasty. Fresh vegetables, flavoursome herbs, garlic, onions, chicken protein, pepper, and salt each have their own healing properties, and combined in chicken soup, their powers are magnified beyond measure. The smell alone stimulates a person's appetite and the salty broth warms the tummy and the heart. Recalling the magickal truism "like attracts like," serving an ailing friend chicken soup is a spell that says "as this soup is packed with flavour and herbs and nutrients and healthy ingredients, so may you be well and full of health." The act of caretaking and showing a person they are loved by providing them with a hot, healing meal goes a long way. If the message "I'm loved, I'm taken care of, I'll get through this" is evident, the healing process can begin in earnest, under better conditions.

Chicken soup is renowned throughout history as a healing meal and, interestingly enough, science knows this to be true, but hasn't quite figured out why just yet. The steam from the soup is thought to open the nasal passageways. That makes perfect sense. The salt and the broth replace vital fluids and electrolytes, keeping the ill person well hydrated. Pretty obvious. Here's where it gets a little mysterious. Chicken soup stops, or at the very least, slows down a barely understood process in the body known as neutrophil migration. Neutrophils are leukocyte cells, which arrive first on the scene to ward off infections, neutralize harmful bacteria, and begin the repair work on bodily injuries.[35] Something in chicken soup helps these cells stave off inflammation in the respiratory system, and that helps you recover from colds and flus more quickly. Chicken soup is proven to be effective but we just don't totally know why. I'm okay with that because, like many magick workers, I don't need to know how something works to see that it does work. Chicken soup works, so I'll keep making it, eating it, and serving it.

---

35. Carlos Rosales, et al. "Neutrophils: Their Role in Innate and Adaptive Immunity." *Journal of Immunology Research* vol. 2016 (2016).

There's a method to making a really good chicken soup. In an old French cookbook, the title of which is lost to me, I learned that good soups are made from fresh ingredients and time. The cookbook goes on to rebuff the quaint old notion of a cook standing over a bubbling cauldron on the kitchen hearth, filling and refilling the pot with ingredients that were about to spoil or were left over from a previous meal, to keep the soup cauldron going and ever full. Instead, the cookbook suggests that the better fable to reference is that of two Jesuit priests who come to a village with nothing to eat and convince the local children that they have a fantastic recipe that starts with a stone, a fire, a pot, and some water.[36]

You may be familiar with this story, known in countless countries and with all sorts of local variations, as the tale of stone soup. The story was first published in 1720 in a collection of letters by the French journalist Madame Du Noyer, but in less than fifty years many variations of the tale had spread throughout Europe and the Americas. What remains the same in every version is the hungry person (or persons) convincing the locals to contribute the tools and ingredients needed for the meal. The soup is layered, first with a stone, then water, then salt, then vegetables, then herbs, then … well, you get the point. What makes a great soup is layering in the ingredients and building a base of flavours. This is where the true magick of chicken soup comes from. I believe the slow process of extracting the nutrients from each ingredient added to the pot, plus time, makes healing magick.

Imagine being sick in bed. Actually, let's not imagine that. After all, we are magick workers, so perhaps not focusing on illness is the better course. Try it this way instead.

Imagine you are making soup. You have all day. You have bundles of fresh and dried herbs and an abundance of celery, onions, carrots, chicken, and spices. Maybe your soup has even more ingredients or uses different proteins. What's important is that you have enough of everything you need to make a wonderful soup. The onions and garlic hit the bottom of a heated cauldron (or Dutch oven or stock pot) and begin to sizzle. Your mind follows the scent to the garden or farm where the onions and garlic were grown. You add water and imagine the water cycle. Raindrops falling from the clouds, making their way to a puddle, a stream, going deep underground to a subterranean aquifer, eventually coming out of your kitchen faucet. As you add salt, perhaps you're reminded of tears

---

36. Du Noyer, Anne-Marguerite. *Lettres historiques et galantes de deux dames de condition dont l'une étoit à Paris et l'autre en province.*

you've cried, or the circle you recently cast, or that time you were in Texas and a friend gave you salt from their coven's altar as a thank you gift.

As herbs and spices and chicken and vegetables get added one at a time, find yourself offering thanks to the plants and animals. Picture who you might share this rich, warm, healthy soup with. See their face, their smile, and imagine the conversations you'll have or the quiet moments you'll steal away with each other. After a while the whole house is filled with the aroma of your stone soup (or chicken soup, whatever you want to call it). In no time at all, in the time between beginning and ending, in your kitchen and in the "no place" that magick happens between the worlds, you've created a magickal elixir indeed, filled with sweet memories and happy futures and healing magick.

Included here is a starter recipe for chicken soup. Think of this as a basic spell kit, because your chicken soup will eventually be much different and better than this recipe will ever be. The reason for that, of course, is that you will add your magick to it every time you make it, with the ingredients you have on hand that you love to cook with.

A Starter Recipe for Chicken Soup

A cooking note: My recipe suggests using chicken breasts and store-bought chicken stock. Usually, I break down a whole chicken and make the stock myself. It's a longer, more involved process and I wholeheartedly encourage you to try the "whole chicken, make the stock from scratch method" yourself at some point. But this recipe is a good place to start your magickal cookery experiments.

Serves 6	Prep Time: 20 minutes	Cooking Time: 1 hour and 15 minutes

3 tablespoons oil (vegetable or olive)

3 skinless, boneless chicken breasts

1 large white onion, chopped

3 sticks celery, diced

3 carrots, chopped (like thin coins)

4 cloves garlic, minced or chopped finely

2 medium potatoes, diced and with the peel still on (I use Yukon Gold potatoes)

1 tablespoon salt

1 teaspoon black pepper

2 teaspoons ground coriander

2 teaspoons ground cumin

1½ teaspoons ground turmeric

1 teaspoon ground cinnamon

1 bay leaf

7 cups water (I like my soups thicker, so you might want to add 1 extra cup)

2 cups chicken broth (or vegetable broth)

Grab a large soup pot and put it on medium heat for 2 minutes. Add the oil and leave for 1 minute. Add the chicken breasts to the pot and cook on each side for 4 minutes. Remove them to a separate plate and let them cool down. We'll come back to those beauties in a while.

Add the onion, celery, and carrots to the soup pot and let cook for 5 minutes, stirring occasionally. Next add the garlic, potatoes, salt, pepper, spices, and bay leaf. Stir everything together so the spices are well mixed into the vegetables (be careful not to break up the bay leaf). Immediately add 7 cups of water and 2 cups of broth. Give everything a quick stir and cover the pot.

Cut the three chicken breasts into 1-inch cubes. It's very likely that the chicken is not fully cooked at this point. That's okay, it will finish cooking in the pot. Just remember to wash your hands and utensils thoroughly after handling undercooked chicken. Carefully remove the cover from the pot and add the chicken to the soup. It's best if you use a ladle or big spoon to do this so the broth doesn't splash about and burn you. Cover the pot, bring to a boil, then reduce to a slow simmer and leave for 1 hour.

Remove and discard the bay leaf and grab a ladle. Fill four bowls with your chicken soup and enjoy with crusty bread…and white wine…and friends…or just eat it by yourself with crusty bread and your favourite binge-worthy program.

There's No Place Like Home

Homegrown foods and locally produced foods have many health benefits, not the least of which is promoting a thriving green economy and preserving open spaces dedicated to food production. Small farms, farmers markets, and seasonal fruit stands all serve as magickal reminders that food does in fact grow on trees or vines or bushes or skips about the field before making it to our tables.

Herbalists and naturopathic practitioners cite all sorts of health benefits to eating local foods, reintroducing heritage grains, using fresh spices, extracts, herbal supplements, and the like. Much of their wisdom comes from reclaiming ancient or long-standing cultural practices. There's a lot to learn and tons of anecdotal evidence supporting their claims. Modern science is starting to agree as well, especially when science looks at the differences between foods that are grown or produced at home from basic ingredients versus mass-produced foods made in factories. The most compelling case for this is bread.

——————— Wisdom from the Community Pantry ———————
THE LONG TALE OF INDUSTRIAL AGRICULTURE
BY SRCERER. BAKER AND SORCERER

A kernel of wheat is perhaps one of the most perfect food sources we have. It can be soaked, sprouted, stone-milled whole and with the addition of only salt, water and a long fermentation produces a magickal loaf of bread that satisfies all the senses.

Researchers in Jordan have just discovered the remains of flatbread that predates agriculture by 4,000 years.[37] The remains of flatbreads were found in many old archaeological sites around the world. At some point, someone stumbled upon fermentation and learned they could hold some bread back for the next loaf, allowing the new bread to expand, grow, and take on new textures and flavours. Bread has been a big part of our community and rituals, bringing people together to bake bread in communal wood-burning ovens. People also came together to "break bread" and share in communion. Bread is referred to as the "stuff of life" and is considered essential to our culture and our lives.

The advent of industrial agriculture gave humans a way to grow grains and create something like bread in an efficient manner. Bigger, faster, better, more. Through the years, wheat has been hybridized to grow uniformly. Its chromosomes have changed. Wheat is now being genetically modified and treated with pesticides so it can grow even more efficiently and in places it does not naturally grow. Bread is created in an hour and mass produced to feed as many people as possible. Instead of dealing with a population that is out of control, wheat is the answer to feeding billions more people without regard to the dwindling resources of our planet. Wheat is considered to cause inflammation.[38] Wheat and other grains contain phytic acid. With the high rate of autoimmune disorders and celiac disease, people are being forced to abstain while scientists try

37. "Archaeologists Discover Bread That Predates Agriculture by 4,000 Years." *HeritageDaily - Archaeology News*. July 18, 2018. https://www.heritagedaily.com/2018/07/archaeologists discover bread that predates agriculture by 4000 years/120954.

38. Hannah Nichols. "Wheat proteins may cause inflammation beyond the gut." *Medical News Today*. October 17th, 2016. https://www.medicalnewstoday.com/articles/313514.php.

to cure celiac and/or create digestible bread in a laboratory.[39] Wheat has found its way into a lot of products, from condiments to lotion. How can we possibly think we can feed billions more when we continue to make people very sick? While there are positives that came from the industrial agriculture revolution, there is now a lot to clean up and heal.

But when wheat is properly soaked and fermented, that phytic acid becomes inactive. Similarly, cassava root is poisonous if not prepared properly. The root, which is known as tapioca (or yuca or manioc in various parts in the world), is a popular gluten-free flour. Cassava flour can be used for wonderful cakes and amazing bagels. In attempting to find wheat alternatives, a whole host of nut, grain, and even insect flours and starches are being discovered and rediscovered, including almond, chestnut, plantain, rice, sorghum, teff, arrowroot, potato, sweet rice, and cricket! Bakers have slowly been successful with the alchemy of flours and starches in the arena of gluten-free desserts. When it comes to bread, however, while one can attain a "sourdough" taste, there is currently no way to reproduce the singular process and magick that gluten provides in order to transform itself into a baguette, country loaf, or levain. Perhaps by returning to old-world strains of wheat and processes, some people beset with a wheat intolerance could once again enjoy the real thing.

Lost in the years since industrial agriculture took hold are the heritage grains people grew up with and survived on around the world for thousands of years. Heritage grains are finally having a renaissance. White sonora wheat is the oldest variety of wheat in North America.[40] Milled whole, it has an amazing texture and heady aroma. It makes an incredible loaf of bread and an equally amazing carrot cake. Italian heritage wheat is finding its way to far-away places so farmers can rediscover what they have to offer and make sure the grains aren't permanently lost. Professional bakers are now challenging each other to ditch white flour and discover ways to make whole grain breads and pastries, which were for years nearly impossible to do well.

Breadmaking is a journey of love, trust, time, patience, and a little magick. Like a good spell, real bread is slow bread. One creates a starter, or mother,

39. Katy Severson. "How Sourdough Bread Is Helping People Eat Gluten Again." *HuffPost.* June 26, 2018. https://www.huffpost.com/entry/sourdough-bread-gluten-celiac_n_5b213232e4b0adfb82702959.

40. Slow Food USA. "White Sonora Wheat." https://www.slowfoodusa.org/ark-item/white-sonora-wheat.

and carefully feeds it, witnessing the daily rise and fall before attempting to make any bread. The starter takes on its own life, consuming the wild yeasts from the air and creating its own kind of *terroir*, the literal flavour of the land. One kneads or turns the bread by hand and transfers useful bacteria from our microbiome, which the dough uses when fermenting. Temperature plays a major role, and you must be curious and observant to know when it is time to move from one step to the next, when to add flour or water. The careful shaping of pillowy bread, the fall and rise all helps the wheat break down and become more digestible, nutritious, and flavourful—something to swoon over. The smell of baking bread is grounding and deeply connects us with our ancestors, much the way cooking with fire does. It takes incredible patience to wait for bread to cool and cure before breaking it open and ravishing it.

Magick in the City

Cooking and eating meals that you've had a hand in creating is nearly always best. If you are someone fortunate enough to have land for a garden, growing your own veggies, raising chickens, and having herb plants is undoubtedly the way to go. But it's not the reality for the vast majority of folks. Living in urban areas, sprawling suburbs, or apartments close to work isn't exactly in alignment with a magickal healing garden or the witch's hut in the woods you've always dreamt of owning.

So, what can you do to participate in your local, natural environment? Buying local foods and supporting local farmers is one way. Eating as many fruits and vegetable as possible, no matter where you buy them from, is another good way. Growing your own window box of herbs is another way. Putting your hands and feet in the soil, leaves, and grasses wherever you live works too.

A RITUAL WITH THE ELEMENTS

You can do this in your apartment, on your balcony, or just about anywhere.

Make your space sacred. This could mean sweeping the ritual room; lighting candles; turning off any devices that are likely to ring, buzz or chime; washing yourself; wearing your ritual clothing or jewelry; or lighting some incense. Whatever sacred space looks like for you and anyone joining you, know that you are stepping into that liminal place where magick happens.

Come to Stillness

You might know this as grounding or centering yourself. Whatever you call it, bring yourself present. I start with my feet on the earth. Sending my energy downward, as far as I need to in that moment, to anchor myself, recognizing that I am of the earth. I shoot my awareness upward to the stars, opening to the infinite, recognizing that I am of the stars. I stand in the knowledge that I am the living embodiment of the elements, right now, right here.

Create a Container

Just like you need a pot to hold the ingredients of a soup you are making, so you'll need a container for your magic. You might do this by casting a circle, by drawing a temenos line and stepping across it, or by asking the spirits of place to bless and accept this work. In my case, I offer libations to the spirits of my place, name my ancestors, and cast a circle, starting in the center, then moving north, east, south, west, north, then above and then below. I say the words that are sacred to me.

Welcoming the Elements

AIR

Hold a small flowerpot, looking at its shape and colour. Perhaps you notice that it appears empty and recognize that it is actually surrounded by and filled with Air. Focus on your breathing. You are surrounded by and filled with Air. Feel the breeze on your skin. Can you hear your breath? In and out. In and out. For several minutes, sit and experience the Air in all of its forms—wind, birdsong, breath, rustling leaves. After some time, thank the Air, blow into the flowerpot, and set it aside.

FIRE

Grab a packet of seeds. Look at their shape and their colour and imagine the plants they will become. Although you can't see any Fire, know that these seeds contain the spark of life inside of them. Fire takes many forms and some of them are not so obvious. Right now, inside of you, is that same spark of life. Your body is creating heat in the form of calories. Your breath is warm and so is your skin. You may be aware that there is sexual energy rising in you at this moment. Creativity and passion and action are burning in you too. For several moments, sit and experience all of the forms of Fire that are in and around you. After some time, thank the Fire and set the seeds aside.

WATER

Fill a small glass of Water and look at it. Can you see the light dancing on the sides of the glass as the Water moves around? Water rarely has its own form and is shaped by the container it is in. Remember that Water also shapes the containers it is in, cutting through rocks, bursting banks, flooding plains. Think about your own precious fluids—the aqueous humor in your eyes, the saliva in your mouth, sexual fluids—and how your life, all life, would be impossible without these waters. Recall the deep wells of feelings and emotions and memory. For several minutes, sit and experience the Water that is in and around you. After some time, thank the Water and set the glass aside.

EARTH

Collect a small amount of rich, fragrant soil and look at it. It is black and brown and warmed by the sun. It smells like forest floors and summer vegetables and dogs' paws after a good dig. There is a solidity to your body, just like there is to the Earth. You are host to a million creatures that live in and on your body. You are the entirety of existence for more than a thousand species of bacteria, viruses, and microscopic bugs. Take care of the Earth as you might tend to your own body. For several moments, sit and experience all of the forms of Earth that are in or around you. After some time, thank the Earth and set the soil aside.

CENTER

Look around. The Center is all around you. Over there and under that and just around the corner. I think about my own Center. Think about what keeps you centered, who keeps you centered. Imagine being the hub at the center of a wheel that spins. The outer edges travel a long way, but the hub stays in the center. Recall the lessons you've learned, from teachers, from your own explorations, about sitting in the Center of your own existence and finding power there. For several minutes, sit and experience the Center in all of its forms—your Center, *the* Center that is all around you. After some time, thank the Center.

Dedication

Retrieve the small flower pot and once again breathe air into it. Fill the vessel with life-sustaining soil. Place the seed, full of its own potent energy, into an indentation you make with your thumb. Pour water into the soil and over the seed and place the pot in the center of the kitchen window. Air. Fire. Water. Earth. Center. Sing and chant and move your body in some way and raise energy. Give this energy to the planting.

If you work closely with a particular deity, you could dedicate this magick to them. Ask them to watch over the seed that has been planted just as they watch over you. If you don't work with any gods, dedicate the work to the earth.

With the working complete, thank the elements and release the Center, Earth, Water, Fire, and Air from this place and this magickal working. Open your sacred space and spend time in silence.

Then, tend to the seed and to the plant it will become. Tend to the magick of being in relationship with the elements and listen to them as they speak to you each day.

May this work be blessed. May your work be blessed.

Chapter 8
Food and Grief

There's an old expression, "Eventually some rain will fall on everyone's parade." Grief is an inescapable part of life. The sun rises and it also sets. Grief is not confined to one day or even a particular season, nor is grief limited to physical death either. Folks grieve for lost animal companions, open spaces turned into shopping malls, the ending of covens or magickal traditions, community betrayals, and relationships that ended too soon or never really quite got started. Grief has no expiration date, no matter what the bereavement policy is where you work. Grief is simply a part of life, and, as with many parts of this incredible whirl around the planet, one must dance with grief at some point.

There are many flavours of Paganism, and generally speaking there's a built-in orthopraxy to honour grief and death. Samhain is a well-known holy day. Samhain is most often celebrated on October 31, but depending on the magickal traditions you've engaged with, Samhain may fall on the full moon in November. My practice acknowledges Samhaintide as a season stretching from October to December, ending on the night of the Winter Solstice. Samhain practices are often marked with remembrances of the recently departed, the Beloved Dead, as they are frequently referred to. Ancestors of bloodlines and magickal lineages are called upon as special guests at meals and rituals. Pioneers of the Craft are remembered for their contributions to modern Paganism.

It's my belief that modern Paganism and modern witchcraft prepare adherents for dealing with grief and death in all its forms, better than most other practices do. Not because Paganism has a monopoly on wisdom concerning the afterlife, reincarnation, or the lack thereof, but because many of our practices celebrate life, the turning of the seasons, and the eventual passing of all things. Generally speaking, Paganism is more concerned with this lifetime rather than focusing on the next lifetime, and because of that there's a shift in perspective. Death and grief are part of what happens in this world and must be dealt with, or, at the very least, paid attention to. And as with every other part of life, grief and death have their own food rituals.

A Place at the Table

Let's start with grief. Just looking at the dictionary definition of grief is likely to cause you more grief. Grief is defined as deep sorrow. Sorrow itself is no picnic either. Sorrow is the deep distress caused by disappointment, misfortune, or loss. Grief and sorrow aren't particularly treatable, from a medical perspective anyway. The lessening of grief and sorrow have more to do with time than with treatment. There's an old axiom that says you don't get past grief and sorrow, you get through them and learn to live life *with* them.

Grief and sorrow tend to have physical symptoms too, one of which is a lack of appetite, which can lead to weight loss and decreased energy. It makes sense, right? If your stomach, brain, and heart are all tied up in knots over a loss, you're unlikely to want to fill your body with food.

One thing I've found that helps to manage grief (and notice I said *manage* grief, not cure it completely or make it go away) is to set a place for grief at the table. It's a fairly common practice to set altars for spells, to mark the seasons, or to remember loved ones. It's less common to create altars specifically for our grief. Part of setting up an altar for grief or making space for grief at the dinner table is to give grief a place to go that isn't in the body. Giving grief a place to go beyond your body can help remind you that grief is happening *to you*, *with you* even, but it doesn't make up the entirety of who you are. If grief has come to visit you, purposely and intentionally invite grief to dinner. Here's what I do. See if this might work for you too.

A RITUAL WITH GRIEF

Figure out what you most want to eat right now. If you're experiencing grief, this could be a giant bowl of ice cream, cheese and crackers, dry toast (my go-to grief food), or a big heaping plate full of "nothin' sounds good.

I don't want anything. I guess I'll have cereal." Whatever it is, do what you can to prepare it or have someone help you prepare it. Go to the kitchen cupboard and pull out two plates or bowls, knives, forks, glasses, and whatever you need to serve the food you're going to eat. Enlist a housemate, friend, or family member to do this for you if you're just not up to it.

Set the table for you and for grief. If you have beloveds that are also experiencing grief, have everyone participate in this process. One person can grab the plates, another can start cooking (or scooping out ice cream), and someone else can set the table.

Have a conversation over a meal, with grief. A conversation can take many forms. Perhaps you sit in silence and acknowledge that grief is there with you. Maybe you tell grief what's going on for you in this exact moment. Crying might be involved; so might laughing. Expressions of grief show up in lots of ways. And then, when your dinner with grief is just about done, announce that the meal is over. Tell grief that you're going to clear the table, do the dishes, scrape the leftovers into the compost bin, and put everything away. Invite grief to leave.

Repeat this ritual as often as you need to until the day that grief forgets to show up or just pops by for coffee but doesn't stay too long.

Riding the Food Train

Grief, sorrow, loss, and death aren't easy to deal with for anyone. Doing much of anything while you're experiencing any of these things quite often feels completely impossible and not worth the effort anyway. You're not alone. Most everyone feels this way; even the person that fills their every moment doing a million things to avoid grief and sorrow will eventually run out of distractions, plop down on the sofa, and realise that loss has been sitting in the living room just waiting for them to show up.

Food keeps us alive. Food connects us to the land of the living. Food is often the last thing someone thinks about when sorrow and death show up at the front door. Making sure that food is available to sustain those in the throes of grief, sorrow, loss, and death is critical and, maybe more importantly, it's an act of compassionate service. Which means it is time to ride the food train.

A food train is nothing more than a group of people providing meals for folks in need until they get back on their feet and can manage by themselves again. I agree to cook/

bring dinner on Monday night. You agree to cook/bring dinner on Tuesday. Another person cooks/brings dinner on Wednesday and so on and so on. The folks in crisis get fed and the workload is spread out over several people, so no one person must do it all. Once upon a time, food trains were called "everyone else in the village doing their part and taking care of each other." The reality today is that most people live fractured lives, away from family, friends, and meaningful, supportive community. Close-knit covens and other magickal communities can be a great place to find respite and resources in times of need. Before a crisis happens,[41] it's not a bad idea to put a food train plan into place. Here are a couple of tips and tricks for setting up a great food train.

> *Tip #1:* It needs to be more than just you. Yes, I'm talking directly to you. You're very generous, I'm sure, and a wonderful cook to boot, but food trains work best when other people share the load.

> *Tip #2:* Reread tip # 1 and then enlist coven mates, friends that love to cook, and members of your local Pagan community that can be counted on in a pinch.

> *Tip #3:* Food trains can be really simple. Keep a list of phone numbers and email addresses handy and share the list with at least one other person. Alternatively, there are lots of online food train resources out there that have done the hard work of setting up schedules and spreadsheets for you.

> *Tip #4:* Spread the word throughout your community that a food train exists. Invite people to join the cooking team and let folks know how to contact you if they are the ones in need.

> *Tip #5:* Practice. This is my favourite step. Even if there's no crisis at the moment, test how the food train works by selecting one person in your group and providing them a week's worth of meals. It's a nice thing to do anyway. It's fun to share food with friends, but it also gives you an idea of whether your food train is working. Your friend Helen might like lasagna, but she might not like it seven days in a row. A test run will sort that stuff out.

> *Tip #6:* Once a need does arise, check in with the person you're providing for or with someone close to them and find out if there are dietary, health, or religious restrictions to the foods they can eat. Showing up with five pounds of pulled

---

41. A quick author's note: This section of the book is about grief and death, but food trains are excellent for happily overwhelming occasions too, like folks becoming parents.

pork isn't going to go over well at your vegan friend's house. Seriously though, ask questions about restrictions, favourites, meals the kids love, anything that makes eating easier for the person on the receiving end of your generosity.

Tip #7: Heat-and-serve or ready-to-go meals are best. Your community member is dealing with a lot. Remember, they don't have the time or the energy to read complicated instructions or cook for themselves. Help them out by making meals that just need heating or putting on the plate. Give them any basic instructions, like "microwave for 2 minutes" or "put in the oven at 350° for 20 minutes" or "the salad dressing is in the jar marked with an V for vinaigrette."

Tip #8: Don't stay unless you're invited. I know it's super tempting to hang out, check in, and see if there's anything else you can do. Of course you should ask, but be prepared for a no or even a non-answer. Remember, you're there to make things easier, and talking about the situation isn't always as helpful in the moment as you might think. Drop off the food. Say hi and skedaddle out of there toot sweet.

Tip #9: Do magick. Stir in your compassion. Dice up vegetables with care and attention. Boil pasta for the recipient's highest good. Call on deities of tranquility as you transfer a favourite casserole dish from the oven to your car. It all helps.

A Meal to Heal and Say Goodbye

Many years ago, I was invited to a meal. I was asked to wear red clothing and encouraged to bring a dish of red foods. The evening was equal parts celebration of life, an acknowledgment of sickness and disease, and a memorial for those that had died. Every course that was served featured red sauces, red vegetables, red drinks. As the meal progressed it became evident that the purpose of serving red foods was to represent our blood. Don't panic! This wasn't some super-secret, occult, vampire-impersonating gathering. We were asked to imagine the red foods, the blood-red foods, as representing everyone's healthy, disease-free blood.

This dinner was not a singular event. Many such meals have happened since the early 1990s, and they continue in some form or other today. A common toast, repeated often throughout the meal is "Hail to the red dragon! Hail to our red, living blood." What a beautiful piece of magick this is. What made this gathering so impactful for me when I first attended, and why it continues to be impactful today, is that the folks gathered know that one day toasts may be made for their good health and healing or to remember them after they've died. While sobering to think about, it's also incredibly comforting to know that there are communities working magick for healing and life all over the world, at any given time.

Now, while it's true that a bowl full of borscht or a platter of pickled red peppers isn't going to cure you of everything that ails you, planning meals with community, however you define that, certainly adds to your mental well-being. Meals designed around a specific intention (and healing is a great intention) have health benefits beyond the vitamins and nutrients in the dishes served. Healing meals reduce stress in sick and dying people, not because of the food but because there's a strong association of eating with loved ones, being honoured, feeling taken care of and supported.

There comes a point when healing the physical body is no longer an option. Meals, especially community and family meals, give us the sad and necessary opportunity to say goodbye. The dying person participates in the act of eating, which is an activity the dead do not need. Eating reminds everyone at the table that we're not dead yet. Mealtime is a good time to recount stories of a life well lived. Tales of how the dying person's actions have positively impacted the lives of their friends, family, or coven members can be shared. Engaging in storytelling is often left to obituaries and eulogies, but there's tremendous value in honouring a person's life while they're still alive to hear it. The dying person may have stories to tell as well, and they may wish to give advice or share wisdom of the situation they find themselves in now.

Of course, a life full of regrets and unfinished business is pretty common too. Gathering and dining together can be a time to foster apologies and offer forgiveness. Hospice and palliative care workers offer this advice to the dying and those they leave behind. They strongly suggest saying five things to each other: Thank you. I love you. I'm sorry. Please forgive me. And goodbye.

And while Samhain night is a perfect time to reconnect with those that have already passed through the veil, having such conversations before someone crosses has a particular healing magick all its own, for everyone involved.

Ancestor Dinners

Much like setting a place at the table for grief, we can make a place at our tables for those that have died. If you are new to the idea of ancestor work or ancestor veneration, it can seem a bit daunting at first. Where do you start? Who are your ancestors? What does veneration mean to you or them? Think about the typical scene from your favourite holiday movie or Hallmark commercial when the whole family gathers in the dining room around a beautifully set table and has a jolly time telling stories from the family's past. Now imagine that scene with a lot more black clothing. Instead of Great-Aunt Maude sitting over there at the head of the table with Great-Uncle Tom by her side, there's an urn with their ashes, lovingly placed next to a picture of them in happier times. That's how I do ancestor dinners. Lots of great food. Toasting the dead. Remembering their names and telling their stories.

The word *ancestors* could have several meanings for you. There are actual relatives, with whom we share DNA, who have passed through the veil and into history. Our Beloved Dead, those we've known personally that have preceded us in shuffling off their mortal coils. And our Mighty Dead, those of the Craft that have influenced us, taught us, continue to teach us, and work with us from another place. These powers combined represent all our ancestors: those of blood and bone, of breath and spirit, of lineage and cause. My beloved grandmother, Lillian, died in 2003. I was with her almost to the very end. In our final conversations, she asked to be remembered. She loved lavender. I have lavender around me always, in the form of oil, the plant itself, or incense. She also wanted a simple honouring at family gatherings or special dinners, a toast to "absent friends." That's a promise and practice I've kept ever since. I've expanded that practice to include other family members, friends, mentors, teachers, and witches that have helped shape my life and understanding of the world.

I'm lucky in the sense that I can trace my family lineage back many, many generations. Being from England helps. Our little island is well known for keeping all sorts of records, mundane and otherwise. For the vast sweep of history, my family has been toilers and tailors, mill workers and land workers. There's a strain of travelers and entertainers. There are the privateers and pirates. As far as I can tell, I am not the direct descendant of King Harold or Charles Dickens.

I am proud and tickled pink at some of the characters my family has produced over the centuries, and I wonder about those that were involved in colonialism and empire-building. There is no known family member that single-handedly started imperialism or thought that it would be a good idea to export slaves. But surely my family members worked in the foundries that made the munitions that fueled an empire and built ships that carried people away from their homelands.

A practice I'm developing involves learning as much as I can about the life and times of my ancestors of blood and asking them questions about what they might see as the result of their time on the planet. This is difficult, raw, and experimental magick for me, but it seems like it is serving some of the work I do (or want to do) in the world today. My ancestors of blood have been as much rowdy as gentile, artistic as bawdy. If we were all present in one place at one time, the stories we could tell would be epic. That's true of my magickal ancestors too, those from the Craft that have gone before me. I can only hope to do them justice by having a few stories of my own to tell when I'm an ancestor.

In our house and in our circles, we share the tales of our ancestors. We laugh with our ancestors. We sing their favourite songs, eat foods they loved, mimic the singular way they did invocations and magick. We keep them alive by calling their names and telling their stories and honouring their memories. There's a line from a Pagan song, "Bone By Bone," written by Phoenix LeFae and Sephora, that goes "I lay you down and promise to remember you," and that's what we do—we remember them.

What Is Remembered Lives

There are recipes that are special. Not because they are difficult to cook or take precise kitchen techniques, but because of who you learned the recipe from. There's a dish in the in the back of this book called "A Winter's Feast: Shepherd's Pie to Live For." It's my grandmother's shepherd's pie recipe that I've tinkered with over the years. I think it's the best shepherd's pie you'll ever taste. It's a humble meal that connects my family to our dear ancestor. I'd say the delight in making and eating this meal absolutely comes from my memories of sitting in her kitchen, watching my grandmother cook.

Similarly, for very many years I've attended a witch camp. It's exactly what you think it is. One hundred and twenty or so witches gather deep in a forest for a week of ritual, community, myth, and magick. There's a team of cooks, many of them chefs in their own right, and they participate in the magick too. It's important to note that they are not "the staff." Each member of the Hearth Team plays an integral role in how witch camp unfolds. The menu varies every year, depending on the cooks present and the myth the camp is working for the week. For instance, if the witch camp theme is "the Descent of Inanna," the meals feature dishes associated with modern-day Iraq and ingredients Inanna would recognize. Each meal is vegetarian, with options for gluten-free and vegan folks. Breakfast is hearty and simple. For lunch and dinner, you could expect an exquisite soup, rice, grain, salad, and main dishes all made lovingly from scratch each day.

Every year I've attended witch camp there's one special soup dish I look forward to. It's often served as part of the first night's meal. There's a story that goes along with the soup that's been told and retold for many years, and I imagine it will be passed along for many more years to come. The culinary genius who created this soup was named Willo. Willo died at an early age. I never met Willo, but I've eaten her soup. I've made her soup. And I've passed along the story as it was told to me. Carin McKay, one of my kitchen heroes, knew Willo well. It was she that first shared the story with me.

What follows is a recipe, or an un-recipe. This is the only recipe in this book that is entirely someone else's recipe. However, there isn't actually a recipe for you to follow, which means that it's your recipe and it's never been made before, because you haven't made it yet. With deep gratitude for Willo's gift and to all the cooks that have made Willo soup and have told the story of this recipe, thank you. For in making and remaking this soup, year after year, we honour Willo's life and her memory. As you embark in creating your version of Willo soup, offer the phrase "what is remembered lives."

Wisdom from the Community Pantry
WILLO SOUP
BY CARIN MCKAY, CHEF AND OWNER OF CULINARY MAGIC

Willo was one of my greatest culinary teachers, an she taught me how to make this soup. The thing is, Willo refused to use recipes, so this soup comes out different every time. She would simply pat the side of the pot and say "it's a good one." In honour of Willo's teaching, I am only going to give you a basic ingredient list for this soup, and I will only offer the principles of how to make it.

For the dish, there is a very important balance of sweet, salty, and sour. Thai cooking has lots of sweet added to it, as well as lots of sour. Toasted sesame oil adds a great touch to this recipe, and feel free to salt to taste. When I make this soup, I constantly adjust the flavourings to get it right for however I'm feeling at the moment. Willo taught me to use a variety of each type and flavour to make this soup so magnificent and rich. Have fun!

Serves 4	Prep Time: 30 minutes	Cooking Time: 30 minutes, plus a little bit until it's just right

1 cup red lentils

1 can coconut milk

2 cups water

1 onion, diced

2 cloves garlic, minced

2 inches fresh ginger, minced

¼ teaspoon cayenne pepper

2 sprigs cilantro, de-stemmed and chopped

2 sprigs mint, de-stemmed and chopped

2 sprigs basil, de-stemmed and chopped

1 lime, sliced into thin wheels

Sour Options: lemon juice, lime juice, rice vinegar

Sweet Options: Sugar, honey, agave

Salt Options: Soy sauce, sea salt, sweet miso (make a paste with miso and water before adding)

Oil Options: Olive oil, toasted sesame oil

In a pot, place the lentils, coconut milk, and water, and bring to a boil. Reduce heat and simmer. Add the onion, garlic, ginger, cayenne. Stir. Do not cover. Once the lentils are cooked and not firm (about 15–20 minutes), add one thing from the sour category, one from the sweet category, one from the salty, and some oil (add about a teaspoon of oil at a time). Taste. Repeat with a different item from each category. Garnish with sliced wheels of lime and minced-up basil, mint, and cilantro. Enjoy![42]

---

42. Excerpted with permission from Carin McKay. *Culinary Magic at the Regenerative Design Institute: Creating Community through Food, Farm and Permaculture.* Self-published, 2013.

Chapter 9

Food and Community

You might have heard the old saying "ask ten Pagans one question and you'll get twenty different answers!" Ask Pagans to define the gods, magick, or community and you can multiply the answers by at least a factor of one hundred. Community viewed through your lens may appear radically different compared to how community looks to me. The good news here is that as long as your chosen community provides a place to gain and share knowledge, receive and offer support, and ultimately practice the kind of magick that aligns with your purposes, then how that community is defined doesn't really matter too much.

For the purposes of our explorations, we'll focus on community as people that you gather with. That could be a coven, a monthly meetup group, folks that gather at public rituals, friendly Pagan faces you see once a year at a festival or conference, or even non-magickal people. The important premise here is that from time to time you find yourself in the actual physical presence of folks and share time and meals with them.

Don't Wait for Cakes and Ale

In Wicca and many Wicca-influenced eclectic magickal traditions, there's a ritual custom of sharing cakes and ale. Depending on the particulars, cakes might be muffins and ale could be apple juice, but the common factor is that at a designated point in the proceedings, everyone shares food and drink. I suspect there are as many ways to share cakes and ale as there are Pagan traditions. Food and drink may be offered only to the deities being honoured, for instance. The cakes and ale become physical representations of devotion and are meant only to be consumed by the gods themselves. Throughout history, there are examples of the priestly caste or temple attendants eating offerings after the various rituals and ablutions were finished and the food transformed from its coarse, physical form to a divine essence that the gods could consume. In other cases, cakes and ale are meant to be shared by everyone attending the rite, accompanied by the common Pagan food blessing "may you never hunger, may you never thirst."

Without suggesting that you disregard the tenets of the magickal systems you subscribe to, what would it be like if we expanded the notion of cakes and ale? Is there a place, beyond the confines of ritual, where sharing cakes and ale becomes part of how a community interacts? I think there is. Again, let's agree that cakes and ale, as a practice, is part devotion, part offering, and part sharing food with community.

Devotion is often thought of as a religious act, but it doesn't have to be. If your flavour of witchcraft doesn't include deities, you can still practice acts of devotion. Simply stated, devotion is dedication or commitment to a specific purpose. Sharing food with your coven or cooking food for your community could easily be an act of devotion, on several fronts. Preparing and cooking for another person or many other people takes time, effort, and dedication, not to mention a certain amount of vulnerability. It's a scary thing to make food for a community, because food is such a core need for us humans. There will always be questions and comparisons, right? Did you make enough? Will people like your meatloaf as much as they liked the meatloaf that Twinkle Fairydust made last month? Did you use too much pepper? And then there's the feedback you might get! If you can, I highly recommend setting all of that aside and just sitting with yourself for a moment, to acknowledge the act of service and devotion you performed for community. Whether you did this by yourself or with a crew of people, the community was fed and you helped that happen.

Devotion can also look like sharing beloved, magickal recipes with new members of your community. You are simultaneously honouring your elders or ancestors by sharing meals that mean something special to your tradition, and showing devotion to the folks that are coming into the group after you, by enfolding them in your practices.

—————— *Wisdom from the Community Pantry* ——————
IMBOLC BAKING DAY

By Tegan Ashton Cohan, High Priestess Rose & Antler

As an urban Pagan running a British Traditional Wiccan coven in sunny Southern California, the Wheel of the Year is more of a concept than an environmental reality, something to be observed astronomically, but otherwise emotionally removed from the agricultural roots from which it sprung.

Our seasons are Sun, Fire, and Mudslide. Even in the depths of Winter, we have access to an abundance of fresh fruit and vegetables; we are very blessed. The magickal tradition I practice, which has covens in all climes, values feasting above almost all else, and honours the Wheel with what we choose to prepare and eat, and when.

One food tradition that profoundly connected me to the Wheel through food is Imbolc Baking Day. My tradition uses Imbolc as an opportunity to clear the cupboards of any dried fruit and nuts, anything preserved, canned, or frozen, in an act of faith that the growing season is returning and we can afford to start eating through the winter stores. Imbolc Baking Day is unique to my coven in my tradition, and preceeds Imbolc itself by a day or two. It came about as a solution to what to do with the dried fruit and nuts that had accumulated over the course of the year.

Quick breads (those requiring no yeast, kneading, or rising) are an easy and delicious use for these ingredients. I have made as little as a single loaf, up to the current record of seventeen Imbolc loaves in one particularly nutty, fruity year.

Imbolc Baking Day is an opportunity for the coven to get together outside of a formal esbat or sabbat, to engage in a different kind of ritual of collaboration and creation. It's become our way of saying to the gods that we trust them to bring back the light and the warmth, and that all things green will grow again come spring. By clearing the cupboards, we ask the gods to believe in us, that they may give us the great gifts of light and warmth and food, so we may worship them in health and strength, able to do their work in the world as a testament to our gratitude. When the loaves are done, we have a physical manifestation of this covenant.

The Imbolc loaves are now ready for the sabbat and will be used upon the altar as our cakes. Ideally, there are loaves to share.

Viewing cakes and ale as a practice, rather than as solely a part of ritual, allows you to move your magick beyond the circle. Imagine if cakes and ale included an offering of service for community, and remember, you get to define just what community means here. Creating a service-oriented offering is much easier than you think. Let's look at three distinct options for taking cakes and ale out into the world. For ease, let's consider these offerings broken into different categories: individual, local, and global.

For the individual offering, ask yourself, "Which person in my immediate community has needs or wants concerning food?" Notice that needing help with food is not necessarily the same thing as having a lack of food or being hungry. Certainly, your offering could mean buying them a week's worth of groceries but it could be that you have their kids over for dinner one night because you know your friend has an important meeting to go to on Tuesday. You are offering help with food—providing it, cooking it, buying it, sharing it, whatever form that takes. The idea here is to make a difference in the life of one person you know. We're not talking about a life-altering commitment or a big showy act of generosity, but rather you taking time to move the magick by working with a friend or family member who has a specific food need and helping them with it.

This really could take a million different forms. Perhaps this person wants to know more about eating a vegetarian diet and you've been a practicing vegetarian for a decade. Maybe you're a great family cook and really know how to stretch the budget and can offer tools to making meals go a little further. It could be that you have the best garden in the neighbourhood, always have a bountiful harvest, and they've always wanted to know how to can and preserve food. Your version of cakes and ale, outside of the ritual room, might indeed include providing a meal from time to time. It could entail teaching this one person how to cook lasagna or coming over after your dinner is done and making school lunches for their kids because your friend is going back to school themselves and spends their nights studying.

Thinking locally, ask yourself the question, "Who in our community has food wants or needs?" Notice it's basically the same question but with a slightly broader scope. Now you or your coven or your magickal group are looking at taking cakes and ale farther afield and impacting more people. Like the suggestions for working with an individual, there are permutations after permutations for exactly what you decide to do to impact your local group or community.

Three ideas that come to mind immediately are kitchen witch gatherings, sharing meals together, and feeding the community. Imagine if your local group offered magickal lessons on how to plant a medicinal herb garden or prepare foods with magickal intentions. Sharing meals together is such a simple way to move cakes and ale out of the ritual circle. Imagine if a magickal group intentionally and magickally created a meal together. The meal could be for a specific, magickal purpose (we'll dive into that subject in more detail later) or simply for the sheer pleasure of providing a meal for folks you are in community with. A local coven could create a schedule whereby each member of the coven was responsible for cooking a meal for another coven mate and, in turn, would have a meal cooked for them by their other coven mates. Broadening the idea to encompass a larger vision of feeding a magickal community, what would it be like if prior to a public ritual, Pagan Pride event, or "outer court" gathering, folks prepared a welcoming meal for anyone that attended? Leftover food could then be doled out to anyone that wanted or needed to take food home.

Finally, we can imagine cakes and ale moving out to the community at large, beyond the magickal community even. Ask yourself the question "Where is there a need or want for food beyond our local community?" City or county food drives come to mind here, but I bet you can think of other ways that you or your local magickal group can provide food or food-related offerings for homeless shelters, schools, and organizations like Food Not Bombs.

A magickal community I've participated in for years made the decision to donate the proceeds of a public ritual to a local food-based organization. Attendees were asked to donate as little or as much as they could to attend the rite. Everything, excluding the rental fee for the public park the ritual was held in, was donated to the Ceres Community Project. Over the course of the next several months, our local Pagan community received updates on how the monies were being spent and how many families were being fed in our local county because of our donation.

As magick often works in mysterious ways, it turned out that a much-revered, ailing Pagan elder and their family benefited directly from our donations, by receiving meals from the Ceres Community Project. We had no idea that they were using the services provided by the Ceres Community Project until several months later. They had done magick asking for their food needs to be met and, without prior knowledge, our community was able to fulfil that spell for them. Of course, the fact that the organization is named after the Roman goddess of agriculture was not lost on anyone! Magick is real. Cakes and ale moved out of ritual and into community and nourished those that needed it most.

Outside of actually providing food for people or donating money to groups that work within certain at-risk communities, there's also the practice of shopping locally. Can your magickal community agree to buy bread for rituals from a local bakery? What about milk from a local dairy or cheese from an artisan cheesemaker? Are there local farms that provide CSA boxes? In case you are unfamiliar with a CSA, it stands for "Community Supported Agriculture," which pretty much sums up their mission and what we're discussing here. Local farms provide local food, produced by local labor, for local people. The magick here is about conservation, not necessarily about eating locally grown food purely for health reasons. More food produced from local sources reduces traffic and pollution, promotes a seasonal diet, and connects folks eating the food to the rhythms and flavours of the place they live and the very spirit of the land they inhabit.

So, we find ourselves coming back to ritual again. Cakes and ale move out into the community in all sorts of wonderful and creative ways, only to return to us and connect us back to the place and people we care about. Now that's magick worth doing.

Eat Your Way through a Ritual

We eat and do ritual all the time. We might not realize it, but we do. Think about a birthday celebration or a favourite sporting event you watch with a group of friends. Are their pregame chips and salsa? What about a birthday potluck at the office that ends with candles, a cake, and a song? We know anytime we gather together with other people for more than five minutes, someone breaks out the food, and if we do that on any kind of regular basis, it becomes a ritual.

Just as we took cakes and ale out of the confines of ritual, what if we did the opposite with meals and made an entire ritual out of eating? Certainly, the sensual food practices mentioned earlier point to ways that we can enjoy food *with* ritual, but what if the ritual was about food? Entirely about food. There are as many ritual practices as there are ritual practitioners, so ritual components will vary from tradition to tradition. What follows is one suggestion for a ritual to celebrate food, following a common ritual format found in Wiccan-based and eclectic traditions. Of course, feel free to experiment, add what serves you, and omit any part that doesn't. Like any magickal ritual, you can do this alone, with a coven, or with a larger group. The key here is that with each part of this rite, you'll be eating something and connecting food and magick and the magickal properties of these foods. Read over the ritual below, as this ritual involves lots of food choices and plenty of eating. You can moderate the amount of food you eat during this ritual. One bite or sip for each segment of the rite could be plenty, or you can create elaborate dishes and feast for hours.

AN EATING RITUAL

Create an environment where you can do magick and eat for a significant portion of time without being interrupted. Set a blanket on the floor where you serve the food or decorate your dining table or even clear a spot outside and enjoy this meal out in the open. Use your favourite bowls and plates, bring out the candlesticks, maybe make a centerpiece out of raw foods and flowers. This is a ritual feast, so make it as sumptuous as you like.

Magickal Intention

The suggested intention or purpose of this meal is this: *"I eat this food as a magickal rite. I honour this food and every being that made this food possible. I acknowledge how food impacts my life, sustains me, and nourishes me."* State this intention out loud. I like to say an intention three times to make it a spell. Feel free to add a *"so mote it be"* or *"let the magick begin"* after you state the intention.

Cleansing

Collect culinary herbs, like bay leaves, basil, lavender, rosemary, and oregano. If the herbs are fresh, bundle them together like a bouquet. If you don't have fresh herbs, raid your herb rack and mix herbs in a bowl. Fill a glass bowl with water and pour in the dried herbs. If you're using a bundle of fresh herbs, dip the herb bundle into the water. Move about the room, flicking herb water in every corner and over anyone gathered—don't forget to give yourself an herb cleansing too. Notice how the energy in the room changes as you cleanse the space with fragrant herbs. You're inviting the very walls to participate in this meal with you, by sharing the herbs with them.

Invoking the Gods

A word about inviting deities to the working. Often, gods are invoked later in the ceremony, but as you're going to be eating your way through this ritual right from the beginning, I'm suggesting inviting them right at the outset too, immediately after the ritual space is cleansed. If you work with a specific deity connected to food, feasting, harvests, or abundance, you can call on them to watch over your ritual.

Ceres, goddess of the harvest and abundance, we call you here to witness our rites. We celebrate the harvest and abundance we have before us. We fill the first plate for you as an offering. Stay with us and enjoy this feast.

Two quick magickal tips here: Remember to actually give the gods the first offering. Sounds simple, I know, but you'd be surprised how often you get halfway through this ritual and realise there's an empty plate that was supposed to be filled with offerings. Secondly, if your Craft doesn't include gods, call upon your ancestral lineage, or acknowledge this big, whirling, blue and green planet we live on.

Grounding

For this portion of the ritual, choose carrots, radishes, mashed celery root, turnips, parsnips, or potatoes. You may associate other foods with being rooted in the ground—add those to your list too. The idea here is to eat foods that help you ground and center into the present moment. The carrots or potatoes or root vegetables you are about to eat know something about being rooted. Tap into the magick as you enjoy them.

You may know grounding as centering or being in the moment. No matter the name you use, begin to feel your feet on the ground or your butt in the chair where you are sitting. Eat one of the root vegetables listed above or one from your list and say,

As I eat this _____ I am connecting to this place, in this moment. As this _____ moves across my tongue and down my throat, let me remember that this food was once rooted in the earth as I am rooted to the earth right now.

Eat the food and feel yourself becoming rooted in this ritual.

Casting a Circle

Not every magickal working needs to take place in a circle, but go ahead and cast a circle for this rite. Pick up an apple and slice it in half. Be careful to cut across the apple horizontally, not vertically from top to bottom. As the two halves fall open, you'll see a star or pentacle in the center. The apple forms a circle. Walk the apple around the room creating a circle, or pass it to anyone participating in the ritual with you. Alternatively, if there are folks with you, have them cut their own apple. As you do this, say,

Let this apple represent a circle, a cycle, a complete magickal act where fruit and seed are present, united in one place. Within this circle, all manner of magick is possible. As I eat this apple, may I remember that I too carry within me the fruit, the seed, the edges, the center, the places between the edges and the center, the pentacle, the star, and the sweetness and tartness of this life. As I eat this apple, may I know the circle is cast and I am between the worlds. What happens in this circle affects all the worlds.

INVOKING AIR

The element of Air is connected to communication, the sky, breathing, smell, and hearing. To connect Air and food, use ingredients with distinct aromatic fragrances that please your olfactory senses. Popcorn comes to mind first. It's airy and fills the room with an unmistakable and irresistible scent. And it makes popping sounds as it cooks. If corn isn't part of your diet, try puffed rice. You could get *really* creative and make a meringue, which is nothing more than sugar, egg whites, cream of tartar, salt, and lots and lots of Air.

Whatever food you choose to represent Air, bring it close to your mouth and take a big inhale. Let your nose tell your mouth what's coming. Breathe in deeply and say,

As I eat this _____, may I be reminded of sweet aromas, and sweeter memories. Without Air I cannot be. Let this food remind me of each precious breath, good times filled with laughter, and moments of exquisite beauty when my breath is taken away. With this food I invoke Air and welcome Air to my circle.

INVOKING FIRE

The element of Fire is most often associated with inspiration, passion, love, and transformation. To connect Fire and food, select red foods like beets or pomegranates, spicy red peppers and chilis, juicy blood oranges, ripe cherries, and fire-roasted salsas. Be careful which foods you eat here, because your energy is about to shift. Your tongue might tingle, your hips might sway, the fire in your belly will brighten your imagination and inflame your spirit. As you ingest these fiery, red, flavourful foods, exclaim,

As I eat this _____, may my body be filled with heat, passion, and inspiration. As I transform these foods into calories, which are units of heat and energy, may I remember that I am energy in motion. With this food I invoke Fire and welcome Fire to my circle.

INVOKING WATER

The element of Water connects us with the flow of life, emotions, and the deep wells of memory. To connect the element of Water with food, choose foods that are mostly liquid. The simplest choice here is to pour yourself a tall glass of clean, clear, cool water. Drink it in and feel how the Water rejuvenates you almost instantaneously. For an equally satisfying watery treat, try watermelon, salmon, cranberries (they grow in bogs, you know), clams, oysters, mussels, spinach, celery, or iceberg lettuce. As you eat or drink, say,

As I eat/drink this _____, may I remember that this planet and I are mostly made of Water. Water is life and without it there is no life. May every being have access to free, clean Water. With this food I invoke Water and invite Water to my circle.

INVOKING EARTH

The element of Earth connects us with bones, foundations, stability, and the source of our existence. To connect the element of Earth with food, select bone broth, meat, or salty foods like preserved fish. If meat isn't part of your diet, choose earthy foods like burdock root, potatoes (with the skins still on), dandelion greens, truffles, and pungent cheeses. Of course, all food comes from the Earth, so really you can eat anything for this part of the ritual, but focus on items that give you that earthy, weighty, full-mouth feel. And as you eat your earthy foods, say,

As I eat this _____, May I remember that the Earth is the source of all food and all life. This _____ is part of the Earth as I am. Today I feast on this _____, knowing that one day the Earth will surely feast on my bones. With this food I invoke Earth and invite Earth into my circle.

INVOKING CENTER

The fifth element is Center, Ether, Spirit, the invisible and always present, ineffable Mystery. Ether connects us with potential, with the process of continually becoming, with magick happening all the time, in the unseen places and ways. To connect the element of Spirit or Ether with food, select foods that rely on a hidden or unseen force. Two foods come to mind here immediately: mushrooms and yeasted breads. Just beneath the surface, a few millimeters below the soil, you see a vast mycelial network of fungi toiling away, supporting healthy forests, transporting vital minerals, composting and repurposing everything. The most visible aspect of this network is mushrooms. Also embodying this mystery, bread is possible, in large part, because of microbes and yeasts floating about in the air. The magick involved in breadmaking is mind dizzying. Choose bread or mushrooms to connect you to the invisible nature of Nature.

As you eat, say,

In eating this _____ I acknowledge that all food is potential. All food nourishes the spirit. All food depends on interconnected and unseen processes. I am the result of millions of unseen and unknowable circumstances. I am the mystery of the universe, of spirit, of potential made manifest. With this food I invoke Spirit/Ether/Potential/ Mystery and welcome Spirit/Ether/Potential/Mystery into my circle.

The "Tofu" of the Ritual

By now, you've had seven opportunities to invoke and eat and you may decide that's quite enough food for one ritual. But there's still a bit of magick left to be done, and one more piece to your ritual.

You've cleansed, grounded, invited, invoked, and eaten your way through a ritual. Now look at your table (or wherever you've been eating). Spread out before you are dishes, fishes, meats, beets, breads, bites, and nibbles, or at least whatever is left over from your feast. Take a few moments and remember what you did to make this ritual possible. If it makes your efforts more real, say everything you did out loud. You shopped, chopped, sliced, diced, opened packages, set out cups, bowls, forks, spoons, knives, cooked, boiled, broiled, basted, and tasted. No matter how meagre or completely over the top your feast was, you made food sacred today. As you ate your way through this ritual, you wove each ingredient and bite into a spell that magickally nourished your being, that fed your body with calories and magick, honoured the gods or ancestors or the living earth we all walk upon. Reflect on the magick you are making here.

Remember the Wonderwerk cave in South Africa, where 1.8 million years ago our most ancient of ancestors gathered to eat around a fire? Their meal and your meal are connected. Without their feast, your feast would not be possible. Without your feast, the memory of their feast would not be possible. Let that sink in for a moment.

When the time feels right, and you're finished, release each element in reverse order and thank the gods or invited guests (like your ancestors or the planet). You might quickly say,

"Stay if you will. Go if you must. Hail and farewell, _____"
(fill in the element or god).

After all, you've spent a long time in this ritual eating and such. I'm a fan of brevity with impact, especially at the end of ritual. You can open your circle and put on your ever-so-comfy after-dinner pants. Leave that one special plate with the offerings on it out for the night, or put it in the backyard, or place it on an altar. Let those invisible allies do what they will with it.

The Incredible Edible Harvest Altar

You know what I love most about harvests? Different fruits, vegetables, herbs, flowers, and livestock are harvested at different times, meaning that if you're lucky enough to live where agriculture and farming are still visible, thriving enterprises, then it's quite possible to enjoy seasonal foods when they are in season. I like fresh peaches, but not in December when they've been imported from another country. Don't misunderstand me, I think it's amazing how many seasonal fruits are now available year-round, and yet what an exquisite pleasure it is to pluck fresh peaches and ripe apples straight from the tree. Is there anything finer than a summer garden, resplendent with runner beans, peas, peppers, and edible flowers?

Over the past few years a spectacular harvest tradition has taken root in the magickal circles I travel in. Magickal people and local covens gather with loaded bags and baskets of local fruits, vegetables, and flowers picked from their gardens. They come bearing breads, jams, spreads, and wild blackberries gathered from hedgerows, and all manner of other tasty seasonal treats. Depending on the circumstances, there may be a ritual that focuses our magickal attention on gratitude for what we have, or recognizing that there's abundance in community, or noting that magickal work begun in the spring is now ripe and ready for harvesting.

The very best part about this community ritual is hanging around in the sunshine with likeminded folks, all willing to share their bounty. The second-best part of the harvest ritual is the altar that is created. Picnic tables are covered with coloured fabrics to match the season, and not much else. As folks arrive they arrange their harvested foods on the tables. As more people arrive, the altar grows, changes shape, is rearranged. Side tables are added to hold huge jugs of lemonade and ice water. Jars are opened, cheeses are unwrapped, cakes topped with berries and cream are carefully set on cake stands, knives are plunged into breads and meats alike. The point of the ritual, abundance, is created by a hundred different food offerings. And when the liturgical portion of the ritual concludes, the real ritual begins, as community feasts on the edible altar. There is something viscerally satisfying about watching friends, beloveds, children, elders, and total strangers filling their plates and bellies with delicious, fresh, juicy, decadent food. When everyone has had their fill, maybe even two or three fills, anything left over is available for anyone to take if they want it, and especially if they need it.

Over the years the ritual has evolved. Participants were asked to bring a magickal item, something dear to them that they've used in their magickal practice, the idea being that passing along magickal tools, be that an athame, a wand, a cherished book, or magickal statuary, is part of abundance too. The magickal items are placed strategically on the food altar, along with the edible gifts. You might reach for an apple and discover the perfect magickal tool you've been searching for.

One year I made a real sacrifice to this harvest altar. I offered a book I've had for nearly two decades, one that I've read and reread more times than I can count. The book, Thomas Moore's *The Re-Enchantment of Everyday Life*, recounts the profound roles enchantment and re-enchantment play in our lives. That hardbound, first edition served me so well over the years, and, as difficult as it was to pass it along, I knew it was the right thing to do. The person that "harvested" this item from the altar mentioned that re-enchantment, the conscious act of making everyday life special, was exactly what they needed.

What's special about this rite is that it doesn't have to happen once a year or only in the summer. Late autumn and early winter harvests happen too. Dried and preserved foods can be shared in the cold months, reminding our taste buds of summers gone by. And, let's be ridiculously practical for a moment, if it's freezing and bleak and grey and blustery outside, and you must eat a strawberry, you can use the magick of the frozen food section at the grocery store and get strawberries whenever you want them.

And you needn't have a huge community to pull this off. A kitchen table or counter-top is a perfectly acceptable altar space. A wooden cutting board, some pickles, a little cheese, a sliced apple, and some prosciutto is a divine altar to abundance. The trick to abundance is to make use of what you have and give thanks to those that provided the feast. Even if—especially if—the person providing the feast is you! There are hundreds of ways to adapt this ritual; a veritable surfeit of options is open to you. In some cases, it's the absence of food, just a well-set table and connection to a million other people that provides the magick.

─────── *Wisdom from the Community Pantry* ───────
THE FAST AND THE END OF THE FAST
By Megan Langley, foodie, witch, and world traveler

The first day of Ramadan I decided to fast. A group of travelers and tourists were traveling out into the desert to camp with Bedouins, friends of our guides, Ghandi and Mohammed. At sunset that first night, as the sun dipped behind the wind-carved sandstone horizon, Mohammed came out of our hosts' tent, a cigarette in his mouth, and offered us dates. I declined the generous offer, and mentioned I was fasting too.

The second day of Ramadan we headed back towards Cairo. By now, most everyone in our group decided to fast along with our guides. We were passing through a village when the call from the mosque signaled an end to the fast. Children ran up to our bus, handing a bag of dates to the driver and passing dates through the windows, from their hands to ours.

The third day of Ramadan we were back in Cairo. It was towards the end of the day and Ghandi was leading us to our favourite Cairo restaurant. The restaurant owners ignored the twelve of us, white and sunburnt, in shorts and tank tops, flip flops and sunglasses, and tried to usher Ghandi to a seat at a table inside. Ghandi said, "No, they are fasting too." In mere moments they had a new table set up on the sidewalk, chairs and a table and place settings, and room for us all to sit together. Bread was laid out on each of our plates.

When the mosque's call came, we all broke bread together, millions of hands and mouths across the city.

The Dude Who Always Brings a Roasted Chicken

Admit it. You know this person. You might even be this person. I'm talking that one coven mate or community member that always shows up to the potluck with a store-bought rotisserie chicken. There's more to say about the potluck chicken-bringing dude, but first let's talk about Thomas Nashe.

It is to the sixteenth-century satirist and collaborator of William Shakespeare and Christopher Marlowe (the other Shakespeare) that we ought to give the dubious accolade for bringing the world the abomination that is the potluck. Okay, that's a bit harsh. Nashe is credited with writing the sentence "That, that pure sanguine complexion of yours may neuer be famisht with potte-lucke" in his book *Strange newes, of the intercepting certaine letters, and a convoy of verses*, published in 1592. And with that one statement, which was strange news indeed, the word *potluck* came into the common vernacular. However, back in the Elizabethan era, the phrase *potluck* really meant something more along the lines of "a pulled-together meal, not thought out or prepared, just whatever was lying about or already in the pot, and so you'll be rolling the dice and it's up to the luck of the pot as to what you'll get." It wasn't until the US depression of the 1930s that the meaning changed to be, "Hey! Everyone brings a dish."

You might have picked up that I'm not a fan of potlucks. I love the idea of potlucks, but not the practice. I've been to more potlucks that resemble "you'll be lucky to find something to eat" than "WOW! You made a great dish too!" You've shown up to the party with your great dish and everyone else has brought a French baguette, am I right?

Here's what I love about the dude who always brings a roasted chicken: they always bring a roasted chicken. Let me explain. If the dude who always brings a roasted chicken shows up with, well, a roasted chicken, then I can prepare a tasty side dish of macaroni and cheese. That way there's roasted chicken, mac and cheese, and the aforementioned ubiquitous French bread baguette. If by the luck of the pot, someone shows up with a bagged salad, we've got a decent meal.

Potlucks highlight the difference between intention and impact, which is an important magickal lesson for sure. The *intention* of a potluck is that everyone attending brings a dish to share, which is a lovely sentiment. The *impact* of folks getting ready to head out to an event, remembering at the last minute it's a potluck, stopping by the local grocery store and grabbing a French bread baguette has a direct effect on what's available for everyone to eat. My own informal surveys of potluck attendees over the years have yielded the general result of "meh! I could live without them."

Believe it or not, the effort that you invest in the meals you bring to potlucks has a lot to do with how you show up magickally. It's that intention-versus-impact thing again. Coven meetings, group rituals, and public magick events are a bit like a potluck. You never quite know who's going to show up and what they're bringing to the magick. The same can be said of personal rituals too. Even though you know that you're going to be there, if you don't have a clear magickal intention for the work, the results might just as easily turn out to be "meh"!

To be fair, I have been to a few spectacular potlucks, but they were, how shall I put it, very well curated. There are two formats for potlucks that work very well, but they are likely to challenge the "bringers of the pots." You'll see the magickal correlations pretty quickly, and you'll learn a lot about yourself and the people you do magick with.

The first model for a successful coven, er ... I mean potluck, involves assigning the roles or, in this case, the rolls. Assuming you know who's coming to the meeting, you can assign a dish or a type of dish to each person. Amy Bright Sparkle is asked to bring the bread. Moonshadow brings beverages. Lord Mikey is assigned the salad. And so on. There's plenty of room for creativity. Lord Mikey can opt to make a spinach, walnut, and cranberry salad or really go overboard and recreate their famous Thai chicken salad from Beltane 2018 or just buy a giant bag of greens and a bathtub of ranch dressing from their local shop. Amy Bright Sparkle is told in advance that they are responsible for the bread. This gives them the option to research where to buy the best breads en route to the meeting, or to spend the afternoon baking a harvest loaf. What they can't do is show up with a roasted chicken because (a) that's the job of the dude that always brings a roasted chicken and (b) chicken isn't bread.

Each person has a role. One person, a committee, or a consensus-based conversation between interested parties determines the needs of the group and delegates responsibilities. Ideally, you take charge for the solstice potluck and another person steps up for the equinox meeting. No matter who steps into leadership, the expectations are clear and the group knows who is responsible for what. Believe it or not, showing up with the food you agreed to provide and seeing that other folks held up their end of the bargain builds trust. Building trust is a key foundation stone for a strong magickal community.

The second potluck model requires a leap of faith, hard work, and trust. Lots of trust. This is my favourite form of potluck, because it's not really a potluck at all. There's more of an element of "the luck of the pot" here, harkening back to the original sixteenth-century meaning. Here's how it works: A number of people agree to cook. Your group can figure out if that's one person per meeting or a couple of people. That's for you to decide. Then, everyone that isn't cooking gives Moonshadow an equal portion of money. That's right. Everyone hands over an agreed upon wad of cash to Moonshadow. Moonshadow's job is now to spend all of the money wisely on food, cakes, ale, and whatever else is needed to construct a feast for everyone. Done well, this is a truly magnificent way to enjoy the luck of the pot. You hand over cash and a plentiful table of morsels appears. Clearly it's important to check in about allergies. "I'm gluten free" or "I'll die if I eat shrimp" is important information to convey. Give Moonshadow basic preferences like, "I'm vegan" or "I follow a paleo diet." That's it though. No details that aren't directly related to health. It's a big deal to be trusted with feeding a group of people. It's weird to spend other people's money, all of their money, on a meal. It's rare to give up control and trust that another person will use the money you gave them well and make great food choices and pull together one delicious dinner and that you will be grateful for their hard work and labour no matter what shows up on the table. It's also incredibly fun and terribly exciting. Think about it. You give over a little cash, that cash is multiplied by the amount of people in your group, and the buying power goes through the roof. The potluck gets elevated from French bread baguettes, bags of Doritos, and a roasted chicken to a Bacchanalian festival with dishes that tantalize the taste buds and excite the imagination.

Which brings us back to the dude that always brings the roasted chicken. Their intention is simple: Bring a hot, nutritious roasted chicken to the share. Their impact is consistency. Everybody knows that there will be at least one meat-based protein and the rest of the meal can be created around that or in support of that. There's an important magickal lesson here that I like to call "What am I contributing to the potluck?"

THE MAGICK I BRING

Find a place to sit where you won't be disturbed for at least ten minutes. Grab a pen and a piece of paper. Close your eyes and imagine a large table. A person shows up, puts down a dish, and says,

This is the magick I bring for the table

and then they name their magick. They look at you and ask,

What magick do you bring for the table?

Sit with that for a couple of heartbeats and ask aloud,

What magick do I bring for the table?

Begin writing everything that comes to mind. Maybe you sing, knit, write spells, brew potions, make soap, have memorized all the words to the ceremonies, provide your group a place to meet, are an elder with lots of answers, are brand new and have lots of questions, or totally rock at advertizing the public rituals. There's some piece of magick that you bring that's uniquely yours. That's your dish for the table.

If you practice magick with a coven or group, try bringing this contemplation to the next gathering. Have everyone imagine the magick they bring to the table. You'll find that everyone has something to offer and that can take any pressure off of one person to be and do everything for the group. You see, if everyone knows that you're the dude that brings the roasted chicken, they'll bring something else. And if everyone brings something, we'll all eat.

Super-Quick Bonus Recipe for Potluck Mac & Cheese

I love me some good mac and cheese. My mother-in-law's recipe is the best because it's light on mac and heavy on cheese. Over the years, I've added ingredients like greens and bacon and Worcestershire sauce, but the key to this recipe is keeping the ratios of mac, butter, and cheese just as they are.

Serves 6	Prep Time: 10 minutes	Cooking Time: 90 minutes

6 cups water

1 tablespoon salt

2 cups macaroni pasta

2 whole sticks butter

½ yellow onion, diced

2 leaves chard or kale, cut into ribbons (chiffonade)

4 cups milk, divided

2 tablespoons Worcestershire sauce

1 pound sharp cheddar cheese, grated, plus 2 cups sharp cheddar cheese, grated (in case you thought we were done with the cheese)

1 pound jack cheese, grated

2 cups sourdough bread crumbs

Preheat your oven to 375° F. Bring 6 cups of salted water to a boil in a large, covered pot. Add the macaroni pasta to the boiling water and cook for 8 minutes. After 8 minutes, drain the water from the pasta using a colander.

Grab a large baking dish, approximately 9" x 12". If you are taking this dish to a potluck, I suggest using an aluminum foil baking dish. Scoop the cooked macaroni into the baking dish. Next, take the two sticks of butter and cut them into 1 tablespoon slices (there's usually a guide on the side of a butter stick, in case you didn't know that!). Evenly distribute the butter on top of the pasta and slowly fold it in so the macaroni gets nicely coated. Fold in the diced onion and chiffonade of greens.

The next part is fun. Add half of the milk, the Worcestershire sauce, 1 pound of sharp cheddar, and 1 pound of jack cheese to the pasta and fold everything together so there's cheese throughout the dish. Now add the remaining milk, but don't stir it in.

Spread the last two cups of cheddar cheese and the bread crumbs evenly over the top of the pasta and bake, uncovered, for 30 minutes. Pull the dish from the oven, stir the whole dish so the bread crumbs become incorporated with the pasta and cheese mix and bake for another 30 minutes until everything is bubbly.

If Everyone Brings Something, We All Eat Well

Carin McKay, author, chef, friend, and all-around kitchen magician, believes that an integral part of food magick is, well, everything. Carin says

> *I'm talking about lineage. I'm talking about people. I'm talking about what emerges when you consciously weave together community, history, health, nature, and a real enjoyment of where you are.*[43]

As a cook and as a kitchen witch, I strive to ensure that the food I prepare is more than the sum of its parts. My favourite meals include four basic components: food, community, shared stories, and time. This is the essence of eating well, of dining rather than consuming, and it requires that every person brings something. Putting that a different way, food is only one component of a meal. Your guests—whomever or whatever they are—and their contributions are just as crucial as salt and pepper. And just to be completely clear, as we're all magick workers here, not everyone present at the meal has to be corporeal. Ancestors, deities, the Good Folk of your land, and the land itself could be (maybe even *should be*) invited as part of your community. It is perfectly fine, polite even, to ask them to contribute too. The food in this equation is the relatively easy part. Vegetables, proteins, spices, sweet notes, savoury flavourings—mix them in interesting combinations, heat them in some form or other, and a meal takes shape.

The community aspect of the meal doesn't imply that every meal you prepare or enjoy needs to be done in the company of other people. Rather, eating with community is an invitation to connect. Asking yourself questions like "where did this food come from?" and "how was this grown?" are good first steps to connecting with your food, but there's more you can do. Every time you eat, even if there's no other person sitting with you, there's an opportunity for engagement with everything that's around you. You might have a dog to share your scraps with. A wasp, a bee, the flowers in the planter box on the patio of your office building where you always eat lunch. The places you eat, the weather, the grass, the sounds, the sights, and the smells are all part of what flavours your meal. There are whole communities to interact with whenever you snack, nibble, or feast.

I used to spend Saturday afternoons in the Mission district of San Francisco. On a hot summer afternoon, the Mission is a veritable feast for the senses. I'd often eat at Taqueria

---

43. Carin McKay. *Culinary Magic at the Regenerative Design Institute: Creating community through food, farm, and permaculture.* Carin McKay, 2013.

Guadalajara, a locally owned, no-frills restaurant. They serve the best tacos in the world. The ingredients are authentic and simple, but what makes the food taste so incredibly good is the live mariachi music being played four blocks away. The music adds spice to the tacos. The telenovelas playing loudly on the TV in the back room and the soccer games being broadcast on another TV in the restaurant absolutely flavour the salsa verde as much as the tomatillos and lime juice. It's as if the entire Mission district, the collective energy of the place, is conspiring with the cooks in the kitchen to perfect every bite. And magickally speaking, that's absolutely what is happening.

When we share our stories, especially our own myths and memories about food, we're doing more than just sharing a recipe or recounting a meaningful meal. What we're creating is greater context for the lives we lead. The story I told about milk sop sits juxtaposed with the orgiastic recipes for wild boar and descriptions of wine-soaked Dionysian rituals. Our tales give us nuance and depth, much like mirepoix adds depth to soups and stews.

Sit with your friends, family, and Pagan beloved and ask them about the foods they love to eat or despise or can't wait to cook. There's always more to the story than just the taste. Watch their eyes, it's like they're replaying a movie. Listen to their words and you'll catch notes of poetry and song. Next time you find yourself with a group of people, ask them to list their all-time favourite meal and why it's so memorable.

Another way we tell stories is by sharing recipes and food lore. There's a recipe in the last section of this book called "A Slow Solstice Supper." A non-food-related memory of this meal involves my grandmother, who was busy raising two teenage boys and a grandson. She was so busy one Sunday afternoon, running around after everyone, that she put the pork roast in the shoe cupboard and roasted her pink fluffy slippers right alongside the apples and pears. I swear, I can smell burnt feathers every time I make this dish. And of course, there are less disastrous memories too.

Do you have a book or file box with index cards of recipes? Where did you get them? Who created them? What else did you learn from your stepmother, Mary, when she taught you how to make tuna noodle casserole? Our food memories aren't just related to the people we know, but can expand out to the cultures we grew up in or inherited from our ancestors. You love pierogi. I love Cornish pasties. Our friend loves empanadas. Pastry and filling make up each of these dishes. Culture and myth and stories change these ingredients into the stuff of legend.

——— *Wisdom from the Community Pantry* ———
CABBAGE IS MY FAVOURITE VEGETABLE
By Elizabeth C. Creely, writer

Cabbage is my favourite vegetable for many reasons, taste and affordability chief among them. It wasn't until recently, however, that I awarded cabbage the highest honour of being my favourite vegetable. My mother once confided to me that a raw cabbage core was a thing she liked to eat when she was growing up in Columbus, Ohio. We—the distributed, shared consciousness between the ancestral and the descended—have always loved to eat it.

Her people set sail from Germany and settled in Auglaize County in the northwestern corner of Ohio, an agricultural area that was—and still sort of is—a German settlement. Before that it was Shawnee territory. Germans settlers, helped by the US Army, killed some and forced the rest out. (Images of that displacement stuck in the ancestral memory of my family. My great-great-grand-aunt Caroline Bechtolt talked about seeing a "starving Indian" going around the small settlement where she lived, spectral and gaunt, asking for food where previously there had been more than enough.)

There's a town called New Bremen in Auglaize County, and I grew up hearing about it, mostly because my fourth-greatgrandfather, Johann Berend Koop, who was born in Lower-Saxony, Germany, settled there after 1831. The really notable feature of this region is a place called "the Great Black Swamp," which is exactly what it sounds like. It was an enormous freshwater swamp, or glacially fed wetland, about one hundred miles long, and full of flora and fauna, including lots of mosquitos. Johann died in 1839 of malaria. (Welcome to Ohio!) Before that happened, he married and had children, and they hung on, living on the edge of the swamp with its miles of waterlogged forests and un-tillable land, until the swamp was drained. Cabbage quickly became the principal crop of Auglaize county.

Potatoes were also grown in that wet ground, and this brings me to this observation. I sometimes feel that there's a mute rivalry between potatoes and cabbage. Both loom large in my family's gastronomic history. Both could claim to be the foodstuff my ancestors depended on—and ate—the most.

As someone who frequently speaks about my Irish-American ancestry, I am often asked about potatoes. *Do I like them? Why did they fail, exactly?*

My answer to the first question is, yeah, sure. Potatoes are okay. I often have them in the house. But I don't love potatoes as much as people think I should. Unless they are pulled straight from the ground, steamed, and eaten with salt and butter (my grandmother once made me this dish, and it was superb), I find them … just okay.

But as far as loving them, nope. They lost the contest for best vegetable in the fall of 1845, the year of the first widespread failure of the potato crop in Ireland. Potatoes are tricksy. Although they are innocent of any wrongdoing and not responsible for the famine that followed the crop failure, they carry such a despairing story with them that I can't help but regard them with the double vision of the ancestor worker. The rage that was directed at the British landlords and Charles Trevelyan, the hated head of the British Treasury and overseer of "relief" efforts in Ireland, were probably directed at the putrid potatoes first.

Cabbage, or *Brassica oleracea*, has never, to the best of my knowledge, let my family down. It had a lower profile than potatoes when I was growing up; it wasn't championed the way potatoes are (French fries! gratin dauphinoise! vichyssoise!). I feel that cabbage has been left out in the cold, somehow. This may have been because of its nineteenth- and twentieth-century association with slums and tenements. M. F. K. Fisher writes about this in her fine essay "The Social Status of a Vegetable."[44]

More for me, as they say. And cabbage is good for you. It has copious amounts of vitamins C and K.

The German settlers knew this. In Auglaize County, there are antique malls lining the streets of the little towns—Saint Mary's, Minster, New Bremen—all of them German and many of them depopulated and forlorn in the quiet way of the Midwest. In these antique malls, you'll see large wooden boards with blades screwed in diagonally across the surface. These are cabbage cutters, and were in use in every kitchen in Auglaize County in the nineteenth and twentieth centuries.

To use them, you brace the board against something, then push a whole head of cabbage over the blades. If the blades are sharp (the cutters in the

---

44. M. F. K. Fisher. "The Social Status of a Vegetable." https://harpers.org/archive/1937/04/the-social-sta tus-of-a-vegetable/.

antique malls never are) you get evenly sliced wedges of cabbage, perfect for sauerkraut.

Or you can work with the wonderfully broad leaves and make cabbage rolls: a savoury stuffing made of ground beef, sausage, onions, and cooked rice (and maybe a bit of parsley) rolled in cabbage leaves, covered in tomato sauce, and baked in an oven until done.

I felt pretentiously retro the first time I did this: was my fascination with cabbage rolls nothing more than a fanciful idea of what used to be eaten? It was a tedious process, too. The cabbage leaves gave a dank odor as I blanched them one by one. *This is hard work*, I thought. I looked up at the framed portraits of my fourth-greatgrandparents, Jacob and Eva Arnett, who lived in Auglaize County 160 years ago, on the edge of the Great Black Swamp. What did they eat? Not much. Cabbage, like most crops, can't tolerate too much water. They were only able to cultivate it after they'd drained the swamp and forced it into the sort of agricultural production that resembled what they had in Germany.

The innocence of vegetable life ends when we produce it, and exists in sharp contrast with its history as a cultivar. Cabbage may have helped my family survive, but potatoes didn't, and both crops entered my family's hearths and kitchens because of some terrible traditions: land hoarding and the displacement of native populations. The need for the food we love can make monsters of us all, even as it connects us across generations.

I have a fat green cabbage in my refrigerator right now, and plan on eating it later. I'll sauté it in olive oil, dash some red wine vinegar across its seared surface, season it with a bit of salt and pepper, pop it in my mouth, and marvel for the thousandth time over the wilted crispness, the sweet yet peppery taste, the goodness of the humble brassica—humble, problematic, yet loved.

The last ingredient to a great meal is time. Time can be measured in two ways: The actual minutes and seconds that elapse, and the quality of those seconds and minutes that elapse. Personally, I think meals should last for at least three hours. In a busy world, that's next to impossible to do on a daily basis. But if we can't stretch every noshing session to many hours, the very least we can do is make the time we do set aside for eating as pleasurable and as sacred as possible.

Think about it. It's likely that you'll eat almost every day of your life. There are precious few actions that you do every day. Like breath, food sustains us. Without it we die. It seems to me that honouring food, making food sacred, and spending time with our food no matter the nutritional value or organic seals of approval, or whether we made it, bought it, stole it, or begged for it, ought to be the one daily ritual we remember to practice. Sometimes you have to eat in the car, in between soccer practice and going to a coven meeting. So before putting the car in gear and pulling out of the drive-through, would it be possible to say, "*This food sustains me. May I never hunger. I am grateful to have this food today*"? It took you a mere few seconds to read that sentence; surely there's time to say thank you.

Sometimes what we bring to a meal is a roasted chicken. Other times we show up with our stories. Making time for a meal with friends or coven mates is like a dish we're contributing to the table as well. Our attention to each other becomes the tablecloth, the plates, the sight of candle flames reflected in a glass of deep, sinfully good red cabernet sauvignon. Food, community, shared stories, and time feeds more than our bodies. They feed our soul and they feed our magick. In fact, I'd posit that they *are* soul and they *are* magick.

Chapter 10

Food and the Kitchen Witch

Here's the really great news about becoming a kitchen witch. As long as you have access to a kitchen you can be a kitchen witch. Now, how you define *kitchen* is totally up to you, but if there are at least a couple of these items somewhere you prepare food, you're well on your way to being an official kitchen witch. Do you have a toaster, a cutting board, a microwave, a fridge, a bowl, a knife, a spoon, a grill on your patio, an oven, a stovetop, or fire? If you checked "yes" to a heat source and at least one tool, it's looking good.

Now that you've got the kitchen part covered, let's talk about the other key component: namely, being a witch. There are many definitions of the word *witch*. No doubt you've heard of or read a few descriptions that sound right to you. Certainly there are traditional witches and self-identified witches and initiated witches. There are hedge witches, green witches, even sandwiches. Each variety of witch has guidelines, rules, ethics, practices, and beliefs, and this is no different for kitchen witches. Practicing kitchen witchery means that you'll work with food and the belief that all food is sacred. As a kitchen witch you may choose to investigate flavours, and you may discover ingredients that open the palate, tantalize the senses, stimulate healing, support love, and create space for conversation between disparate parties.

Being a kitchen witch means utilizing herbs and working with magickal correspondences, and preparing dishes seasonally to create harmony with the places you live. Food will be the most obvious vehicle by which you'll deliver your magick, but being a kitchen witch also asks you to consider what it is to be a storyteller, a passer of lore, a skill-sharer, a listener, a dishwasher, a teacher, a nurturer, a gardener, a keen shopper, and a humble cook (in my case, a humbled cook!). If that's the journey you're looking for or have been on for years, it's time to pass along a ritual to you.

By the power vested in me, I hereby share with you the very secret and holy rite of becoming a kitchen witch. Once you take this step, there's no turning back. Ready? Stand in the middle of your kitchen or a kitchen you have pretty regular access to. Close your eyes, take a deep breath, announce out loud to everyone and everything, "I am a kitchen witch," and go make some food. That's it. You are now an officially ordained kitchen witch. Oh wait! There a few things to know. You'll need some tools, and there are rituals to memorize, and there's a cost to being a kitchen witch that you should probably know about as well. Maybe I should have told you all of that before encouraging you to tell the universe that you're a kitchen witch …

A Witch's Kitchen Tool Kit

Every trade, profession, or craft practice has its specialized tools. Being a kitchen witch is no different. There are basic tools you simply must have. As with every craftsperson, the more familiar you are with your tools, the more you get to know them and the better you can become at wielding them. Magickal tools often look like ordinary household objects. Don't be fooled by their banal and benign outer appearances. It's just a glamour to the untrained eye. In the hands of a kitchen witch, the mundane becomes magickal.

A Tea Towel

The first tool you must acquire is a tea towel. Professional kitchen witches often wear their tea towel over one shoulder anytime they are in the kitchen. I hook my tea towel in the straps of my apron, so it's always handy. While a tea towel might not leap to mind as the foremost tool in your tool kit, it is, and there's one simple reason. It's both a practical item and a symbolic one. Tea towels wipe down countertops. Tea towels transform into de facto oven mitts. Tea towels mop sploshed ingredients from the stovetop. Tea towels clean off knives and steady cutting boards. Tea towels can do a great number of things. I suspect the author of *The Hitchhiker's Guide to the Galaxy*, Douglas Adams, may have been a kitchen witch, as evidenced by the advice to always bring a towel along on your adventures.

There's a symbolic meaning behind a tea towel too. A tea towel conveys the message of "clean as you go." Magickally speaking, and as a piece of kitchen technology, this is sound advice. As you cook, clean. Done with a knife? Wipe it off and put it away or set it aside until you need it again. Finished a spell? Clear away the bits and pieces you used to create the magick. Working on a relationship? Your tea towel comes in handy for dabbing away tears and reminds you that even the most successful relationships need to be wiped down every now and again. Just like life, cooking and magick are messy. There's no getting around that fact. Invariably, countertops become littered with scraps and flour and trimmings, pie casings leak, and magickal spells boil over and get everywhere. Mistakes will be made, fingers will get cut, and spells will catch fire and need putting out immediately. A good tea towel, in the hands of a kitchen witch, reminds us that we can wipe up our messes, whatever they may be, and start again.

A Knife

A good knife is essential for a kitchen witch. Think of your knife or knives as the athames of the kitchen. I was taught many years ago that one's athame was a tool for discernment, and my kitchen knife plays exactly the same role. The practice of discernment, or learning how to judge well, is both a practical matter and a magickal one. How I use my knife to prepare the ingredients has a direct effect on the outcome of the meal. When preparing food, I think about the end result of the dish and what I want to the meal to convey. The flavour and texture of a dish changes substantially when carrots are sliced into medallions, or roughly chopped, or julienned.

As a magickal matter, I suggest consecrating your kitchen knives ritually too, as they play an integral part in the creation of the magick you perform in the kitchen. If you have a "magick only" athame in your everyday witch's tool kit, you can use it to confer power, intention, and discernment into your kitchen athames. Your magickal athame is likely used to draw and direct energy when you're making magick and doing ritual spell work, right? Your kitchen athames do essentially the same thing. A simple consecration ceremony could look like this:

Grab your "magick only" athame and bring it to the kitchen. Clean each of your kitchen knives with your tea towel and place them on your altar (I suggest a cutting board). Touch the tip of your magickal athame to the tip and butt of your kitchen knives and say,

> *One athame to another, magick shared, energy sent. Let the wisdom of knowing whether slicing or paring or chopping or piercing best serves the magick created here. Let discernment be in this blade hereafter.*

A Journal

I know, you were expecting the next tool to be a blender or a cauldron or something like that, but a journal is an extremely important tool for a kitchen witch. Think of it as your kitchen's Book of Shadows. A kitchen journal becomes your repository for recipes, ingredients, preparation techniques, failures, quick fixes when things go wrong, and culinary triumphs. I also like to include how I set the table or what bowls I used or where I first heard about this dish. It's a record of what I made, how I made it, and what made the meal memorable. Memorializing your recipes and food practices becomes the liturgy of your practice. On a moment's notice, you'll be able to pull together a food spell, carefully disguised as shepherd's pie, or create food-based love magick from memory.

Now a word about journals. I'm a terrible journaler, so I also write in the margins of my cookbooks, making notes about alterations in cooking times, whether to add an extra pinch of pepper, and detailing anything that will remind me how to make the recipe just the way I like it. This is part of my journaling practice. Yellow sticky notes can be found all throughout my collection of cookbooks, and I have more bookmarked internet pages than I can count. All these serve as my extended kitchen Book of Shadows.

Measuring Cups & Timers

There are rules to cookery. You can't braise short ribs in fifteen minutes no matter how much you wish it to happen, and a teaspoon of salt is very different than a cup of salt. Magick, I find, works much the same way. Certain spells take careful measurements and time, and there are no good substitutes for either.

I've been cooking for years and I have a pretty good feel for how much is a pinch or a dash or a cupful of any ingredient I'm working with, but until I master a recipe (which is much rarer than you might think) I always measure the ingredients properly. I've watched way too many cooking shows for my own good, so I like to measure the ingredients into little glass bowls or ramekins or measuring cups and set them aside until I need to add them to the pot or pan. The extra step of measuring salt and adding it to a bowl for later does make more dishes to clean up, but it makes for better results, and good results are essential in cooking and magick.

Time is best used in cooking and in magick when we view it as an ally rather than something to run up against or fear we don't have enough of. Every meal benefits from time, whether that's the minutes we spend consuming the food or the hours it takes for the flavours of spices and vegetables, proteins and alcohols to break apart, come back together again, and form deep, nourishing combinations that no amount of laboratory tinkering and genetic engineering can replicate or improve upon.

The correlation of measurements and time in both recipes and magick is obvious. If you have spells that work for you, write them down and, perhaps more importantly, write down exactly what you did, when you did it, what "ingredients" you used, and how long you let the spell "bake" before deciding the magick was done and the loaf was ready to eat. Knowing what makes a meal or a spell work for you is a critical step in making magick. As a side note, knowing what ingredients you used and measuring how long your dish took to cook also allows you the freedom to experiment. What happens if you omit the paprika next time? Does using margarine really make a difference when the recipe calls for butter? Once you understand how a dish or spell is supposed to work and you've experienced it as the original cook or magician intended it to be, then you can begin colouring outside of the culinary lines and making the meal or the magick your own.

A Wooden Spoon

Second only to my knives, the most beloved tool in my kitchen witch's tool kit is my wooden spoon. My favourite spoon is hand carved, red, about twelve inches long, and was gifted to me. The spoon has both the rounded end you'd expect and a slightly beveled area that makes it good for scraping the bottom of pans right before I deglaze them. The spoon, although thoroughly cleaned, somehow carries the memory of every soup, stew, and cake it's ever had the pleasure to have known. I love this spoon. We know each other well.

A good spoon is much like a wand, I think. Wands are often described as an extension of the witch's hand. Wands don't create magick, but they aid in the process of bringing the spell to fruition. My spoon tells me how the spell is going. I like to touch my food when it's cooking to get information about doneness. My fingers tell me a lot about how well-cooked a protein is, for instance. However, it's highly impractical to plunge one's hands into a boiling pot of soup to check the temperature, taste, or consistency. My wand, my spoon, can do that for me. As I stir the ingredients, I learn the feel of when the ingredients of a stew are properly integrated together. My spoon brings me information from the bottom of the pot too, releases aromas as it swirls components together, and delivers the first taste of the dish to my mouth. Most of the food magick I do is inviting, welcoming, rooted in abundance, and concerned with growing a vibrant community, so as a matter of magickal habit, I typically stir deosil or clockwise.

Practically speaking, my spoon also gets used to lift off hot and heavy cast iron lids, spans a pot of boiling water to prevent spillovers, and gets waived disapprovingly in the general direction of people that want to taste my food before it's ready, thus confirming its use as a powerful protective wand. Much like the knives and athames, one could easily consecrate a treasured wooden spoon too.

A Well-Stocked Pantry

In my house there are three magickal cabinets. One houses fabrics, yarn, candles, rocks, a Book of Shadows, pins, flash paper, goblets, wands, runes, and the gods know what else. Just about anything I could need for a spell or ritual lives in that cabinet. There's a magickal herb closet. There are jars filled with lemon verbena, lavender, mugwort, valerian root, rose petals, damiana, belladonna, roots, stems, soil, and that's not to mention the flying ointments and assorted lotions, potions, balms, and salves. Any number of magickal concoctions could be made from this cabinet.

Lastly, there's the pantry. I view the pantry as my laboratory, my magickal cabinet containing the secrets to flavour and teleportation. A well-stocked pantry allows me to transport my guests back in time, across the world, to ancient temples and places locked in myth and legend. I know that sounds awfully grand, but what I'm talking about here is a cupboard in my kitchen with essentials. Here's a good starter list. It's far from complete, but start here and grow as needed:

- Salt: Finishing salt, kosher salt, pink salt
- Fleur de sel
- Pepper: Black pepper white pepper, whole peppercorns, cayenne pepper
- Oregano
- Thyme
- Sage
- Cumin
- Coriander
- Bay leaves
- Rosemary
- Parsley

- Garlic: Garlic powder, pickled garlic, raw garlic
- Onion powder
- Garam masala
- Ginger: Powdered ginger, stem ginger, candied ginger
- Allspice
- Cloves
- Baking powder
- Baking soda
- Assorted flours
- Polenta
- Sugar: Brown sugar, dark brown sugar, white sugar
- Lentils: White, red, and black lentils
- Dried beans: Pinto, black, lima
- Rice: Brown, white, jasmine, wild
- Vinegar: Red, rice, malt, balsamic, distilled white, apple cider

If you have the chance to grow or purchase fresh herbs and then dry them yourself, so much the better. Plus, bunches of herbs hanging in your kitchen makes your dwelling look awfully witchy and just like Baba Yaga's cottage in the woods.

Curiosity

I know it's hard to buy curiosity at the local supermarket or metaphysical store, but get a hold of some wherever and whenever you can. Curiosity is the most magickal of ingredients you can ever hope to cultivate. Curiosity led me to discover sourdough starters and ras el hanout and flummeries and borscht and why our ancestors loved pickled everything. Curiosity and magick have a lot to do with each other as well. When I first discovered magick and magickal practices, I had an infinite number of questions. There seemed to be innumerable paths to run down. Every currently available style of Paganism and tradition of witchery has its own unmistakable flavours and ingredients. I find that endlessly fascinating and exciting. I hope I never run out of questions. I wish that for you too.

The Cost (not actually a tool, but you definitely need to know this)

Being a kitchen witch has a high cost, as well as a veritable cauldron full of rewards. If you are anything like me, you'll be forever buying cookbooks and testing recipes and watching cooking shows and trying new foods and randomly finding yourself in a friend's kitchen cooking at an impromptu gathering and being asked to make success potions and love cookies and healing broths.

You'll come to find that magick and food are obviously and inextricably linked and the practice of making a meal and infusing it with a dash of blessing, a pinch of love, or a spoonful of protection becomes second nature. Being a kitchen witch is an opportunity to practice your art virtually every single day and see magick created and shared up close and personal. Kitchen witchery looks like beautiful meals and cleaned plates. It also comes with the sting of burnt wrists, cut fingers, and an aching back. Oh, also, once you decide to become a kitchen witch, it's basically a lifetime appointment.

A Few Words about Cauldrons

There's one obvious tool that wasn't mentioned in the last section. The cauldron deserves special attention, and no witch, magick maker, or cook should be without one. Witches and cauldrons go together like, well, witches and cauldrons. Whether it's from the ubiquitous "*Double, double, toil and trouble; Fire burn and caldron bubble*" of Mr. Shakespeare or the flaming brazier from the John William Waterhouse painting "The Magic Circle," the image of a witch tending to their cauldron is both ingrained and much beloved. Of course, cauldrons have been part of magickal lore since long before Messrs. Shakespeare and Waterhouse.

Welsh mythology tells us of Cerridwen's cauldron brewing three drops of Awen that magically end up on Gwion Bach's thumb. In the second branch of the Mabinogi, we have the tale of Branwen Ferch Llŷr (Branwen, Daughter of Llŷr) which recounts how a great cauldron brings dead soldiers back to life to fight another day. Medea, from Greek mythology, also had a cauldron of rejuvenation. A vase from approximately 650 BCE depicts a resurrected sheep emerging from Medea's cauldron. The Irish god, Dagda, had a cauldron that was said to be ever filled and never dry. This self-refilling vessel could feed countless numbers of people, and it is said that no one ever left unsatisfied.

Cauldrons serve practical purposes too, of course. Large cooking vessels, especially ones made of metal, have been used in practically every culture, in every time period, throughout human history since the invention of metalcraft. Cauldrons are incredibly sturdy and easy to use. Generally speaking they are portable, which for traveling folk made them super user friendly. Suspend a cauldron over a fire, fill with ingredients, add liquid, and—presto!—you have a meal. Keep the pot hot, add ingredients and more liquid and the cauldron seemingly keeps on giving and giving endlessly. It's not difficult to see where such legendary stories came from. I mean, as a cook, who wouldn't want to knock out a lovely vegetable stew on a wintery Sunday afternoon and have the cauldron continuously reproduce the contents until early spring? That certainly works for me! If a mere human could feed the family for a week or two, surely the gods with their infinite resources and magick would have cauldrons that were self-replenishing and ever full.

My guess is that when you picture a cauldron, you imagine a large, black, cast iron pot. Maybe there's a tripod that goes along with this as well. These days you can order cauldrons online and find them in all sorts of metaphysical shops. They range from quite tiny and decorative versions that have just enough room to burn some charcoal and incense in, to larger iterations with handles, lids, and three legs that look very impressive sitting next to fireplaces. My house is affectionately called "the Cauldron House" because our family has a collection of cauldrons we've amassed over the years. For certain, we have the very typical black cast iron models, but there are copper cauldrons, clay cauldrons, decorative cauldrons, and cauldrons we use every day in the kitchen.

Laura Tempest Zakroff, in her book *The Witches Cauldron: The Craft, Lore & Magick of Ritual Vessels,* devotes an entire chapter to discovering a whole cadre of unconventional household cauldrons and their uses. She astutely suggests that *"If you think magick can only happen with a traditional cauldron, think again!"*[45] Here's a challenge for you. Stand in your kitchen and find three cauldrons. Remember, a cauldron is a vessel that can be heated, holds liquid and other ingredients, and is mostly portable. In my kitchen I found a large, red cast iron and enamel Dutch oven, a crockpot, and a stock pot. What did you find?

My appreciation for the power of the cauldron as a cooking tool, a metaphor, and an indispensable magickal tool came from an unlikely source. I spent years studying Tibetan Buddhism in the Gelugpa lineage. One of the central tenets of Buddhism is *the Heart Sutra,* which deals with emptiness. *Emptiness* is described not as the lack or absence of anything but rather the potential for almost anything to arise from that emptiness. In my witchcraft, the corollary to or symbol of Buddhist emptiness is the cauldron.

There's never a time when my cauldrons are filled with nothing. They might not contain a particular or obvious thing in them, but that's not the same as saying they are devoid of *anything.* There is something in the cauldron at all times. What that something might be

45. Laura Tempest Zakroff. *The Witches Cauldron: The Craft, Lore & Magick of Ritual Vessels.* Woodbury, MN: Llewellyn Publications, 2017.

depends largely on how I approach working with it. Before beginning any magickal under-taking, I ask myself and the cauldron and my guides and my intuition, just what might want to issue forth as a result of the magick that's being called forward. That could be a delicious pot roast, a magickal manifestation, or a pot roast infused with the intention that much magickal manifestation comes to those that eat the contents of my cauldron. Saying that another way, my cauldron has the potential to produce almost *anything*, because just about *everything* is already in it. It's just a matter of reconfiguring *everything* into *one* thing.

Now this filling-of-the-cauldron business occurs on three levels. I do actually take real things like herbs and liquids and bits of this and dashes of that (the proverbial eye of newt and wing of bat) and make a brew or elixir or paste or poultice. In alchemical terms, this is the *prima materia*. When my brewing is done I will have a tangible manifestation of the magick I've been making. Depending on what I've just made, I can apply it, wrap it, or eat it as the spell calls for.

Now the next level is a bit divinatory in nature, I suppose. Looking at what's in the cauldron gives me a sense of how my magick might turn out. I can use what's actually been made in the cauldron as a benchmark for what's occurring in the magickal realm. If my stew looks soupy, my magickal outcome could well be a bit watered down as well.

Lastly, there's the realm of mystery and potential. What occurred during the brewing, stewing, bubbling, heating, combining process that I didn't plan for? Maybe one flavour came through stronger than another. Perhaps the goop was more goo and, as it turns out, adhered better to the thing I was pasting the goo with. See, there's this element of mystery and *something happens here* that I think many witches and magick workers forget about in their spell work. Being a kitchen witch gives you the ability to eat your spell work or share your spell work with others and make adjustments to your recipes and spells as you go along.

Looking back at the many cauldrons we find in mythology and lore, there's often an action that has to be completed to make sure the potion being brewed is effective. In the story of Gwion Bach and Cerridwen, the cauldron has to be stirred three times a day for a year and a day to produce the three drops of Awen. Your cast iron cauldron might need to be seasoned to keep it in good working order. The outdoor fire pit, a cauldron of sorts, will need to have the ashes cleaned out from time to time or the fire won't grow as you intended.

The cauldron then is the both the container of the magick and an active participant in the spell work. One might say that it is actually the most important ingredient in the whole process, for without it there's nothing to put the other bits and bobs into. The mystery of the cauldron permeates all of the work and play I do with magic. One could posit that the cauldron is the absolute quintessential piece of magickal equipment that one needs in order to do effective, practical kitchen spell workings.

Cooking with Intention and Attention

Intention is one key ingredient in magick and meal making. Good magick often starts with a good intention, but just what is an intention? In its simplest form, the intention of a spell is the desired outcome of the magickal working. It's the Love in a love potion or the Healing in a healing broth. The intention is the stated reason for the magick being done. If we know why we're engaging in spell craft or employing our guides to help us with our tasks, the likelihood of the magick turning out remotely how we thought it might increases dramatically.

Before embarking on any kitchen witchery, I go through a type of checklist, if you like. I ask myself, why am I taking on this particular piece of food magic? What might I need to complete this spell? What would this magickal spell look like under ideal circumstances? How would I know the result if, indeed, it comes to fruition? Knowing the *what* and the *why* of the magick determines a lot of the *how* of the magic.

If I want to make a stew, buying the ingredients for a fruit cake isn't going to net the result I'm looking for. If I have all of the correct ingredients for a stew but follow the recipe for a soup, my concoction won't be quite right either. So, knowing what I want the result to be, at least generally, has to be the first step. One way to accomplish this is to craft a good intention, setting the intended result firmly in my mind and letting intention permeate through the ingredients, the mixing, the sautéing, and the meal itself. Now I have my intention and I can proceed with the spell, the recipe, and plan for exactly what I need.

Of course, intention isn't the only magickal ingredient in kitchen witchery. Watch any cooking show and you'll no doubt hear the host say, "You can taste the love in that dish." Love is a bit of an enigma when it comes to cooking. There aren't jars of love readily available on the shelves in my local supermarket, and even if there were, I'm not sure I'd want to cook with prepackaged "Love™ now with 5% less sodium." Love, for me, often falls into the same category as the word *energy*.

Just what are energy and love? Most magick workers recognize energy in some form or another, but explaining exactly what it is and what it does is another matter altogether. It's much the same with love. I believe most people know what love feels like, and will notice the difference in the air when love is not present or has ceased to be invited to the party. But what does love add to food? How does love change the recipe? And what does it have to do with intention and spell craft? A talented chef friend of mine really bristles at the often-quoted cliché "I cooked this meal with love" and goes on to note that over-baked cookies, even when cooked with all the love in the world and chock-full of good intentions, still taste bitter and burnt, and should probably be thrown away.

However, cooking with attention and intention is a better magickal combination. Attention is quite different from intention. Attention speaks to how a meal or spell is crafted and the techniques used to make the food spell possible. Attention moves intention from the ethereal to the manifested.

If you're planning a hearty, warming meal intended to remind you and your guests of home, hold the intention that you're feeding their bodies and also nourishing their longing for connection, safety, and the security of being home (or whatever it is that you all associate with being home). Let that intention inform how you cook, but keep in mind that attention is equally important. It's your attention to the details of the meal and how you serve it that add to the flavour and coax out the magick. If you want to evoke a feeling of home, how are you treating the ingredients? Is it just the food itself or are there other components you need to pay attention to, like what the meal should be served on, or in which order the courses will come out? Will certain spices transport you and your guests across the miles, and possibly the years, to a distant market or favourite uncle's kitchen? The place may no longer exist in real time, but the associated aromas and tastes live on in our memories. This is what attention brings to a meal. It's your intention to serve a good, home-cooked meal that is special to you and your guests. It's your attention that makes the meal authentic, magickal, and tasty.

Fish and chips, a meal I dearly love, is basically just fried fish and potato wedges. Serve me those tasty fried morsels wrapped in greaseproof paper or better yet, wrapped in newspaper, and I'm instantly transported to PJ Starlings chippie at the top of Brook Street in Erith, Kent. I'm handing over a few coins and getting a "penneth of chips" and crackling. Its neither the fish nor the chips that take me back there, but the feel of the newspaper in my hand. It's the attention, not the intention, that does the transporting.

Earlier on I said that intention is a little like a checklist, a shopping list that determines how the magick might turn out. Attention also comes with a checklist:

- What techniques do I need to know to cook this meal?
- How do I prepare the ingredients to best bring out their authentic flavours?
- Who cooked this meal originally and what do I know of them, their times, and how they made this food?

- Are there specific accoutrements that will make the meal more familiar, like using a tagine, a paella pan, baked naan to use as a utensil, or coffee served from a traditional cezve?

- Am I following a traditional recipe? (*Traditional* here could mean culturally correct or could refer to Uncle Mick's lemon tart recipe that's been a closely guarded secret for years and you've finally managed to track down after years of searching.)

- Am I watching the pot? Should this simmer or boil? Do I flash-fry this protein or let it cook down for hours?

Sharing Leftovers with the Earth

Growing up there were rarely, if ever, leftovers. Dinners were made or bought and consumed at dinner time. As food scarcity as a way of life faded into the background and I learned to make meals for a family, leftovers became a cherished gift. Not only was I able to have enough for today, but there was going to be food for tomorrow as well. As a result, I discovered three interesting things about leftovers.

Firstly, they often taste better for having sat overnight. I know the change in taste has more to do with chemistry than magick, but just how flavours and ingredients marry together, given enough time, is truly amazing. Last night's dinner served as breakfast the next day is simply divine. Secondly, having leftovers prepares one for the unexpected. After all, you never quite know when you might need a preprepared spell or an extra meal on just a moment's notice. Most importantly though, having leftovers means ample offerings for the land and spirits of place.

In every single place in this world there are spirits of place. In any given locale, they may be regarded as the "Good Folk" or the Fae. You might imagine the spirits of land as seen and unseen beings that are present in a place when you are not. On a more metaphysical level, the spirits of place might be conceived as the energy signature of a place—you know, that certain feeling that defines a place but you can't quite put your finger on. Broadening the definition could also include the deities that receive devotions or worship in this place.

If you're unfamiliar with the concepts of leaving offerings for the land or the spirits of place, the practice is incredibly simple and there are a variety of ways to leave offerings, in this case, food offerings. To be clear, this practice is about making an offering, not receiving anything back. If you're fortunate, you might begin a conversation with the spirits of your place. Here's one way you can start.

SERVING THE SPIRITS OF PLACE

During cooking or plating, set aside portions of food for the spirits of place. We're not talking about scraps or the rotten end of a stick of celery, but a small plate of food made especially for the spirits of place. Either before or after eating your meal, take the plate outside and carefully put it in a special place. You might fashion an altar from a tree stump or clear a space along a fence line separating your home from the lands beyond it. As you set the plate in your designated space, call out,

Hello, spirits of this place. Here is an offering for you. There is a tasty nibble of (here you can describe your food just as you would to any guest). Please accept this offering. I'd love to chat with you again, so I'll make more offerings. Perhaps we can start a conversation.

If standing in the garden talking with the Fae beings in your neighbourhood doesn't excite you magickally, there are a few exceptionally good practical ways to leave offerings for the spirits of land too.

You might also consider buying a compost bucket and filling it with kitchen scraps, wilted lettuce leaves, egg shells, onion peels, and coffee grounds. If you have a garden or backyard, set up a compost pile and add your food leftovers to it. Compost, as it breaks down and you add the mulch back into the soil, releases vital minerals and nutrients. Those same minerals and nutrients will influence the flavours of next year's crop of zucchini and sweet peas. This is a time magick spell. You'll taste your hard labour and cooking joy the next time you eat food from this part of your garden.

If you don't have a garden of your own you can still participate in this magick. Ask your neighbours if they grow their own food and if they'd want any extra compost. Perhaps you can agree to swap compost for a few runner beans next summer. Connecting with your neighbours about composting may lead to shared meals and recipes. Getting to know your neighbours is a lovely piece of kitchen witchery.

Alternatively, find a community garden in your area and see if they are accepting compost donations. Community gardens and local organic farms often set clear guidelines about what kind of materials they can take and when. This is an incredible piece of community and environmental magick. You are reducing your waste impact on the local environment and turning your leftovers into food for hundreds, maybe even thousands, of people in your community.

Three Speedy Food Spells

Being a kitchen witch means actively participating in spell work. Cooking certain foods with magickal ingredients and making meals with the expressed intention of influencing outcomes, feeding a lover, healing a friend, providing for community, or inviting the spirits of place or your gods to join you in ritual, is all part of what a kitchen witch does. In the spirit of sharing (something kitchen witches are usually pretty good at), here are a few of my favourite speedy food spells.

A CLASSIC LOVE POTION

Yes, I'm sharing a love spell. This is a love spell because (a) more love in the world is usually a good thing; (b) this love spell is simple to make and customize; and (c) as soon as someone finds out you're a kitchen witch they'll ask you about a love spell.

Bring a kettle of water to a boil. Fill your favourite magickal mixing bowl or measuring cup with 6 ounces of boiling water and drop in one tea bag of black tea. Let it steep for 3 minutes. Remove the tea bag. Add one ounce of brandy to the tea. Add 9 drops of the extract of your choice (see options below) to the brandy and tea. Carefully pour the potion into a dark blue or brown glass 2-ounce bottle. The best bottles to use come with a dropper as part of the lid. I recommend drinking four to six drops of the potion each day until it's gone. You can add the potion to a drink, incorporate them into a dish, or just drink the drops straight from the dropper. If you work with deities associated with love, such as Aphrodite, Frigga, or Juno, call on them to infuse your potion with their blessings. You may consider leaving this potion on an altar dedicated to love overnight, right after you make it.

Extracts to use:

- Vanilla for a sweet, enduring love. This is great for folks looking for a long-term relationship or wanting to maintain one.

- Ginger for spice. This version of the potion says you are looking for some hot lovin' right now.
- Strawberry or raspberry for sweetness. Think of this as those lovely, sweet feelings that come along with first love. If you're looking for a love that is sweet and bright and full of joy, this is just the ticket.

CALMING TEA

The world today is a fast-paced place. There's a good chance that you or someone you know is dealing with stress. In a moment of high stress, this simple tea reminds us of the benefits of calmness and ease. Drink a cup of calming tea before bedtime, as a daily practice, or brew it whenever needed.

Brew 2 cups of water in a kettle. While the kettle is boiling, add 2 teaspoons of lavender buds and 2 teaspoons of chamomile flowers to a teapot. Pour the water over the lavender and chamomile. Add 2 tablespoons of lemon juice to the tea and let it steep for 9 minutes. Strain the tea into your favourite tea cup and sip while hot. If you are able, get super comfy. Maybe that means getting under the covers of your bed or changing into your pajamas and snuggling on the couch with a blanket and your cat. Whatever comfort means to you, do that. When you're good and comfy, sip the tea. Recite the following words three times:

I am calm. I am present. The chaos of my day is banished for at least as long as it takes to drink this tea.

If you have someone in your life you associate with calmness, poise, and equanimity, picture them now as you recite the words. Perhaps you associate calmness with a place—a river's edge, a valley of flowers, that bed and breakfast you stayed in recently. Imagine that place as you recite the words. Maybe you're aligned with a god, goddess, or otherworldly friend that exudes calmness. Dedicate your cup of calming tea to them as an act of devotion as you recite.

MAGICKAL PANCAKES

Pancakes, like tacos, are basically perfect vehicles for magickal spells. You create the pancake and infuse the batter with spices that align with the spell you're working. Then you top the pancakes with fruits, sauces, and syrups that match your magickal intention too.

Super-Quick Bonus Recipe for Magickal Pancakes

Pancake recipes are simple, with lots of options. I typically use all-purpose flour, but you can use wheat flour or gluten-free flour. Same with the milk choices. I tend to cook with whole milk, but buttermilk is awesome. If you're lactose intolerant, there are some great substitutes out there.

Serves 4 (about 12 pancakes)	Prep Time: 10 minutes	Cooking Time: 10 minutes

1½ cups all-purpose flour

2 tablespoons sugar (I use light brown sugar)

2 teaspoons baking powder

1 teaspoon baking soda

½ teaspoon salt

1 cup milk (or milk substitute)

2 eggs

¼ cup melted butter

Grab yourself a large mixing bowl and combine all the dry ingredients. Make a well in the middle of the mixture and whisk in the milk, eggs, and butter until everything is incorporated. The mixture should be loose, not at all stodgy like cake batter. Heat a skillet (or griddle, if you have one) over medium heat for 3–4 minutes or until hot. Pour ¼ cup of the mixture onto the hot griddle. Leave it alone until tiny bubbles form over the surface of the pancake. Flip the pancake over and let it cook for another 2 minutes.

My big skillet can easily accommodate three pancakes at a time, which makes cooking a bit faster. I keep my pancakes warm by putting them on a plate in a preheated oven, but most of the time they go straight to a plate and get eaten immediately. Top with magick and enjoy.

Love Pancakes: Mix a half teaspoon of cinnamon into the batter recipe you're using. There are all sorts of fruits associated with love, some quite esoteric in nature, others because they're a bit risqué looking (like figs and bananas). Add fruits that speak of love to you, red berries for instance. Remember to top the pancakes with vanilla whipped cream (just add a teaspoon of vanilla extract to your whipped cream). As you stir the batter clockwise, recite the name of your lover, speak aloud a love poem, or sing your favourite love song as loud as you dare. If your spell is more lust than love, mix as many ingredients by hand as possible. Touch everything. Taste everything. Involve as many of your senses as you can as you create these pancakes and, of course, serve hot!

Prosperity Pancakes: Mix a half teaspoon each of allspice and carob powder into the batter recipe you're following. Both allspice and carob are associated with money and abundance. Chop pecans or almonds to top your pancakes. Pecans are associated with money and employment. Almonds are said to aid in healing around past money issues. Pour the best maple syrup you can afford on your pancakes. Here's the most important part of an abundance or prosperity spell: eat as many pancakes as you feel called to, but share at least one of them. You can share the pancakes with someone else in your house or make an offering to the spirits of place or your house gods, but prosperity magick works best when you share the wealth with someone.

Protection Pancakes: Add ½ teaspoon of chili powder to your batter recipe. Chili is a good "keep away" or "get away" spice. Cube one medium potato and sauté it in 1 tablespoon of oil for 10 minutes. Remember to move the potato chunks around the pan to keep them from sticking. Dice one small red onion and add it to the potato. Add another half teaspoon of chili powder if you can stand the heat. Cook the potato and onion for another 5 minutes. Remove the potato and onion to a paper towel to soak up any excess oil and spoon on top of your pancakes. The magick here is that you're making pancakes with a kick. It's as if you are saying, "I've got a full belly. I'm spicy and I'm recommending that you stay away from this heat." Consider using basil, garlic, black pepper, and salt, or any other protection herbs and spices you work with. If you're looking for folks to stay away from you, stir the ingredients counterclockwise.

Food Blessings

This book began with a brief and incomplete tour through food history. In each of the early cultures discussed, and in many countries around the world today, there's an understanding that food connects us. Food is a storyteller, reminding us of our cultural identity. Food anchors our religious and kitchen witchery practices. Food offerings and rituals inform the gods that we are still here and they are still a vital part of the human experience. Food is another word for love, because when someone takes time to prepare and cook food, no matter how humble or exotic the ingredients, they are saying, "You are important to me. May this food keep you alive and healthy and vibrant."

The food on your table came from somewhere, whether you grew it yourself or hundreds of people played a part in transporting it to your local food shop. Getting food out of the ground, off of the trees, into packages, loaded onto trucks, driven across counties and countries is honest, arduous work. And hard work often goes unnoticed. An elegant, simple way to remember why we eat together and honour those who helped the food on our plates come to be is to offer a blessing.

Here are some examples:

> "May this food nourish your body today. May this food remind you that you are loved today. May you never know days without food or love."
> GWION RAVEN

> "Come, spirits of my food. And feed my life. We will live our lives together from now on, you living in me."
> A PAGAN BOOK OF PRAYER[46]

> "Our hands will work for peace and justice. Our hands will work to heal the land. Gather round the harvest table. Let us feast and bless the land."
> HARVEST CHANT[47]

---

46. Ceisiwr Serith. *A Pagan Book of Prayer.* Boston, MA: Weiser Books, 2002.
47. Thorn T. Coyle. *Harvest Chant.* Reclaiming Campfire Chants, 2016, compact disk.

"I am food, I am food, I am food. I am the food eater,
I am the food eater, I am the food eater."
MYSTICAL CHANT FROM THE UPANISHADS[48]

"Over the lips, over the gums. Look out stomach, here it comes."
ANONYMOUS

"YUM! YUUUUUM! YUUUUUUUUUUMMMMM!"
A RECLAIMING TRADITION food blessing

"We receive this food in gratitude to all beings who have
helped to bring it to our table and vow to respond in
turn to those in need with wisdom and compassion."
BUDDHIST BLESSING

"In this plate of food, I see the entire universe supporting my existence."
ZEN BLESSING

"Spirits of this place, accept this offering of food and drink.
Make use of it as you will and know that it is given
with love and gratitude for all that you have provided."
GWION RAVEN

"May you never hunger. May you never thirst."
OFT-QUOTED PAGAN FOOD BLESSING AND QUOTE FROM
STRANGER IN A STRANGE LAND BY ROBERT HEINLEIN[49]

---

48. The Taittiriya Upanishad 3–10, Translated by Alladi Mahadeva Sastry.

49. Robert A. Heinlein. *Stranger in a Strange Land.* New York: G. P. Putnam's Sons, 1961.

Section III

All the Recipes

Many, many years ago I learned that you should always follow a recipe exactly as it's written the first time you try it. The practice of cooking and serving the ingredients as described is an act of respect and gratitude. Following a recipe is a way to honour those that have passed their knowledge and wisdom to you. Imagine the cooks that created the recipes sitting there with you, and imagine you thanking them for discovering such wonderful combinations of spices and vegetables that you might not have ever put together on your own.

There's a moment of connection that happens when you realise you are cooking wat just like an Ethiopian grandma did or baking bread as ancient Sumerian women did before heading out to sing praise songs to Inanna. I love the practice of following the recipe and believe this is great advice, and so, in the tradition of many cooks, I'm passing the advice along to you.

Of course, once you've tasted my version, you can start adding, deleting, or substituting ingredients, or change the cooking times so the food matches your palate and cooking style. Raise a glass and toast the name of the cook (or cookbook, or culture) that inspired your new dish, as a sign of respect, and then tuck in to your meal with great gusto.

All of the recipes that follow are my own creations, but that doesn't mean I originated the dishes. The combinations of ingredients and cooking instructions are my versions of recipes handed down to me by friends and cooks I know, or learned from cookbooks long ago, or a few made up because I had certain ingredients in the pantry and figured I'd try something new.

Whenever possible, I choose organic vegetables and locally sourced meats. That's a privilege I currently have and am grateful for. That wasn't true for much of my life and who knows what the future may bring. For many years, I bought as much food as I could for the least amount of money, so I could feed myself and my family. Your food choices and circumstances are unique to you, and I invite you to play with these recipes and make them your own.

Every one of these recipes can be made from ingredients found at most large supermarket chains. If you're vegan or vegetarian, you probably know more about great protein substitutes than I do. If you're following a paleo-style diet, omit what doesn't work for you or change up the recipe until it feeds your needs. If I call for a whole suckling pig to be roasted over a spit, feel free to buy a pork loin and oven-roast it instead. The flavour profiles will be similar if the ingredients are similar.

Chapter 11
Everyday Food Magick

The best thing about being a kitchen witch and practicing food magick is that you can do it every day. Magick and cooking are so easily intertwined that the magick can happen in plain sight and yet never be discovered. Here are a few of my favourite everyday food magick spells.

The Salmon of Wisdom: Salmon with Hazelnut Topping

In the Welsh tale of Cerridwen, Gwion Bach transforms into a salmon and swims in the deep pools, gaining knowledge of the watery realms. Irish lore tells us of an ordinary salmon who feasted on nine hazelnuts and gained all the wisdom there was to know. Offerings of fish were made to the Sumerian god Enki, the god of water and of wisdom. Clearly there's something about fish and wisdom.

More recently, modern science has shown solid correlations between eating a diet high in omega-3 fatty acids, found in fish, and good brain health.

This recipe doubles as a spell for your health (or the health of the people you love). Along with the fish, there are herbs long associated with memory and wisdom, like lemon balm, which grows practically everywhere.

Serves 4	Prep Time: 15 minutes	Cooking Time: 20 minutes

4 salmon fillets (if you're using frozen fillets, make sure they are thawed before cooking)

½ cup toasted hazelnuts

¼ cup plain breadcrumbs

½ teaspoon salt

¼ teaspoon pepper

1 teaspoon lemon balm, finely chopped

3 tablespoons olive oil

1 lemon

1 tablespoon honey

If you're unfamiliar with cooking fish, let me start by saying that this recipe is really simple. The trick to cooking fish is timing. Most folks overcook fish, and overcooked fish is dry and bland, no matter what herbs and spices you put on it. Make sure that your salmon is fresh or, if frozen, fully thawed before you start cooking.

Another tip: preheat your oven for at least 10 minutes before you put the salmon in to cook. I know a lot of people see the instruction "preheat your oven" and read it as "turn your oven on and put food in it right away."

Preheat your oven to 375° F. While the oven is heating, pour the hazelnuts into a sealable bag and bash them silly with a rolling pin, so they are all crushed up. Alternatively, you *can* put them in a food processor and pulse them, but bash them with a rolling pin! It's more fun. Pour the crushed nuts into a bowl and add the breadcrumbs, salt, pepper, and lemon balm. Mix until combined and then add the olive oil, stirring the whole time. The mixture should become a bit clumpy and sticky. This is perfect. You'll be topping the salmon fillets with this paste in a few minutes.

Slice the lemon in half and squeeze the juice from one half into a bowl. Add the honey and mix the two ingredients together. Using a basting brush, paint the salmon with the honey and lemon drizzle. Then top the fillets with the hazelnut mixture. Use the back of a spoon to pat the mixture down a little bit to coat the fillets.

By now your oven should be good and warmed, so put the four salmon fillets on a lightly oiled baking tray (or you can use parchment paper) and cook for 20 minutes. The hazelnut mixture should be golden brown and the salmon will be flaky.

Serve with a fresh green salad, lightly tossed with oil and vinegar. Quarter the remaining half of the lemon so folks can squeeze it over their salad and fish. While you're eating, tell stories about times when you learned something. Maybe a hard-won lesson, or one of those lovely "aha!" moments. Share your wisdom and your memories. If you're a fan of mythology, read the tale of Gwion Bach and put your thumb in your mouth just once during the meal, like Gwion did. You never know what you might learn!

The Thermos of Gratitude: A Spell with Bone Broth

Once upon a time, when I when was very young person, my dad would take me fishing. It was frequently cold and often raining. Such are the woes of angling in England. He'd pull out a thermos flask, pour the contents into a cup, and I'd take a few tentative sips of the steaming, thick, brown but almost black liquid. The beefy, salty concoction would instantly warm my mouth and, soon thereafter, my toes, my ears, and the tip of my nose. Every part of me was warmed through and through and the grey skies and my wet socks seemed much less of an inconvenience. I learned that the best part of fishing with my dad was hearing his stories and drinking "beef soup." I'm inordinately grateful to my dad for his patience and skill and wise words. A cunning man if ever there was one. This recipe and spell are for him (and you, but you'll need your own thermos!).

A few words about beef broth or bone broth or beef bone broth. First of all, bone broth isn't really broth, it's more like a good stock. Good beef stocks are made from vegetables and beef bones and tend to be pretty thick. Stocks get their rich flavours from time in the pot. Broths by comparison are thinner and are truly the product of just water and meat.

This recipe makes a lot (it varies based on your cooking time, but figure about 8 cups of broth)	Prep Time: 30 minutes	Cooking Time: 8–24 hours

3 pounds beef bones (ask the meat department for soup bones)

1 large yellow onion, peeled and roughly chopped

3 carrots, roughly chopped

2 stalks of celery, roughly chopped and with the leaves left on

12 brown mushrooms, halved

6 cloves garlic, peeled and halved

1 bay leaf

1 tablespoon pepper

1 tablespoon vinegar (white or apple cider)

4 tablespoons Worcestershire sauce

12 cups water

1 tablespoon salt

1 notepad or journal (don't worry, you won't have to cook the journal)

Preheat your oven to 450° F. Place the bones, which should be a good mix of knuckle bones, tail bones, and rib bones, onto a baking sheet or roasting pan and roast for 30 minutes. While the bones are roasting, chop the onion, carrots, celery, mushrooms, and garlic. Grab a stock pot, preferably 5 quarts or bigger. Toss the veggies, bay leaf, pepper, vinegar, and Worcestershire sauce into the stock pot over high heat. Give the ingredients a good stir and then leave on the heat just long enough for you to retrieve the bones from the oven and toss them in the pot too. Make sure you add any juices and brown bits that are on the baking tray too. Those are chock-full of flavour. Now add enough water to cover the bones and the vegetables. 12 cups of water usually does it for me, making sure there are at least a couple inches of space between the top of the water and the rim of the pot. Now add the salt.

Bring the whole thing to a boil. It takes a while for 12 cups of water to come to a boil, so clean your countertops, pour a nice glass of your favourite beverage, and grab your journal because there's spell work to do.

Answer this question: Who are you grateful for? Get really detailed here. It doesn't just have to be the obvious people; anyone that's contributed to your comfort, your health, your home, your income, or your understanding of the world as it is today can make you feel grateful. Write them all down in your journal.

Next question: What are you grateful for about the building you live in? Again, really dig deep here. Is it safe? Is it beautiful? Close to schools? Affordable? Where your grandparents lived? The first place you moved to after that terrible breakup? Your coven meets here? Write down everything in your journal.

Third question: Who lived on this land before you? Did they build bridges or dig canals? Were they farmers? Did they live in this place for centuries or millennia before you? Do their lives and ways influence you today? Maybe their influence lies on in the names of places, the physical landscape, or the traditions you uphold. Write down what the ancestors of this place have created or sacrificed or gifted you.

Last question: What does the land provide for you? You might consider the land to be the place you inhabit, or the where your foods grow, or the fresh air you breathe, or the lakes and rivers you visit, or the gorgeous sunsets you see, or the tall trees around you. What does the land provide for you? Write all of this in your journal. Reflect upon it and add to your answers if more answers come.

By now, it's probably a good time to check the water. If it's boiling, go ahead and turn the pot down to a low simmer, then let it bubble away for 8 hours. If it's not yet boiling, go back to your journal and write a little more. When you lift the lid, you'll see a brownish foam forming on the top of the liquid. Get a wooden spoon and skim that off. You might have to do that a few times while the bone broth is cooking. You can continue to simmer the broth for up to 24 hours, but definitely give it at least 8 hours. It's okay to turn the stove off and start again the next day, but please do refrigerate in between for food safety reasons.

The next bit can be awkward. You'll need to strain the broth liquid into another pot. The best way is to put a new pot into the sink and pour the contents of the cooking pot through a sieve or colander. You'll end up with a pot of broth and a colander full of bones and very mushy vegetables. Discard the vegetables and bones, leaving you with a pot full of bone broth. Put the pot of broth on your counter. There's a little more to do yet.

Remember your journal entries? Get your biggest, most favourite mug. Fill it to the brim with hot, delicious bone broth. Open your journal and read aloud everything you are grateful for, every person you are grateful for. State aloud your gratitude for the land, the earth, the peoples that lived here, the cow that gave its bones to make your broth, the vegetables, and the folks that picked those vegetables. Give a nod of gratitude to every living being, rock, hill, teacher, mentor, friend, lover, goddess, or god that shapes who you are. And sip the broth. Notice that the broth you take in is more than just its components. Think of everyone and everything that has contributed to this broth. Drink more. You are transforming this simple beverage into a spell of gratitude, and it is transforming and nourishing you.

Oh! Then transfer the rest of the bone broth into sealable containers. You can keep it in the fridge for up to 5 days or the freezer for up to 3 months. A layer of gelatinous collagen (that's fat to you and me) will form when the broth cools. You can skim that off before reheating the broth. Drinking the broth and repeating the spell daily is a lovely practice.

Keep 'em Sweet: Honey Shortbread for Love

Be honest. The first spell you were asked to do by someone else was a love spell, right? Maybe the first spell you ever did for yourself was a love spell. Love, money, and protection are probably the three most commonly asked-for and performed spells. Interestingly enough, honey has long since been associated with offerings to the gods, the Fairy Folk, and use in magickal spells across many cultures. Honey is frequently an ingredient in love, money, and protection spells. Using honey as an ingredient in a food spell or ritual offering is one practice that truly is ancient. Sumerian clay tablets dating back five millennia record honey, milk, and butter being given as ritual offerings to the gods in the Sumerian pantheon.

As a food witch, the ingredients you choose to cook with and the intention you put into your food magick will certainly impact the results of your magick. "Keep 'em sweet" could just as easily be a love spell, sweetening the love as you sweeten the cake. "Keep 'em sweet" could entice someone to part ways with their money and give it to you. "Keep 'em sweet" might soothe a person's bad temper, thereby offering a little space, time, and protection. Your mileage may vary and so will your magickal ethics. But this spell is called "keep 'em sweet: honey shortbread for love," so let's stick with that for now. Every time you add an ingredient or stir the mixture, say "let the sweetness of this food add to the sweetness of the relationship with my partner(s)."

Serves 4	Prep Time: 30 minutes	Cooking Time: 30 minutes

4 tablespoons softened butter

3 tablespoons honey

1 teaspoon vanilla extract

1 teaspoon + ¼ teaspoon lemon extract

¼ cup brown sugar

¼ cup powdered sugar

1 cup all-purpose flour

Preheat the oven to 350° F. Lightly grease a 9-inch springform pan with butter (or cooking spray, but I like butter best). Set the pan aside. Into a large mixing bowl, add the butter, cutting it into small slices. It's important that the butter is soft, but not runny. If you take the butter out of the fridge 30 minutes before you need it, you should be just fine. Add 2 tablespoons of the honey, 1 teaspoon of vanilla extract, and 1 teaspoon of lemon extract to the butter. Pour in the brown sugar and the powdered sugar. Now it's time to mix it all up, and the best way to do that is to use your hands (you can use a hand mixer if that's easier for you too). I use my fingers to incorporate the ingredients together. The mix will look a little crumbly. If you are using a hand mixer, beat for about a minute. Add the flour, half a cup at a time, and beat it into the mixture too. Again, I like to use my hands, and I'm looking for the dough to be crumbly, without any obvious clumps of flour, sugar, or butter.

Take the crumbly dough and pour it into the greased pan. Flatten the dough down with the back of your hand or the back of a spoon, so it's spread evenly throughout the tin, going right up to the edges. Prick the dough all over with a fork, nine times. Pop the pan into the oven for 30 minutes. Just before taking the shortbread out of the oven, pour the remaining honey and lemon extract into a small bowl and mix well.

Take the shortbread out of the oven and immediately paint the honey and lemon extract mix onto the hot shortbread. I like to paint heart shapes, or spell out the word *love*, or the name of the person(s) I want to be sweet with. The honey-lemon mixture isn't actually that great for spelling or writing with, so this is more of an exercise of your magickal intention at work, rather than actual cake decorating. Let the whole thing cool for about 5 minutes and then remove the springform pan. Carefully, using a spatula, remove the shortbread to a serving plate and cut into eight slices with a pizza wheel or thin, sharp knife.

Make a lovely cup of tea or pour a tall glass of milk and enjoy your sticky, slightly chewy, slightly crumbly, lemony-sweet shortbread and talk about love with whomever you're with. I highly recommend concentrating on fun, playful, flirty, sweet love, rather than, say, your deep and abiding love for all humanity. Oh! And have seconds, thirds even, if you're feeling sassy.

Chapter 12
Magick Potions

A great number of witchcraft books, especially the "how to" variety, list pages of correspondences. The idea of this is that the efficacy of spells is enhanced when as many favourable conditions as possible are brought together at once. Typically, days of the week, herbs, colours, crystals, and moon phases are detailed, but I rarely find alcoholic beverages listed. I find that odd, as alcohol has been part of humanity's personal, magickal, and religious life since the first records of humans engaging in personal, magickal, and religious acts.

Since times well out of mind, alcohol has been offered to the gods, local spirits, and ancestors. There are wine gods and beer goddesses. Magick workers employ alcohol to appease gatekeepers, honour the dead, and cleanse ritual spaces. "Cakes and ale" plays an integral role in many Wiccan-based traditions, toasting is practically a given in Heathen groups, and a fair number of Druids I know single-handedly account for a high percentage of whiskey sales worldwide. Simply put, alcohol always has played and likely always will play some role in the magick of a great number of traditions. Jason Mankey, a Pagan author and Wiccan, notes: "Human beings have been using altered states of consciousness in the pursuit of the spiritual for tens of thousands of years. Even something as simple as locking yourself in a pitch-black cave for twelve hours will produce an altered mental state. Alcohol does that far faster, and in a shorter period of time. Certainly, alcohol and other intoxicants are not needed to produce an altered state of consciousness, but as long as something is used in a responsible and safe manner I think it's fair game. Alcohol can fit that criteria.

"But why enter an altered state of consciousness? I think the easy answer is that while we are in an altered state we are more open and susceptible to outside forces. Signs that we might have missed while completely sober are more readily apparent, and I think it's often easier to achieve a state of religious ecstasy while in an altered state. Alcohol can help turn off the over-thinking, over-analytical parts of our brains and open us up to new experiences, just like many other drugs and some mental disciplines. Can I enter an altered state without gin? Certainly, but sometimes I think using alcohol in such a way has its place in my life as a Witch." [50]

Having said that, it's also true that there are magickal traditions that absolutely do not condone the use of alcohol in magickal space. The Reclaiming Tradition of witchcraft specifically states that their public rituals and classes are drug and alcohol free, as a conscious act of solidarity and inclusiveness, standing with folks that are clean and sober and need magickal spaces to support their sobriety. Individual witches within the Reclaiming Tradition need not practice sobriety—it's not a "dry" tradition—but Reclaiming events are drug and alcohol free.

Imbibing alcohol before, during, or after a ritual is, of course, a matter for one's own ethics, boundaries, and self-care practices, and these should be prime determining factors about your alcohol usage.

A word about the following recipes. Cocktails contain booze. Mocktails don't. A few of these concoctions could certainly be used in a ritual setting or as an offering to a deity or to the land. Mostly though, these drinks are meant for the very sacred ritual of consuming and enjoying, and the holiest of offerings, that of sharing them with friends.

50. Jason Mankey. "Alcohol Before and During Ritual." *Raise the Horns* (blog), *Patheos*. http://www.patheos .com/blogs/panmankey/2016/12/alcohol-before-and-during-ritual/.

Cocktails

Cocktails and magick go hand in hand in my craft practices. Let's brew up a concoction or two and celebrate life!

While witchcraft and magick are often thought of as somber undertakings, there's nothing that says there can't be a whole lot of fun involved, and these cocktails will add a little extra kick to your workings (or playings).

Gin and Cthonic: An Underworld Cocktail

Underworld and death deities abound in classic mythology and Pagan lore. Hades, Persephone, Arawn, Hel, and Ereshkigal are just a few that spring to mind. Wherever it is we go, these folks will be waiting. Toast the work they do and drink up. It's later than you think.

1 drink	Prep Time: 5 minutes

3 ice cubes

2 fluid ounces gin

2 fluid ounces tonic water

½ fluid ounce absinthe

½ fluid ounce pomegranate juice

Add the ice cubes to a tall glass. Pour the gin, tonic water, absinthe, and pomegranate juice into the glass and stir. Call on your favourite Underworld deity, reflect on mortality, and drink up. Repeat responsibly.

Baba Yagatini: A Sorting Cocktail

I've experienced Baba Yaga as a kindly older woman who winks at me from her flying mortar and pestle until I pay attention to her. Before I know it, she's got me in a chicken-footed house sorting seeds for my dear life. This cocktail is like Baba Yaga herself. It seems harmless enough, and then it's too late to do anything but sit and sort through your life.

1 drink	Prep Time: 5 minutes

3 ice cubes

2 fluid ounces vodka

2 fluid ounces cranberry juice

2 fluid ounces orange juice

Chilled sparkling wine to fill

Add 3 ice cubes to a cocktail shaker. Pour the vodka, cranberry juice, and orange juice over the ice. Shake vigorously. The mixture will get a little foamy. That's good. Strain into a tall glass and top it off with the sparkling wine. Pour a shot glass full for Baba Yaga and welcome her to your rites. Drink two or more of these and prepare to spend the night sitting on the floor, sorting everything!

Cerridwen and Cassis: A Spell for Transformation

Cerridwen brewed an elixir for her son, Afagddu (pronounced Ah-vahg-thee). Her cauldron bubbled for a year and a day, transforming all of the herbs and plants Cerridwen gathered into a powerful brew, containing the full knowledge of the universe: Awen. Young Gwion Bach, employed to stir the cauldron, accidentally drank three drops of the Awen brew, and after being chased by an angry Cerridwen, eventually became the bard Taliesin. When you sip this brew, will you find the Awen and begin a journey of transformation? If you're ready for change, drink up.

1 drink	Prep Time: 5 minutes plus 30 minutes to make the lavender syrup

2 fluid ounces brandy

1 fluid ounce cassis (blackcurrant)

1 fluid ounce lavender-honey syrup

1 tablespoon lemon juice

Dash of bitters

3 Ice cubes

To make the lavender-honey simple syrup, pour ¼ cup of boiling water into a bowl. Add ¼ cup of dried lavender and ⅓ cup of honey. Stir these three ingredients together and let steep for 30 minutes. After the 30 minutes are up, strain the syrup through a sieve or strainer to filter out the lavender bits. Extra lavender syrup can be stored in an airtight jar in the fridge for up to two weeks.

Add 3 ice cubes to a cocktail shaker, pour in the brandy, cassis, lavender-honey syrup, lemon juice, and bitters and give everything a good shake. Serve in a tumbler or stemless wine glass (because they look like little glass cauldrons). When Cerridwen shows up in your life, it means profound changes are on the near horizon. Raise a glass, bid her welcome, and invite the wisdom that comes with transformation.

Mocktails

Here are my favourite mocktail recipes. These magickal drinks, filled with intention and great ingredients, are perfect for summer coven gatherings, dinner parties, or midnight meetups.

Melon Pomona: A Spell for the Joys of Summer

Melons have existed forever—well, at least for the last five thousand years or so. It's likely they originated on the African continent and spread from there. Watermelon seeds, specifically, were discovered in Egyptian tombs, including none other than that of King Tutankhamun.[51] Roman accounts show that melons of several varieties were a regular part of the diet for wealthy folks. I think the Roman goddess Pomona, who oversees the successful burgeoning of fruit, orchards, and abundance, would love this concoction. It speaks to long, hot summer days and says, "Yes! Summer is wonderful and life is a sweet, treasured gift."

Serves a bunch	Prep Time: 30 minutes

2 medium melons (cantaloupe, watermelon, or honeydew)

3 tablespoons lemon or lime juice

4 tablespoons sugar (or your preferred sweetener)

3 cups tonic water (you can use lemon-lime soda instead of tonic water. If you do use soda, you won't need the sugar. You can always add sugar to taste, if you think the drink needs it)

This recipe starts out with a choice: pulp or no pulp? A true agua fresca, which is what this recipe is based on, usually requires straining out the solids and just using the juice. I like to keep the pulp and make this more like a slushy. If you're a "no pulper," simply strain the solids through a sieve or a cheesecloth after blending and use only the juice. If you're a "pulper," ignore everything I just said.

Slice the melons in half and scoop put the seeds. Cut the melon into cubes, remembering to remove the rind. Run the cubed melon through a blender just until smooth, about 30 seconds. Unless you have a giant blender, you'll have to repeat this step a few times, so pour the blended melon into a punch bowl or large pitcher and blend the rest in batches. Add the juice, sugar, and 3 cups of tonic water and stir. Fill a tall glass with ice

51. "The 5,000-year-old secret of the watermelon." https://news.nationalgeographic.com/2015/08/150821-watermelon-fruit-history-agriculture/.

and serve the Melon Pomona immediately. As you drink this thirst-quenching glass of veritable summer sunshine, recount all that is good and sweet and delicious and abundant about your life right now. If life is tough and not particularly sweet for you at the present moment, use this drink as a siren call to attract the sweetness and abundance you want. Magick is rarely an instant undertaking, but sipping this mocktail brings immediate sweetness. Hold on to that.

Metamorphoses Mojito: A Spell for . . .
(this one really depends on you)

Ovid's Metamorphoses introduces us to Menthe, a beautiful nymph who fell head over heels in lust with Hades and decided to seduce him. Hades was rather attracted to Menthe, and so they began a love affair. Persephone, Hades's wife and Queen of the Underworld, was none too pleased at this, and transformed Menthe into a plant and crushed her beneath her feet. Every time she stepped on the former nymph, a sweet fragrance was released. And that's the happy tale of why mint smells so fragrant. Maybe your magick is about seducing someone you lust after. Maybe your magick is about crushing your enemies underfoot. Maybe your magick is picking mint from your garden, window box, or grocery store, adding it to a mojito, and reveling at just how versatile mint is.

1 drink	Prep Time: 5 minutes

1 dozen mint leaves

1 tablespoon lime juice

1 tablespoon honey

Ice

Sparkling water, tonic water, or lemon-lime soda

1 slice of lime

Get yourself a tall glass. Add the mint leaves, lime juice, and honey and muddle it. To muddle ingredients means to crush them a wee bit so they release their oils and flavours. So, for a brief moment or two, you can pretend to be Persephone and crush Menthe under your feet or, in reality, just use a wooden spoon and squidge everything together for about 5 seconds. Add ice, your sparkling water of choice, and a slice of lime, then enjoy.

Midnight Margaritas: A Spell for Hangin' with the Coven or Other Magickal People

Okay. There's no ancient myth that goes along with this drink recipe, but there is a story. I like magick. I like magick that is practical. One could say I like practical magick. It's seems perfectly practical to me to have the coven over to watch movies during Samhain-tide, and I have a couple of favourite movies I watch every year. It's not practical magick to have friends and coven mates drive home inebriated, so mysteriously and completely independently I came up with a non-alcoholic margarita drink that we sometimes drink late at night, usually around midnight.

Serves 4	Prep Time: 30 minutes

2 cups frozen strawberries

7 tablespoons orange juice

4 tablespoons lime juice

2 tablespoons sugar (or agave nectar)

2 cups ice

Salt or sugar for the rim of the glasses

Pause whichever magickal movie you're watching with your coven. It could be practically any magickal movie. Everyone assemble in the kitchen and chatter and laugh and help. Someone get glasses, another person get out the salt or sugar, you grab the blender. I think you get the picture here.

Add the strawberries, orange juice, lime juice, sugar (or agave), and ice to the blender. Blend until smooth. While you're blending, someone else can pour out salt or sugar onto a plate, dab their finger in agave nectar or honey or lime juice, and run their finger around the rim of each glass. They then turn the glass over into the sugar or salt so it sticks to the rim of the glass. Share the blended strawberry margarita mix with everyone and dance in the kitchen as witches often do.

Magickal Libations

Libations are liquids offered to the gods, ancestors, spirits of place, and the newly dead. Virtually every culture, from the ancient to the modern, employs the practice of pouring libations. I've raised a glass for a dearly departed loved one and tipped it out onto the land so they could join with the living and enjoy a drink too. After certain rituals, I go to a favourite lemon tree and pour offerings for the deities I've been working with. And at one infamous revel for Dionysus, several bottles of wine were upended into a huge vessel, one glass at a time, in honour of the god. Many more cases of wine were consumed by those in attendance at the same ritual in the name of Dionysus, and what happened next was... um, nevermind. I swore an oath of confidentiality. Libations can be given in their entirety to those being remembered, or shared with those pouring them. Here are two libations to share.

Hot Toddy: A Libation for Health

*A hot toddy is a classic drink, with roots dating back to eighteenth-century Scotland.[52]
It's the go-to remedy in my house. If you are feeling run down, have a chill, or feel as
if a cold is coming on, this drink will soothe what ails you. I consider this a libation,
as I call upon the knowledge of my ancestors who worked the land and used natural
remedies before there was an alternative. I call upon the wisdom encoded in the very
genes of my own body to know how to rest and heal. Pour a drop or two on your ancestor altar if you have one, or share a small portion with your preferred healing deity.*

1 drink	Prep Time: 5 minutes

1 cup hot, brewed black tea

1 fluid ounce whiskey

1 tablespoon lemon juice

2 tablespoons honey

Boil water in a tea kettle. Pour the water into a large mug, leaving enough room for
the whiskey. Add a tea bag of black tea to the mug. If you prefer loose-leaf tea, add the
leaves to the mug in a diffuser or pour through a strainer. Let the tea steep for 3 minutes
and then remove the tea bag or leaves. Pour in the whiskey, add the lemon juice, and stir
in the honey.

52. Kat Eschner. "The Hot Toddy: A 'Medicinal' Drink That Might Actually Work." *Smithsonian.* https://
www.smithsonianmag.com/smart-news/hot-toddy-medicinal-drink-might-actually-work-180961714/.

Mulled Wine: A Libation for the Gods

The Romans are responsible for a great many contributions to civilization—culinary arts, medicine, aqueducts, and the roads. Of course, the roads. That goes without saying. The Romans would transport legions of soldiers, along with their swords and spears and other weapons that made the Pax Romana so appealing to those that were being "paxed." They also brought all sorts of exotic foodstuffs, ideas, new gods, and wines. It's widely thought that mulled wine was brought to the provinces of the Roman empire in the second century of the common era.

There is a slew of Roman deities that love offerings of wine, and just as many non-Roman ones too. Generally speaking, if you're pushed for an offering and aren't quite sure what to use, milk, honey, or wine are pretty safe bets. And, let's be honest for a moment, if you're the one who is going to share in the offering, a nice warm glass of spiced, red wine might be preferred to a bowl full of milk. The addition of spices and the warmth of the wine itself add to the health benefits associated with mulled wine, so the gods will be happy and so will your constitution. So, hail the gods of your choice, share with them, and drink heartily! I mean, drink responsibly and with much deference…

Serves a bunch	Prep Time: 10 minutes	Cooking Time: 1 hour

1 medium orange

2 cinnamon sticks

12 whole cloves

4 tablespoons dark brown sugar

2 750-ml bottles red wine (or a 1.50-liter bottle)

1 tablespoon lemon juice

There are two important points to know about this recipe. First, your home will smell great. So great, in fact, that you'll be tempted to make mulled wine even in the heat of summer. Mulled wine may end up as the go-to "ale" in the cakes and ale portion of your rites, and you'll find yourself making mulled wine just to use as a nice drinkable pot-pourri. Second, please do use the dark brown sugar. I've tried this recipe without sugar or by substituting honey for dark brown sugar. It just doesn't have quite the same "oomph!" if you swap out the sugar for something else. What makes brown sugar brown is molasses.

The darker the sugar, the more molasses it contains, about double the amount of light brown sugar. It's the richness of molasses that takes this mulled wine right over the top.

You can make mulled wine in a large pot or in a slow cooker. I'll make it in a slow cooker if I'm having folks over, as it looks nicer than my stock pot. Plus, that way you can move it around and plug it in elsewhere to keep it warm.

Slice the orange into thin rounds and put the rounds in the bottom of your slow cooker (or stock pot). Add the rest of the dry ingredients. Pour in the 2 bottles of red wine and the tablespoon of lemon juice. Give everything a gentle stir. Turn the slow cooker onto the low setting, cover, and leave for an hour. If you're using a stock pot, place the heat on a low simmer, cover, and leave for an hour.

It's important not to bring the wine to a boil, as you'll burn off the alcohol and, in the case of this recipe, that completely obliterates the magick you're doing. Okay, I made up that last bit about ruining the magick, but you really don't want to burn off the alcohol.

After an hour, remove the lid, stir the mulled wine, and lower the setting on the crock pot to warm. Again, if you're using a stock pot, keep the wine warm by setting the heat to the lowest setting you can. Other recipes call for you to strain out the fruit, cloves, and cinnamon. I don't because I like the way it looks in the pot, but you do want to be careful when you serve the mulled wine not to get any cloves in the glass or cup. You can strain the whole thing if you like or pass the wine through a tea strainer as you transfer a ladleful of wine from the pot to the cup.

Chapter 13
Food Magick for Special Occasions

It doesn't take much convincing to get me in the kitchen to work magick. Kitchen witchery is pretty much an everyday event at my house. But there are special times when it's important to put on my big witch apron and turn out something extraordinary.

For example, most modern Pagan traditions have designated certain high days and holidays throughout the year. There are seasonal shifts to take note of and festivals dedicated to the gods. This makes menu planning easy, because you have plenty of time to research the upcoming event and create a stunning meal for yourself... oh, and anyone else you might invite over.

What follows is a collection of recipes that you can return to over and again. I believe cooking food to celebrate the gods is a time to pull out all the stops, so I've included four recipes that might give you a little inspiration. There are eight more recipes based on the Wheel of the Year. Lastly, there are four recipes for very, very special occasions. That's right, I'm sharing my favourite aphrodisiacs.

Eating with the Gods

Here are four modern recipes I've created as ritual offerings for the gods. When I cook for the gods, I imagine the flavours and foodstuffs they would recognize or at least appreciate. You can employ these recipes for your rituals, offerings, or just to have an incredible meal for you and your beloveds. As a magickal act and a sign of respect for the gods you might be inviting to dinner, consider making a place for them at the table and serving them first. Also, just in case you're tempted to give the gods the leftover fatty pieces of meat or the burned veggies, I have it on good authority that they'll know ... just sayin'.

In Praise of Inanna: A Modern Take on a Traditional Sumerian Recipe

You might recall a recipe for Tuh'u broth in the Sumerian section of this book. This is my modern adaptation I mentioned. I suspect that Inanna has changed and evolved over the millennia and perhaps her tastes have too. This recipe stays true to the spices the Sumerians would recognize, but is updated to reflect what you can find in just about any grocery store.

Serves 4	Prep Time: a few minutes or 2 hours if you make your polenta from scratch	Cooking Time: 1 hour

FOR THE POLENTA CAKES:

3 cups water

½ teaspoon salt

⅔ cup polenta

1 tablespoon olive oil

FOR THE LAMB:

1 pound cubed lamb

1 small yellow onion, diced

2 cloves garlic, crushed

½ teaspoon coriander

½ teaspoon cumin

¼ teaspoon cinnamon

Pinch of salt

1 cup red wine (I like to use tawny port)

⅓ cup water

Salt and pepper to taste

Making the polenta is the only part of this recipe that takes any real time. I like to make my polenta cakes from scratch, but you can buy plain pre-rolled polenta at many grocery stores. If you want to make your own, it adds a few steps and a fair bit of effort. If you buy pre-rolled polenta, you can skip all the polenta steps except the sautéing.

Bring 3 cups of water to a boil and add ½ teaspoon of salt. Stir in the polenta and mix until combined. Turn the heat down to a gentle simmer and cook until the polenta thickens up. You'll have to stir the polenta mix frequently so it doesn't stick to the bottom of the saucepan. Trust me on that part. I've ruined good polenta and a few saucepans by burning the polenta because I forgot to stir it. Cook for approximately 30 minutes, stirring frequently.

Grab a 3-quart casserole dish (8" x 13") and grease it with a little butter or cooking spray. Then line the dish with clear plastic wrap. Pour the thickened polenta into the dish and smooth it out with a spatula or wooden spoon. Cover the top of the polenta with more plastic wrap and place it in the refrigerator for about 2 hours or until the polenta is chilled and firm (ish). Once your polenta has chilled for half the time, about an hour, it's time to start making the lamb and broth.

Sprinkle your cubed lamb with salt and sauté over medium heat until browned. Once browned, set it aside on a plate. To the same pan you just cooked the lamb in, add the onion, garlic, coriander, cumin, cinnamon, and salt. Cook over medium heat for about 5 minutes, stirring frequently. Add the wine (or port) and the water to the sauté pan, then add the lamb. Stir to make sure everything is nicely combined. Once the liquid starts to boil, reduce to a slow simmer. Cover and simmer for about 1 hour or until the lamb is tender. During this hour, I recommend singing songs to Inanna, reading one of her many stories, and beautifying wherever you're going to enjoy this meal. If you are having wine with this dish, which I do recommend, open a bottle of red wine and let it breathe a bit. A Shiraz will work quite nicely.

At the two-hour mark, pull your polenta out of the fridge. Take hold of the plastic wrap and gently coax the hardened polenta out of the casserole dish and onto a cutting surface. Discard the plastic wrap and cut out four round polenta cakes. I use a ramekin for my guide, but you can eyeball it or use a cookie cutter.

Get a sauté pan big enough to hold all four of the polenta cakes at one time. Heat the pan over medium heat and add a tablespoon of olive oil. Cook each cake for 4 minutes per side. They should have a little golden-brown crust on either side. (See, with the pre-rolled polenta, all you have to do is slice four 1-inch slices and add them to your hot pan.)

Place one polenta cake in the center of a plate. Divide the lamb into four portions and pile one portion of lamb onto each cake. Spoon the braising liquid, which should be reduced down and fairly thickened, around the polenta cake and over the lamb.

Goat for a God: Roasted Goat Leg with Grape Molasses

Roasted goat leg? Yes! You read that correctly, this is a recipe for goat. Depending on where you live and your circumstances, getting ahold of a goat leg might not be as easy as, say, popping to the local grocery store and buying a bag of potato chips. You might have search around a bit. If your local shop has a good butcher department they might be able to order a goat leg for you. The folks in the butcher's department generally love eating meat, so if their store can't order goat, ask them if they know of a good source. There's a good chance one of the butchers will know where to get goat. If there's no goat to be had, check in with Pan or your favourite goat-footed gods and ask them if a leg of lamb will do for this meal.

Speaking of gods—the reason this recipe is called "goat for a god" is because I like a bit of indulgence every now and again. I find gods like Dionysus, Pan, and Thor respond approvingly of goat dishes and they love attending rollicking, decadent, sumptuous feasts that feature eating without utensils; getting our hands right up in our food; letting the juices run down our arms as we quaff copious quantities of wine; partaking in conversations covering all manner of topics; and enjoying the pleasures of being a living, breathing, embodied person. But before we can get to the revelry, we need ingredients.

Serves 6	Prep Time: 30 minutes	Cooking Time: 2 hours and 30 minutes

1 goat leg (about 3 pounds)

2 teaspoons salt

2 teaspoons black pepper

2 cloves garlic, minced

2 sprigs fresh rosemary

1 bay leaf

2 large carrots, chopped into 1" chunks

1 celery root, peeled and chopped into 1" cubes

¼ cup + 1 tablespoon olive oil

1 cup white wine + one glass for sipping and toasting while cooking (use mead if you're cooking this for Thor)

4 tablespoons grape molasses

1 teaspoon coriander

1 teaspoon cumin

First step: Open the bottle of white wine or mead and take a hefty drink. Cooking goat is easy, but there's something about it that just says "YES! Drink much," so I like to get the proceeding off to a rollicking start. If you have a Bota bag or a drinking horn, use those, because, really, we don't use drinking horns nearly enough these days.

Now to the goat. Preheat the oven to 375° F. Liberally season the goat leg with salt and pepper. Rub the minced garlic all over the goat leg too. If it helps, poke a few holes in the goat leg so you can get the garlic right into the meat. Place the rosemary sprigs and bay leaf in the bottom of a large roasting pan and put the goat leg right on top. Add the carrots and celery root around the edges. Pour the olive oil all over the goat and rub it around. Coat the carrots and celery root too. Looking at these instructions, I'm remembering that you will also need an apron or plenty of kitchen towels, because this does get a little messy. Pour the white wine around the bottom of the roasting pan. Loosely cover with kitchen foil and put the whole pan into the oven for 2 hours.

About an hour and forty-five minutes into the cooking process, it's time to make the glaze. Mix the grape molasses—which is a super-condensed syrup made of grape must—in a bowl with a tablespoon of olive oil, the coriander, and the cumin. A quick side note: You can make your own grape-must molasses, but it's a really difficult process. Mediterranean and Turkish food stores will carry grape molasses. Again, if this meal is in honour of Thor, you can substitute honey for the grape molasses. It will pair well with the mead.

At the two-hour mark, pull the roasting pan out of the oven and paint the goat with the grape (or honey) and spice glaze. Pop the goat and veggies, uncovered, back into the oven for another 20 minutes or until the internal temperature reaches at least 145° F.

When you're ready to serve this dish, scoop the veggies into a bowl (for now) and put the goat leg on a platter. If you have access to one, get a cedar plank and serve the goat on it. There's no culinary reason for this other than it looks fantastic and, remember, we eat with all our senses, so why not treat the eyes? If there's room, surround the goat leg with the vegetables. If not, serve in your favourite rustic bowl.

Baskets of bread with bowls of olive oil and balsamic vinegar are great side additions for this meal. A crisp sauvignon blanc or well-chilled pinot grigio are splendid wine pairings for the aromatic goat meat. The ancient Greeks and Romans would have consumed red wine cut with water. I like a light, fruity pinot noir. The pinot noir stands up well to the "goatiness" of the meat and brings out the sweetness of the carrots and celery root. Working with Thor? Mead. Lots of mead. Was there a question about that?

Demeter's Vegetarian Feast: Lentil and
Olive Salad with Cabbage and Carrot Slaw

The ancient Greeks almost certainly used lentils throughout the year, but they were mostly eaten during the winter months when fresh vegetables were less plentiful. Lentils store for a long time and are incredibly versatile. They make a great base for soups, stews, and salads.

I imagine, as the spring returned and spices and vegetables began to make an appearance, this dish, or one like it, might be served. Cabbage and carrots were also part of the Greek diet, and this quick slaw recipe fits right in with the fresh, springtime theme.

Serves 6	Prep Time: 10 minutes	Cooking Time: 30 minutes

FOR THE CABBAGE AND CARROT SLAW:

4 cups cabbage, chopped thinly (I stick to green cabbage, but a combination of red and green cabbage is nice too)

1 carrot, cut into thin medallions and then sliced into thin sticks

2 tablespoons apple cider vinegar (or any other vinegar, like red wine, rice wine, or white wine)

1 tablespoon olive oil

Salt and pepper

FOR THE LENTILS:

2 cups black lentils

4 cloves garlic, chopped

1 medium red onion, diced

1 cup finely chopped mint

½ cup kalamata olives, chopped

1 medium cucumber, diced

3 tablespoons olive oil

1 tablespoon vinegar (I like apple cider, but balsamic, white, or rice wine vinegar also work)

Salt and pepper to taste

½ cup feta cheese (for something a little more decadent, try a gorgonzola dolce)

Make the cabbage and carrot slaw first and put it in the fridge while you're making the lentil salad. The slaw is really delicious when it's chilled.

Add the cabbage and carrots to a serving bowl. Shake the vinegar and oil together in a mason jar and pour over the slaw. Stir to coat the cabbage and carrot with the vinaigrette. Add salt and pepper to taste. That's it. Takes less than 5 minutes.

The lentil salad is also quick and easy, only taking about 30 minutes from start to finish, and it goes a long way. Try this version first, then experiment by adding other seasonal vegetables. (It's kind of nice with fresh, steamed asparagus too!)

Pour the lentils into a medium saucepan and add enough cold water to cover the them. Bring the lentils and water to a near boil, on high heat, and then reduce the heat to a low simmer. The lentils should simmer for about 25 to 30 minutes. While the lentils are cooking, there's time to chop up the garlic, onion, mint, olives, and cucumber. Pour the lentils into a colander and rinse in cold water. Add all of the chopped and diced ingredients to the lentils. Stir gently until everything is combined. I use a big wooden spoon to stir and I use a folding motion so as not to smoosh the lentils too much.

Grab your mason jar again and combine the additional oil and vinegar. Give it a good shake, but remember to make sure the lid is secure. And yes, before you ask, I have thrown oil and vinegar all over the kitchen because I didn't check that the lid was secure. Pour the oil and vinegar mixture over the lentils and give the whole thing another gentle stir. Add salt and pepper. Finally, add all of the lovely feta and serve.

If you have time, you can totally make the lentils ahead of time, chill them in the fridge, and add the rest of the ingredients when you're ready to serve. If there's any leftovers, this dish will keep for several days in the fridge.

Boar for Bacchus: Boar Tacos with Spicy Berry Salsa

Yes! This is a taco recipe featuring boar. Tacos are quite possibly the world's most perfect food. There's an infinite number of ingredients you can use and a handy serving plate—the tortilla—is included. Tacos are meant to be eaten with your hands and are deliciously messy. Basically, everything I like about food. Now to be fair, there is no ancient Roman recipe for boar tacos or any mention of Bacchus being partial to boar tacos, but if Bacchus and I were hanging out in the kitchen wondering what to eat on a Saturday night, I'd suggest boar tacos. Bacchus would love boar tacos, right?

Let's talk about Bacchus for a minute, while the images of boar tacos are sending your salivary glands into overdrive. Look up Bacchus and you'll mostly see references to Dionysus. That's understandable, as the Romans certainly borrowed heavily from the Greeks, but I like to think of Bacchus a little differently. Almost every statue or painting of Dionysus shows him to be youthful and thin. The Flemish artist Peter Paul Rubens (1577–1640) painted Bacchus, and the art and figure of Bacchus was later described as such:

"Seated on a wine-barrel as if on a throne, one leg resting on a tiger, Bacchus looks both repulsive and majestic. Bacchus was conceived by the artist as the apotheosis of earth's fruitfulness and the beauty of man and his natural instincts."[53] There are statues and sculptures of Bacchus that show him bearded, a little softer around the pectorals and abdominals, and clearly more mature. When I see that Bacchus, I can relate, because I'm a little older, a little wiser, and there's a bit more of me to love than when I was younger.

Ready for those boar tacos? Me too.

---

53. Pieter Paul Rubens. "Bacchus." https://www.arthermitage.org/Pieter-Paul-Rubens/Bacchus.html.

Serves 6	Prep Time: 15 minutes	Cooking Time: 6 hours

1 tablespoon salt

1 tablespoon pepper

1 tablespoon cumin

1 tablespoon brown sugar

½ tablespoon dried chipotle powder (this has a kick, so adjust the amount as you like)

1 tablespoon marjoram or oregano

3 pounds boar shoulder

2 large yellow onions, chopped roughly

3 garlic cloves, peeled and halved

½ cup blueberries

½ cup zinfandel wine (or cabernet sauvignon)

Tortillas

FOR THE SPICY BERRY SALSA:

2 cups blueberries

1 cup raspberries

1 small yellow bell pepper

1 jalapeño

½ cup red onion, chopped/diced

¼ cup cilantro, chopped

Salt to taste (I use about ½ teaspoon)

1 tablespoon olive oil

1 tablespoon vinegar (white or apple cider)

¼ cup lemon juice

This recipe takes 6 hours and 15 minutes to complete, so start early in the day. Six hours is waiting for the boar to be done, the other 15 minutes is in the preparation time. Preheat your oven to 225° F.

Mix together the salt, pepper, cumin, brown sugar, chipotle powder, and marjoram or oregano and rub the blend onto your boar shoulder. Set aside for a few minutes. Peel the onions and chop them roughly. Peel the garlic and chop the cloves in half. Add the onions and garlic to a Dutch oven or other ovenproof pot. Add ½ cup of blueberries to the Dutch oven and pour in the zinfandel. Take your well-seasoned boar shoulder and put it on top of the onions, garlic, blueberries, and zinfandel. Put a lid on it, pop it in your oven, and dream of boar tacos for the next six hours.

Making the salsa is really simple. I usually do this right before I pull the boar out of the oven, but you can do it ahead of time and chill the salsa in the fridge. Use a big bowl because there will be a fair amount of stirring going on. Pour the berries into the bowl. Cut the pepper in half. Remove the seeds and then dice. Add the pepper to the bowl of berries. Slice the jalapeño in half, lengthwise, and scrape the seeds out. Then dice the jalapeño and toss into the bowl with the berries and pepper. Stop what you're doing and go and wash your hands again. I mean it. Touching your eyes, which you'll probably do in a couple of minutes from now when you start chopping the onions, is a really bad idea if you have jalapeño oil on your hands. Dice the onions and chop the cilantro, then add them to the bowl too. Sprinkle in the salt. Give the whole thing a gentle stir—more of a folding action, really—to get all of the ingredients mixed together.

In a separate bowl, combine the oil, vinegar, and lemon juice. Whisk them up and pour over the salsa, again stirring gently and making sure all the ingredients are nicely coated.

Open the oven door and carefully remove the Dutch oven. Lift the lid and take a long, full sniff. I have no idea what the Otherworld smells like, but I imagine it smells like slow-roasted boar. Grab a meat thermometer and check the internal temperature. You want the boar to be at 200° F to ensure that the meat is tender and all of the connective tissue has broken down. The boar should be completely tender and shred easily as you run a fork through it. With a fork or a pair of tongs, pull the boar apart and let it mix with the onions, garlic, zinfandel, and pan juices. Remove the shredded boar into a serving dish and grab some warmed tortillas (I prefer corn over flour) and the salsa.

Think of Bacchus, make a plate for him first, pour a glass of zinfandel for him, and then feast. Feast like you're Bacchus. When you've satiated yourself on boar tacos, berry salsa, and red wine, put your feet up for fifteen minutes and then get another taco. Bacchus would approve.

A Year of Food Magick

Each witchcraft or Pagan tradition has its own way of marking the important days that make up a year. Food magick fits nicely with the calendar too, as certain ingredients ripen and come into season, are plentiful (or on sale), and then disappear again.

Beyond the choices of ingredients, the time of year influences the types of meals we prepare too. The idea of a light picnic spread out on a blanket and eaten by the lake doesn't resonate quite as much in the dead of winter as it might at the height of summer.

Here are eight of my go-to seasonal recipes. If you live in the southern hemisphere you might have to do a little adjusting to make the seasons line up with the recipes, but my guess is that you're quite adept with that sort of translation magick.

Brigid Bread: Bread Pudding and Whiskey Sauce

Stories of the goddess Brigid are ubiquitous throughout Ireland, England, and parts of France. Add in the tales of St. Brigid and it seems she rivals practically any deity for name recognition. Brigid is often associated with blacksmithing and baking. Her attributes include being an accomplished poet and orator. In her spare time, Brigid is a midwife and healer. Brigid's feast day is celebrated in early February. If you stop and think about the weather in early February, especially in the ancient British Isles, you'll discover it was bleak and miserable. Life through the long, cold winter was arduous and precarious. Brigid's association with Imbolc, with cows, with the heat of the forge, and the not-too-distant return of spring has contributed to her longevity, I think.

When I think of cold, dark, dreary February nights I want to be comforted by the notion that better times are coming, that spring is returning, and that I will play in the sun again soon. Bread pudding, made with whiskey and cream and leftover bread, is extremely easy to make and even easier to eat. Trust me. You'll have seconds.

Serves 6	Prep Time: 10 minutes	Cooking Time: 45 minutes

2 cups milk

¼ cup butter

2 eggs

2 tablespoons vanilla extract

½ cup sugar

1 teaspoon cinnamon

1 teaspoon nutmeg

¼ teaspoon salt

6 cups bread, torn into rough
    cubes

½ cup raisins

FOR THE WHISKEY SAUCE:

½ cup butter

½ cup heavy cream

¼ cup whiskey

Preheat your oven to 350° F. Pour the milk into a large saucepan over medium heat. Add the butter and stir until the butter is melted. You want the milk to be hot, but don't let it boil. In a separate bowl, mix the eggs, vanilla extract, sugar, cinnamon, nutmeg, and salt. Tear the bread into rough cubes and place it in a lightly greased 9" x 13" pan.

A quick note about the bread: I'll pretty much use any white bread for my bread pudding. My preference is brioche, but French bread is great, and so is plain ol' sliced bread.

Sprinkle the raisins over the bread, then pour the milk mixture over everything, making sure to soak all the bread. Pop the pan in the oven for approximately 45 minutes. You'll know your bread pudding is done when you can insert a knife in the middle and pull it out clean. Just before the bread pudding is done, combine the butter, cream, and whiskey in a saucepan over low heat. Keep stirring until the sauce is just boiling. Pour it over the finished bread pudding and serve.

This is a dense, sumptuous dessert, so I recommend eating smaller portions. Who am I kidding? Sometimes my bread pudding never makes it out of the pan and into a dish. Enjoy it however it makes you feel good!

Equinox Eggs: Fresh Vegetable Frittata

Eggs and the vernal equinox go together like, well, eggs and the vernal equinox. In many Pagan traditions, the spring equinox is celebrated as Ostara. Eggs are decorated, and the return of the spring is heralded. There's really very little information on the roots of the goddess Eostre, and there's an incredible amount of terrible information circulating that links Eostre, Easter, and the Akkadian goddess Ishtar together.

One potential link to the tradition of colouring eggs does come to us through the Persian celebration of Nowruz, a thirteen-day New Year's festival that spans the spring equinox. The festival reaches back into Persia's ancient history and the rites connected to Zoroastrianism. Nowruz is still celebrated today all throughout the world. Coloured eggs represent fertility, coins bring wealth, and mirrors give one a reason to reflect on the coming year.

Celebrating the spring and the coming abundance seems like a good idea to me. Spring vegetables like asparagus and new potatoes easily combine with eggs to make a tantalizing, simple-to-prepare dish, with about a zillion variations depending on what your tastes are. The recipe I've included below is more of a template than a full recipe. I've given you the basics and you get to develop it from there. One note about the vegetables, though. If you choose veggies with a lot of moisture, like zucchini for instance, slice them, salt them, and let them sit for 10 minutes. Then dry them on a paper towel before adding them to the skillet. The salt will draw out the excess water. Too much liquid being released will make everything else you're putting in the dish too mushy.

Serves 4	Prep Time: 10 minutes	Cooking Time: 10 minutes

8 eggs

Salt

1 cup cheese, shredded or
  crumbled

Any of the following: Spinach,
  arugula, asparagus, chives,
  celery root, mushrooms,
  potatoes, bacon, sausage,
  ham, beef

Preheat the broiler, if you have one, to 400° F. You can also cook this in the oven at the same temperature. It might just take another 5 minutes or so to get good and firm. Crack eight eggs into a bowl and whisk until smooth. Add a pinch of salt. Set aside. If you're using meat, cook it in an eight- to ten-inch ovenproof skillet over medium heat until it's done. Set aside.

Add any firm vegetables, like celery root or potatoes, into the same skillet over medium heat and cook until just underdone. Put the meat back into the skillet, along with any softer vegetables like mushrooms, asparagus, or leafy greens. Cook over medium heat and stir everything together.

Add the whisked eggs, making sure that the eggs reach the outside edges of the skillet. Sprinkle the cheese over the eggs, meat, and vegetables.

Quick tips: For eight eggs, I find an eight-inch skillet to work the best. If I'm making this dish for two people and using only three eggs, I use a six-inch skillet. Don't stir the eggs at all. Don't shake the pan. Just pour the eggs in on top of the meat and/or veggies and leave it well alone.

Cook the eggs for 3 to 5 minutes until they form a solid edge. The top will likely be runny still. This is perfectly okay. Carefully transfer the hot skillet into the oven and cook for 10 minutes or until the egg mixture is fluffy and firm. You can put a toothpick into the eggs and if it comes out clean, your frittata is done.

Some ovens have a broiler tray or a grill. It's best if you put the skillet under the broiler or grill, as it turns the top a lovely golden brown. If you do use the broiler or grill, you only need a couple of minutes at most to finish the cooking and don't need to put the mixture in the oven for 10 minutes at all. Keep an eye on the skillet, because it can go from tasty frittata to burnt offerings in about 10 seconds!

I recommend eating Equinox Eggs in bed. If there's someone next to you, ask them to feed you (if you like that sort of thing) or chat about what you'll do together throughout the spring and coming summer months. The spring is the perfect time to plan for long days and long meals to come. If you're by yourself, take your time. Eat breakfast in bed slowly. Think about what is coming back to life or just beginning to sprout for you. Oh! And have seconds. It's okay.

Summer Passion: A Flummery of Fresh Fruit

You might be asking, "What on earth is a flummery?" The simple answer is that a flummery is a little like pudding or a stiffened smoothie. A flummery is either sweet or savoury, which is not uncommon with many British desserts. Flummeries were particularly popular in the British Isles in the seventeenth century. The first recorded usage of the word flummery appears in 1615 in Gervase Markham's book The English Huswife: Containing the Inward and Outward Virtues Which Ought to Be in a Complete Woman. Allegedly, the name derives from the Welsh word llymru which is approximately pronounced phonetically as lum-ra, except that in Welsh, the LL sound is made by placing your tongue up behind your two front teeth, exhaling, and saying "Lah." However, according to my Welsh dictionary, llymru means stomach in modern Welsh, so clearly there's a linguistic mystery to solve there.

The summer, in most regions, is a time of activity. Flowers are blooming, fruits and vegetables are growing and being harvested, meals are eaten outdoors as the evenings stay brighter, longer. In many Pagan traditions, especially those influenced by the Wheel of the Year, Beltane is celebrated in May, which might be the late spring or early summer depending on exactly where you live. Nothing speaks of summer quite like a dessert of fresh berries. There's something deliciously sensual about eating berries and freshly made whipped cream on a warm summer's afternoon and taking in the breathtaking beauty that is life in full bloom. And to that end, the flummery is the perfect dessert.

Serves 4	Prep Time: 10 minutes	Cooking Time: 30 minutes, plus 12 hours in the fridge

1 pound mix of fresh berries
(blackberries, raspberries,
strawberries, blueberries)

2 cups + 3 tablespoons water

2 tablespoons butter

½ cup sugar

2 tablespoons all-purpose flour

1 egg yolk

1 teaspoon lemon juice

1 egg white

Place your mixed berries in a medium saucepan with three tablespoons of water, and cook over medium heat until they are soft (or about 7 minutes). Stir frequently, but gently. The fruit will begin to give up their juices just a little bit. Remove from the heat and puree the berries in a blender for about fifteen seconds, just enough to get everything good and sloppy, but still have a few chunky bits. Set the puree in the freezer while you're making the rest of the flummery.

Add the other two cups of water and the butter to a saucepan (it can totally be the saucepan you just used to soften the berries). Heat until hot, but not quite boiling. The butter should be melted. Remove from the heat and mix in the sugar and the flour immediately. Whisk until the water, butter, sugar, and flour make a smooth slurry, making sure there aren't any bits of unincorporated flour floating about. Put the saucepan back on medium heat and whisk in the egg yolk. Whisk this mixture for approximately 5 minutes, keeping the heat even. It's important not to let the mixture boil, so you may need to lower the heat or lift the saucepan up from the heat from time to time. Remember to keep whisking. After the 5 minutes are up, remove the saucepan from the heat.

The next step is fun. Well, I think it is. Grab the chilled berries from the freezer. Add the lemon juice to the berry puree and pour the puree into the hot slurry mix. I like to use a folding motion here rather than a stirring motion, but the idea is to incorporate the slurry and the puree into one pot of purple-red goodness.

Now it's time to whisk your egg white for a few minutes until it just begins to form soft peaks. Fold the whisked egg white into the berry mixture. The trick here is to fold the egg white in gently and slowly, because you want to maintain as much of the air you just whisked into it as possible. You might notice little trails of foamy egg white running through the mixture. That's totally okay.

Lastly, pour the berry mixture into a shallow serving dish and chill it in the fridge overnight (at least 12 hours, but maybe 24) until it sets. The flummery will firm up. It won't be solid exactly, but it shouldn't be runny either. Right before you serve it, top with fresh berries and healthy-sized dollops of fresh whipped cream. If you're feeling extra special and fancy, you can pipe whipped cream on the flummery and make the dessert all pretty like.

Grab spoons. Savour the tart and sweet summer berries. Put whipped cream on someone's nose. If you are by yourself, still put whipped cream on your own nose. Maybe ask to lick the whipped cream off someone's nose. You never know what eating a good flummery might lead to.

A Slow Solstice Supper: Slow-Braised Pork with Fruit and Onion-Bacon Jam

Summer Solstice. The longest day of the year. A time, in an ideal world, when we languidly wile away the entire day and long evening with nothing to do but simply enjoy the company of friends, family, and beloveds. A slow, long, laid-back affair honouring the very apex of summer and all that's good about life. A platter of food appears, seemingly out of nowhere, wine is poured, a solstice bonfire is lit, and folks tuck into a meal with full abandon, using their fingers for cutlery and their jeans for napkins.

I love slow meals. I mean meals that last a long time. Not because there's so much food that it takes forever to cook, serve, and consume, but because there's absolutely no hurry to eat everything and get anywhere else. I adore dining without a time limit, when conversation and laughter are equally important ingredients as salt and pepper. I like meals that tiptoe right to the edge of gluttony, consider whether less is in fact more, and then decide without haste that more is more and more is better.

And this recipe typifies summer solstice, slow eating, and great company. It is best to cook this recipe early in the day, hours before you'll want to eat it. There's no cookery reason for making the dishes early, but there is a magickal reason. Preparing everything ahead of time gives you the ability to laze about, participate in conversations, and enjoy the solstice with your guests. Time is a precious commodity, and this is a meal to be enjoyed slowly with others.

Serves 8	Prep Time: 30 minutes	Cooking Time: 2 hours

FOR THE PORK:

2 teaspoons salt

2 teaspoons pepper

2 teaspoons allspice

3 tablespoons olive oil

3 tablespoons honey

5 pounds pork shoulder (pork butt is the same thing)

3 firm apples, cored but not peeled; sliced

3 firm pears, cored but not peeled; sliced

1 12-ounce bottle of crisp, hard cider (apple or pear) or apple juice if you prefer

1 cup vegetable broth or water

3 tablespoons flour

FOR THE JAM:

2 slices platter bacon (I like cherrywood smoked bacon, but whatever you have is good)

4 medium red onions, peeled and diced

2 cups red wine

½ cup honey

½ cup red wine vinegar

3 tablespoons brown sugar

It's time to cook some pork butt! Preheat your oven to 400° F. Combine the salt, pepper, allspice, oil, and honey in a bowl. Paint the pork shoulder on all sides with the honey, oil, and spice mixture. Then place the pork shoulder on a wire rack in a roasting pan, and put it in the oven for 20 minutes. After 20 minutes, reduce the heat to 350° and roast the pork shoulder for another hour.

Pull the roasting pan out of the oven, place the pork on a plate, and pour any cooking juices into a bowl for later use. Add the cored and sliced apples and pears to the roasting pan, underneath the rack, and pour in half of the cider (or apple juice). Reserve three tablespoons of the remaining cider for later use, and drink the rest, because cooking is thirsty work. Place the pork shoulder back on the rack and pop it into the oven for another 30 minutes or until the internal temperature reaches 160° F. Get your favourite big serving platter. Put the pork slap-dab in the middle and use a slotted spoon to arrange the apples and pears all around it. There should be some juices on the bottom of the roasting pan (cider, liquid from the fruit, and maybe some pork drippings). Pour these juices into a saucepan. Add the vegetable broth or water. Whisk in the reserved pan juices (from earlier), and the three reserved tablespoons of cider. Once the liquid is hot but not boiling, remove a couple of tablespoons to a bowl and stir in the flour, making a roux (a thin paste). Add the roux back into the saucepan and set over medium heat until the liquids come to a boil. Turn the heat down and simmer for 2 more minutes. Pour the sauce over the pork roast. Depending on when your meal begins, cover the roast and leave it alone until you're ready to eat it. Now let's make the onion-bacon jam.

Technically speaking, you could make the onion-bacon jam way ahead of time. I'll often make a batch and keep it in the fridge for up to a week. Okay, that's a total fib. I do make it ahead of time, but it never lasts a week. I eat it on everything, so the onion-bacon jam might last for two days if I'm lucky!

Start with your favourite skillet and the platter bacon. Cook the bacon until it's done but not overdone. In fact, you can undercook your bacon a little because it's going back into the skillet in a little bit. Remove the cooked bacon from the skillet to a paper towel. Peel the four onions and then halve them. Dice the onions and toss them into the skillet with the bacon drippings, on high heat. Stir for 5 to 7 minutes, coating the onions, until the onions start to give up their juices.

Next pour two cups of red wine (minus a sip or two for the cook, of course) into the skillet with the onions. Let the wine reduce for 20 minutes, stirring the onion and wine mixture frequently. Slice the cooked bacon into small strips and combine again with the onions. Add the honey, red wine vinegar, and brown sugar and stir until incorporated into the onion mixture. Turn the heat down to medium-low or simmer and cook for 30 minutes. Every 5 minutes or so, give the mixture a good stirring, folding everything over itself. You'll start to notice the difference in colour and consistency, as the onions, bacon, honey, wine, and vinegar all meld together and form a sweet, sticky jam. Remove from the heat. Scoop the jammy goodness into a sealable container and pop it into the fridge until cooled. The onion jam can stay in the fridge for up to a week.

When your guests have arrived and you've chatted for a bit and it's getting to be time for food, dash into the kitchen and uncover your platter of pork, pears, and apples. Pull your onion jam out of the fridge and scoop it into your favourite serving bowl. Bring everything outside, or wherever you're eating. Get your biggest carving knife, some spoons, small plates, napkins if you're delicate, a little bread, some cheese maybe, bottles of your desired beverage, and your appetite all ready. Be the first person to cut a chunk of the pork and greedily eat it, making sure to lick up the juices that are running down your fingers. Next hunk of pork gets a huge dollop of onion jam on it. Eat, drink, talk, and laugh until the solstice sun goes down, the platters are empty, and everyone is full.

High Summer's Bread: Garlic and Herb Focaccia

Baking bread is a magickal process, and generally a long process too. This recipe is quick, tasty, and you make it your own by adding your favourite herbs, spices, and toppings to the mix. Also, it's wicked easy to make for your Lammas celebrations.

When I think of Lammas, I think of bread and sharing a bountiful harvest with friends. In Anglo-Saxon times, loaf mass commemorated the wheat harvest. Bread was shared, and some say the loaf was imbued with magick and that the magick was spread about the community either by breaking pieces of the loaf off and secreting them about the village or by eating the bread and sharing the magick, quite literally.

As you gather the ingredients, focus on your own harvests, literal and spiritual, and how you send that magick out into the world. And then rip this thin loaf into pieces, dip it in olive oil or balsamic vinegar or even ranch dressing, and rejoice in your creation. Share it if you have any left.

Serves 4	Prep Time: 30 minutes	Cooking Time: 30 minutes

⅓ cup warm water

1 package dry active yeast

1 tablespoon sugar or honey

3 cups flour (all-purpose or bread flour)

1 teaspoon salt

4 tablespoons olive oil

4 teaspoons garlic, minced

1 tablespoon fresh sage, chopped

1 tablespoon fresh oregano, chopped

2 heaping tablespoons parmesan, pecorion Romano, or other hard cheese

Combine the water, yeast, and sugar (or honey) in a small bowl. Let the yeast activate for about 10 minutes. You'll know the yeast it doing its microbial thing because the water will start to look frothy. You'll want the water to be about 100° F; any hotter and you can damage the yeast.

The next step is to combine the flour and salt in large bowl and add the yeast mixture. Using your hands (you know I'm a big fan of using hands to cook), combine the water, yeast, sugar, flour, and salt until you have a nice dough. What you're looking for is to have all the flour incorporated. You might need to add a little more water. If you do, add a teaspoon at a time. When you've got your dough, plop it out onto a floured surface and knead it for a couple of minutes. You don't want to overwork this dough.

Oil a bowl with 1 tablespoon of olive oil, get it right up to the edges and all around, and put your dough in it. Turn the dough over once to make sure there's oil all over it. Cover the dough with a tea towel and leave it in a warm place for 30 minutes or until it has doubled in size. My trick here is to turn the oven on and preheat it to 475° F. I put the bowl of dough on the stovetop for 15 minutes and then set it next to the stove for the last 15 minutes.

Once the dough has risen, punch it down and place it on a lightly floured surface. Take the garlic and herbs and knead them into the dough. Again, don't overwork the dough, just knead it enough to get the herbs and garlic distributed evenly. Now roll the dough out into a rectangle and place it on a baking sheet. Using the butt end of a wooden spoon, make dimples in the dough. I do this in nice even lines, like 4 dimples across by 5 dimples long, but your dimpling numbers may vary. Brush the dough with the remining olive oil and top with the cheese. Pop the baking sheet in the oven for 10 minutes. If you like crunchier focaccia, bake it for 15 minutes.

When it's done, cut the bread into 2-inch-wide strips or use a pizza wheel and cut into 2-inch squares. Eat. Dip. Do that again and again until the bread is all gone.

A Bowl Full of Autumn: Butternut Squash and Ginger Soup

The autumn equinox is often referred to as the second harvest. Early summer fruits and vegetables are slowly giving way to autumnal delicacies like squashes and gourds. The equinox is another one of those balance points in the magickal year, a space between summer and winter. Depending where you live, the warmth of the sun still blesses your bones and the heat clings about you, reminding you of the full summer sun. On the wind though, there's a certain chill, a sense that winter is just around the corner. The oncoming winter might not have the same "You'll freeze, starve, and die" imperative that it may have had for our ancestors of just a few generations ago, but there's always uncertainty and risk and, perhaps, a deep-seated memory that it's possible the sun won't come back for us after all. And that's where this recipe really comes in handy. When I eat a huge bowl of autumn soup, I can taste the heat and sweetness of summer and my belly knows that there will be warmth when I'm cold.

Serves 4	Prep Time: 15 minutes	Cooking Time: 30 minutes

2 pounds butternut squash

3 tablespoons butter

1 medium yellow onion, sliced into half-moons

2 cloves garlic

1 teaspoon ground ginger

1 bay leaf

Big pinch of salt

1 tablespoon lemon juice

3 cups vegetable stock

½ teaspoon dried marjoram

1¼ cups milk

Pepper

Several snips of fresh chives

Peel the butternut squash and scoop out the seeds. Here's a good tip for peeling butternut squash: Slice the squash in half lengthwise, scoop out the seeds, and place the flat side of the squash on a cutting board or other flat surface. This keeps the squash really stable as you peel it. Use a vegetable peeler or sharp knife and peel away from yourself. Alternatively, some grocery shops sell peeled and cubed squash, which makes this dish even easier to cook. Once you've peeled your squash, cut it into 1-inch cubes.

Grab your biggest saucepan or an eight-quart stock pot. The eight-quart pot is a little too big really, but I like it because I can stir the ingredients without worrying about splashing stuff over the sides of the pot and onto the stove. Melt the butter over medium heat and add the sliced onion and crushed garlic. Give the onions and garlic a good 3 to 5 minutes to cook so they get soft, but don't let them brown. Then add the cubed butternut squash. Stir everything together. Add the ginger, bay leaf, and a good pinch of salt. Give a quick stir so the spices get distributed about. Add the lemon juice and the vegetable stock and bring everything to a boil. Once the soup has come to a boil, cover the pot, reduce to a simmer, and go do something fun for 20 minutes, like setting the table with red and orange fabrics and finding those handmade soup bowls you bought last year and haven't used yet.

The next bit is a little tricky. Discard the bay leaf and pour the soup mixture into a food processor. If you don't have a food processor or blender, strain the mixture by pouring it through a sieve over another saucepan and use a wooden spoon to push everything through. Whichever way you do it, what you're looking for is a smooth puree. Pour the puree into a saucepan. Add the marjoram and the milk and heat the soup until it's the temperature you like.

Ladle the soup into your bowls or one big bowl if you want to be fancy about it. Add a little pepper if you like, as well as the fresh chives. Serve with crusty bread and do remember to lick the bowl clean. I know some people would frown on this last step, but really, give it a try. There's something deliciously decadent about bringing the bowl up to your mouth and getting the very last drops of soup all over your tongue and lips. Encourage anyone eating with you to do the same. It's fun. Give it a whirl.

Samhain Pot Roast for One

Without a doubt, this is one of my all-time favourite recipes. There's enough food to feed four people, but sometimes I make this just to eat all by myself. I'll eat pot roast for breakfast, lunch, and dinner for a few days. When it comes time to scrape the last few precious morsels out of bowl, I've been known to cut a slab of sourdough bread and pile on whatever is left for an open-faced sandwich fit for the gods.

I associate pot roast with Samhain because it reminds me of the foods my grandparents made. This is an ancestor meal, of sorts. There's nothing "officially" Pagan about this meal, except that a witch is cooking it and at least three witches besides me will be eating it. Whenever possible, the ingredients are locally and ethically sourced. I prefer knowing that the cow led a lovely life right up to the moment that it didn't (which is a spell I hope we can all say about our own lives!). And the national chain supermarkets often have chuck roast on sale, so buy the best meat you can, wherever you can get it. Remember, all food is sacred, and sacredness has precious little to do with the price tag.

Serves 4 (or one)	Prep Time: 20 minutes	Cooking Time: 4 hours

5-pound chuck roast

Kosher salt and ground black pepper

3 tablespoons olive oil

2 medium onions, peeled and cut into large chunks

6 medium carrots, cut into chunks (you can throw in three cups of baby carrots if you don't have whole carrots)

3 celery stalks, cut into chunks

12 small Yukon gold potatoes (red bliss will work too), unpeeled

2 rutabagas or turnips, peeled and with the hard end bits cut off

1 cup red wine for the deglazing + 1 extra cup for drinking

3 cups beef stock, mushroom stock, or veggie stock

5 dashes Worcestershire sauce (that's about a tablespoon)

2 sprigs fresh thyme

1 tablespoon dried savoury

1 tablespoon dried oregano

1 bay leaf (remove before serving)

Salt and pepper to taste

I get started by heating my oven to 275° F. Then I pour a glass of red wine for me, because, you know, standards!

Liberally season the chuck roast with salt and pepper. I like kosher salt and fresh cracked pepper, but whatever you have will work. I set it aside and explain to the dogs that pot roast is not for them, no matter how much they stare at me. Sip wine.

Next, it's time to heat a tablespoon of olive oil in a cast iron skillet or Dutch oven over medium-high heat. I roughly chop the onions and toss them into the hot oil. Is there anything better than the immediate sizzle of onions in a hot pan? I don't think so, and the aroma is a magick all of its own. This is the perfect time to send a quick note of appreciation to whichever god, goddess, or mysterious entity created Amaryllidaceae, and to our brilliant great-great ancestors who first foraged for onions and proclaimed "these we will eat with everything!" Leave the onions for about 5 minutes, giving them time to brown. After the 5 minutes are up, scoop the onions into a bowl or plate and set aside.

While the onions are in the pot browning away, start chopping the carrots and celery into nice chunks. I always split my celery stalks down the middle and then cut them crosswise. There's no real reason for this, except that it makes it look like there's even more celery. Throw the carrots and celery into the Dutch oven for just a few minutes— 5 minutes is just about enough. You might need to add a little more oil, just to keep everything moving. Once they are done, they might have just a bit of browning around the edges, which is what you are looking for.

Next, take the Yukon gold potatoes (skin on if you like that sort of thing; I certainly do) and toss them into the same hot pot that you just cooked the onions, carrots, and celery in. Peel and cut up two turnips or rutabagas. I usually quarter them, depending on the size. Again, give them about 5 minutes, just to get some heat and colour on them. Remove them to a bowl and set aside.

Now, grab the well-seasoned meat and add it to the pot. Sear it on all sides for about a minute per side. Once seared, remove it to a plate. Once you've got your chuck roast resting, pour a cup of red wine, or a cup of broth if alcohol is something you choose not to cook with, and deglaze the pan. *Deglaze* is one of those very cheffy terms for getting the sticky bits of food off of the bottom of the pot.

Pick up the chuck roast and put it back into the pot. I hear you saying, "But I just took the meat out of the pan. What's up with that?" I'm always tempted just to leave the roast in the pan and skip the deglazing, but just trust me and do the extra step. It does really add to the flavour. Pour in the rest of the stock, with a couple dashes of Worcestershire, just enough to cover about half of the meat. Put the onions, celery, carrots, potatoes, and rutabagas back into the pot too, and arrange them around the meat. I like to sort of dunk the veggies under the broth as much as possible. Add whatever herbs you'd like. I've listed my favourites in the recipe list.

Place the lid on top of the Dutch oven or ovenproof stew pot. Carefully put it in your oven and leave it alone for the next 4 hours. No really… don't peek. Don't taste. Just leave it there. The internal temperature should hit 200° F. When you do finally take it out, be prepared to thank Edesia, the Roman goddess of food and feasting, because you are about to enjoy one delicious feast!

The last step, when the cooking time is done and while everything is still in the pot, is to take a couple of forks and pull apart the meat. The chuck roast should pretty much fall away as you pull on it. Serve in the same pot you cooked it in or ladle the contents into your favourite serving dish. Optional: Enjoy the meal with someone else or just fill your own bowl and pour another glass of red wine. Either way, you might want to set a plate for your ancestors to enjoy.

A Winter's Feast: Shepherd's Pie to Live For

Let me start by answering the two most common questions I get about this shepherd's pie recipe: "What is a shepherd's pie?" and "Why is it to live for?" To be called a shepherd's pie properly, the mince mixture must include lamb. Anything other than lamb and it's really a cottage pie. Now, truth be told, I've made this dish with all vegetables, with meat substitutes, or with beef, and I still called it shepherd's pie. It's called "shepherd's pie to live for" because I dislike the expression "to die for." There may be causes I'd be willing to die for, but shepherd's pie isn't one of them and I believe that cooking, eating, and sharing food is best done when we're as fully engaged and present as possible. Live for the food you love. It will taste better.

Shepherd's pie is a winter staple in my house. Truth be told, it's been a constant food throughout my entire life, partly because it's completely scrumptious and filling and partly because if you have a few potatoes, a little meat, some leftover veggies, and a little time, you can turn some pretty meagre ingredients into a piping hot plate of hearth-warming goodness. Depending on your budget, this can be a lifesaver when funds are low or a gourmet experience when times are better. Imagine this dish with venison or slow-cooked boar and exquisite cheeses mixed through the potatoes. It's worth experimenting! But here's my basic shepherd's pie recipe, the version I've shared with my children, which harkens back to my grandmother's kitchen, where I first began to cook.

Serves 6-8	Prep Time: 20 minutes	Cooking Time: 60 minutes

15 medium Yukon gold potatoes (that's about 2 pounds),
peeled

Pinch of salt

1 pound ground beef

1 pound ground lamb

2 medium yellow onions, diced

1 large carrot, diced

4 cloves of garlic, minced

1 cup frozen peas (those 8.5-
ounce cans of peas work
well too)

1 tablespoon fresh thyme

1 tablespoon fresh sage

1 teaspoon pepper

5 tablespoons Worcestershire
sauce

4 tablespoons ketchup (the secret
is out. I do use ketchup!)

½ cup red wine

1 cup beef stock (use 2 cups
of beef stock if you are not
using the red wine)

¼ cup milk or cream

4 tablespoons butter

¾ cup grated cheese (I like
strong English cheddar, but
use what you have)

I start by preheating the oven to 400° F on the broiler setting. Next, I place a pot about three-quarters full of water on a burner and get it to a near boil. Take the potatoes, wash them, and cut them into quarters. Put them in the pot of water, making sure the water covers the potatoes. Add a pinch of salt and cook for about 15 minutes.

While the potatoes are boiling, it's time to start working on the mince. Mince is a typically English term. I don't hear it often elsewhere. Basically, mince is the mixture of meats, veggies, spices, and flavourings, all simmered together.

Add the beef and lamb to a large skillet on fairly high heat. I don't add oil to the skillet, but plenty of folks do. If you use oil, maybe add 1 tablespoon. The key here is to move the meat about the pan, slowly breaking it down to crumble-sized pieces. Once the lamb and beef are no longer pink, remove from the heat, drain off any excess grease, and then return the meat to the heat. (Some use a colander for this; I usually just use a saucepan lid.)

Immediately add the diced onion, carrots, and garlic. Stir everything around for 5 to 7 minutes. Then add the peas, thyme, sage, pepper, Worcestershire sauce, and ketchup all at once and stir for another minute or so until everything is incorporated.

A quick note: Many people struggle with the word *Worcestershire*. In the United States people tend to want to pronounce it "Wer-sester-shy-er" which is a right mouthful indeed. In England, it's typically just referred to as "woosta" or "woosta-sheer." Much simpler!

Add the half cup of wine and let it simmer for several minutes until it's well reduced and almost gone. If you are not using red wine, add half of the stock and let it reduce down too. Really do let the wine (or stock) reduce down. You might think the mince will be too dry, but there's a lot of liquid still to add. The idea of adding the wine or broth is to deepen the flavours of your shepherd's pie, not just about increasing the liquid. Add the stock (or the rest of the stock) and simmer until the sauce has thickened up. This may take up to 10 minutes. Transfer the mince into a deep casserole dish.

By now, the potatoes should be cooked. Strain off the water and add the milk (or cream), butter, salt and pepper, and grated cheese, and mash the potatoes until smooth and creamy. Spoon the mashed potatoes onto the mince mixture, covering the entire surface. I like to take a fork and make little lines and peaks in the mash—when you broil the dish it makes nice crunchy bits. Sprinkle a little cheese on top of the mash too. I love the way the cheese turns the top of the dish a lovely golden brown (or slightly darker brown). Put the casserole dish in the oven for 25 to 30 minutes or until the top of the mash is the golden brown. Usually, I do one last step here, but this is really optional. I transfer the casserole dish to the broiler for just a couple of minutes to get the peaks of the potatoes and cheese a little crunchier and darker. Truth be told, I kind of like the potatoes to be just a little burned ... er ... I mean well done. It's the way I learned to cook.

The hardest part of this recipe? Once you've pulled the steaming dish of potatoey, meaty, cheesy goodness out of the oven, let it sit for 10 minutes. The sauce will set just a wee bit. If there are leftovers, which is highly doubtful, pop everything into the fridge and eat for breakfast, second breakfast, lunch, brunch, or for an in-between meal snack the next day. It's usually even better.

Four Ridiculously Good Aphrodisiacs

While there's evidence that foods rich in certain minerals can boost the libido, aphrodisiacs are, by and large, what you make of them. The recipes in this section certainly contain ingredients often associated with stimulating the, ahem, senses, but there's more to an aphrodisiac than just the ingredients. As you'll find out when you make these dishes, they're hot, sticky, salty, sweet, and best enjoyed in bed (or the kitchen table, no judgement here).

A word about the serving sizes. Generally speaking, these recipes serve two. In this case, that's a matter of practical cookery instructions, not an endorsement of the dominant relationship paradigm. Need three, make three. Aphrodisiac for one? Make two servings anyway. You never know, it might be so good you might want seconds!

Breakfast in Bed: New York Strip, Arugula, and a Poached Egg

It's the egg that gets me every time. The moment my fork pricks the poached egg and thick, golden yolk oozes over a bed of spicy arugula, making its tantalizing journey toward a perfectly seared, medium-rare New York strip, I start to ... perhaps I should just share the recipe and let you experience this for yourself.

Serves 2	Prep Time: 5 minutes	Cooking Time: 20 minutes

FOR THE STEAKS:

1 tablespoon olive oil

2 10-ounce New York strip steaks

Big pinch of salt

Several cracks of fresh, black pepper

1 sprig of rosemary

2 tablespoons salted butter

FOR THE SALAD:

2 poached eggs

2 cups arugula

2 teaspoons olive oil

1 teaspoon lemon juice

2 teaspoons red wine vinegar

Salt and pepper

This dish takes about 20 minutes to make, which leaves you plenty of time to savour it. If you have time, it's best to take the steaks out of the fridge and let them come up to room temperature for 30 minutes before you cook them, but it's not super critical if you are raring to get going.

Heat a cast iron skillet on high heat for a minute. Coat the hot skillet with one tablespoon of olive oil and leave it for a minute or until you see just the faintest wisps of smoke. While you're waiting for the oil to heat up, season the steaks with the salt and pepper. Add the seasoned steaks to the hot pan and cook for 3 minutes. Turn the steaks over just once and cook for an additional 3 minutes. Turn the heat down to low and add the rosemary sprig to the skillet. Immediately add 2 tablespoons of butter. As the butter melts, baste the steaks using a spoon. The best way to do this is to tilt the skillet towards you and scoop the butter over the top of the steaks. Remember, if you're using a cast iron skillet, it's going to be hot, so use an oven mitt. Baste the steaks for 1 minute and then remove the steaks to a plate to rest for 10 minutes. The steaks will be medium to medium rare. Cook a little longer and use a meat thermometer if you like your steak medium well or well done.

Now it's time to poach the eggs. I have a quick method for this. I use silicone egg poaching molds. Heat half an inch of water in a saucepan until it's bubbling. Add one drip of oil to the bottom of each mold and spread around with your fingers. The oil helps the eggs slide out really easily. Crack each egg into the mold, add a pinch of salt, place in the bubbling water, cover the saucepan so the steam stays in, and leave for 3 minutes.

While the eggs are poaching, add 2 cups of arugula to a bowl. Mix the olive oil, lemon juice, and vinegar in a separate small bowl and drizzle over the arugula. Dress the arugula by gently tossing the salad greens with your hands, coating everything lightly. Be careful not to get the arugula soggy or let it become overdressed. Evenly divide the arugula on plates. Add salt and pepper to taste.

Remove the eggs. Tip the molds ever so slightly so any excess water drains out, and then gently upend each egg onto a waiting mound of barely dressed arugula. Slice each New York strip, against the grain, surround the greens and the egg with the steak, and enjoy. Really, really enjoy it.

Aphrodite on the Half Shell: Oysters with Fennel

It's the aphrodisiac section. There had to be at least one oyster recipe, right?
Jonathan Swift, a satirist from the late seventeenth and early eighteenth centuries
wrote an entire poem about oysters and their purported effects.[54] Here's a snippet:

> *"Your stomach they settle,*
> *And rouse up your mettle:*
> *They'll make you a dad*
> *Of a lass or a lad;*
> *And madam your wife*
> *They'll please to the life."*

Serves 2	Prep Time: 45 minutes

Crushed ice

1 small fennel bulb with fronds

2 lemons

4 tablespoons white wine or champagne vinegar

2 dozen oysters

Pepper

Start by crushing ice. My favourite technique is to fill a large freezer bag with ice cubes and bash it with a rolling pin. You'll want enough crushed ice to cover a serving platter that can accommodate 24 oysters. The next step is dicing the fennel bulb. You'll want to dice the fennel quite small, as it will be spooned onto each oyster. The fennel adds a delicate, anise flavour, so big chunks of fennel are way too overpowering. Place the diced fennel in a bowl. You'll only need 2 tablespoons of diced fennel. I never save the leftover fennel; I just eat it while I'm finishing the dish. But if you have leftovers, you can store it in an air-tight container in the fridge for 3 days. The fennel stalks are covered in fine, green fronds. Take one of the stalks and pull the fronds off. You'll garnish each oyster with these later.

---

54. Jonathan Swift. *Poetical Works of Jonathan Swift: With a Life (Classic Reprint)*. Forgotten Books, 2016.

Cut the lemons in half and squeeze the juice into the bowl with the fennel. A quick tip here: Squeeze the lemon halves with one hand and let the juices run over your other hand, positioned over the bowl. This way you catch any of the lemon pips in your hand and you don't have to fish them out of the bowl. Add the wine or vinegar to the lemon and fennel and stir gently, just making sure that the fennel is coated with the lemon and wine or vinegar. Set the bowl aside and begin shucking the oysters.

There are three things you need to shuck oysters easily: A kitchen towel, a firm surface, and an oyster knife. Oyster knives can be found in almost any store that sells kitchen wares. In a pinch, while camping, or when oysters need to be shucked unexpectedly, you can substitute a good penknife blade or even a flathead screwdriver. If you're able to, though, buy an oyster knife.

Place your kitchen towel on a flat, firm surface. Put one oyster on the towel and fold the towel over the oyster. Doing this protects your hands in case the knife slips. Take the oyster knife and insert it in the valve or hinge. This is where the two halves of the shell meet. Pry the shell in a twisting motion, using a fair amount of pressure. As the oyster shell begins to open, gently slide the knife into the oyster, detaching it from the top shell. Place the lower shell and oyster on the crushed ice. Repeat 23 more times. You'll be an expert by the time you're finished.

Spoon your fennel, lemon, and vinegar or wine mix onto each oyster, crack a little pepper, top with fennel fronds, and then bring this silky smooth, briny, anise-infused delicacy to your lips. Toss your head back, open your mouth, and let the oyster slide past your teeth. It's entirely possible that nakedness may ensue sometime after the third oyster.

A quick food safety note here: This recipe calls for raw oysters. Raw oysters need to be bought fresh, used right away, stored on ice, and the shells need to be unbroken. Most importantly, the shells need to be tightly closed. If the shells are open, the oyster is dead. Dead oysters are dangerous to eat. Consuming raw seafood can cause severe stomach issues.

Hot and Sweet: Chocolate Pots

Chocolate contains phenylethylamine. That's a very sexy fact, right? Phenylethylamine, also known as PEA, helps release other chemicals in your body that make you feel good and maybe even a little amorous. The science shows that there's just not enough PEA in chocolate to stimulate a lot of sexual desire, but that's where these hot and sweet chocolate pots come into play. If you like chocolate and you have a special someone (or someones) in your life that also likes chocolate, then this is the recipe for you. But be prepared, this dish is hot and sweet and oh so very messy.

Serves 2	Prep Time: 10 minutes	Cooking Time: 30 minutes

1 tablespoon butter

2 teaspoons cocoa powder (carob powder works here too)

2 ounces chocolate (get the best you can. I prefer dark and bitter. If you like spicy heat, omit the cinnamon and use your favourite chocolate and chili bar)

5 tablespoons unsalted butter

1 egg yolk

1 whole egg (minus the shell, of course!)

4 tablespoons superfine sugar

¼ teaspoon cinnamon

1 tablespoon brandy (totally omit this if alcohol isn't for you.—the dessert is just as delicious without, but I like it with)

4 tablespoons all-purpose flour

Preheat your oven to 325° F. Take 1 tablespoon of butter and liberally apply inside two 3-inch ramekins. Add one teaspoon of cocoa powder to each ramekin. Rub the powder on the bottom of the ramekin and on the sides. Then set aside.

Add ½ cup of water to an uncovered medium saucepan and heat on medium high. Place a glass bowl on top of the saucepan and add the chocolate and butter. Break the chocolate into pieces so it will melt more easily. Once the butter and chocolate are melted together, take the bowl off the heat. In a separate bowl, add the egg yolk, whole egg, and sugar. Whisk these ingredients by hand for about 8 minutes, or until thick and pale yellow. Alternatively, use a hand mixer for about 3 minutes.

Pour the chocolate and butter into the eggs and sugar. Add the cinnamon and brandy and gently stir them together. Lastly, carefully add the flour to the mixture, folding it in rather than stirring it in. Fold just until there's no visible unincorporated flour. Place the greased ramekins on a baking sheet, then fill them equally with the chocolate mixture. Cook in the preheated oven for 18 minutes.

Technically, the next step is to turn the ramekins out onto a serving plate, loosening the chocolate pot with a butter knife. The dessert does look better if you do this. I, however, am partial to putting the ramekins directly on a plate, grabbing spoons, and tucking right in to the ever-so-ooey-gooey, chocolatey decadence sitting right there in front of me. The center of the dessert should be filled with hot, sweet, molten chocolate. Lick the spoon. If you are with another person, feed them a big, delicious spoonful and let them return the favour (if you both agree to that). Oh my! This really is so decadent.

A cooking note: My oven takes 18 minutes. I've cooked in others that only took 15 minutes or as long as 20. A good guidepost to keep an eye out for is that the top of the chocolate pots will appear a wee bit wobbly. If the top is set firm, it's probably overdone. If you've overbaked it, you'll have a delicious brownie, so unless you burn the chocolate pots altogether, practically any result is a good result.

The Platter of Seduction: A New Way to Look at Finger Foods

There's no actual recipe here, rather a suggestion for a seductive meal and a list of foods that might help facilitate that. Here's how it works. Get plates, platters, bowls, and glasses, and find a place to eat. Chop, dice, slice, and peel; open jars, scoop dollops, and generally prepare a feast of raw, pickled, cured, and/or cultured items. This meal is all about your senses, about how certain foods feel in your hands and in your mouth. The coolness of cucumber on your lips, the sweet tang of chutney exploding on your taste buds, the saltiness of olives, the taste of the ocean in anchovies, and how those sumptuous flavours and textures excite and tantalize you.

Try this by yourself or with others you have an intimate, consensual connection with. It's exquisite. It's silly. It's sexy. It's fun.

Create a platter of any of the following, or whatever else comes to your mind:

Lemon	Cucumber	Carrots
Red Bell Peppers	Avocados	Oyster Mushrooms
Radishes	Pickled Kohlrabi	Black Olives
Kalamata Olives	Honeydew Melon	Watermelon
Cherries	Strawberries	Bananas
Figs	Dates	Honey
Honey Pecan Cream Cheese	Hummus	Yogurt
Whipped Cream	Feta Cheese	Triple Cream Brie
Dolce Gorgonzola	Cockles	Smoked Salmon
Prosciutto	Champagne	Prosecco
Sparkling Non-Alcoholic Drinks	Chocolate	

This list is a good starting place. Let your imagination run wild. What would you add? Where will you do this? Where do you *really* want to do this? What will you wear or not wear? A blindfold? Dare to be fed? Dare to feed? Maybe you are the plate. Who knows how this sensual feast will end.

Conclusion

Time to Clean the Kitchen

If you've made it this far in the book there's a good chance you've added a few spices to the cabinet, experimented with new recipes, and yelled at me loudly because I said the recipe needed to be in the oven for one hour and your version took an hour and a half. Hopefully along the way you've discovered or rediscovered that your kitchen, or wherever you cook, is a sacred place and whatever food you choose to eat is sacred too. In case it wasn't abundantly clear, you're sacred as well.

It's my earnest wish that all the days of your life are filled with stocked pantries, filled larders, fridges bursting with all sorts of goodies, and good company to share these gifts with. May you thrive as a kitchen witch and pass along your best recipes and spells to someone you love dearly. May you never hunger. May you never thirst.

And now it's time for me to clean the kitchen.

Bibliography

Bottéro, Jean. *The Oldest Cuisine in the World: Cooking in Mesopotamia*. Chicago: University of Chicago Press, 2011.

Chadwick, Janet. *The Beginners Guide to Preserving Food at Home*. North Adams, MA: Storey Pub., 2009.

Cunningham, Scott. *Encyclopedia of Magical Herbs*. St. Paul, MN: Llewellyn, 1985.

Enheduanna, and Betty De Shong Meador. *Inanna, Lady of Largest Heart: Poems of the Sumerian High Priestess Enheduanna*. Austin: University of Texas Press, 2006.

Faas, Patrick. *Around the Roman Table*. Chicago: University of Chicago Press, 2005.

Fallon, Sally. *Nourishing Diets: How Paleo, Ancestral and Traditional Peoples Really Ate*. New York: Grand Central Life & Style, 2018.

Griffiths, Bill. *Aspects of Anglo-Saxon Magic*. UK: Anglo-Saxon Books, 2012.

Guarnaschelli, Alex. *Old-School Comfort Food: The Way I Learned to Cook*. New York: Clarkson Potter, 2013.

Henderson, Jeff, and Ramin Ganeshram. *America I Am: Pass It Down Cookbook*. New York: Smiley Books, 2011.

Ingram, Christine, and Jennine Shapter. *Bread the Breads of the World and How to Bake Them at Home*. London: Hermes House, 2006.

James, Peter, and Nick Thorpe. *Ancient Inventions*. New York: Ballentine Books, 1995.

Jones, Gwyn, and Thomas Jones. *The Mabinogion*. London: Dent, 1970.

Kornfield, Jack, and Christina Feldman. *Soul Food: Stories to Nourish the Spirit and the Heart*. San Francisco: New York: HarperSanFrancisco, 1996.

Mankey, Jason. *The Witch's Athame: The Craft, Lore & Magick of Ritual Blades*. Woodbury: Llewellyn Worldwide, 2016.

Manson, Mark. *The Subtle Art of Not Giving a Fuck: A Counterintuitive Approach to Living a Good Life*. HarperCollins, 2018.

McKay, Carin. *Culinary Magic at the Regenerative Design Institute: Creating Community through Food, Farm and Permaculture*. Bolinas, CA: Carin McKay, 2013.

Moore, Thomas. *The Re-enchantment of Everyday Life*. New York: HarperPerennial, 1997.

———. *Care of the Soul: A Guide for Cultivating Depth and Sacredness in Everyday Life*. New York: Harper Perennial, 2016.

Oliver, Jamie. *Jamie at Home: Cook Your Way to the Good Life*. London: Michael Joseph, 2010.

Otto, Walter Friedrich. *Dionysus: Myth and Cult*. Bloomington: Indiana University Press, 1995.

Perowne, Stewart. *Roman Mythology*. Twickenham: Newnes, 1983.

Pollan, Michael. *Cooked: A Natural History of Transformation*. London: Penguin Books, 2014.

Pughe, John, and John Williams. *The Physicians of Myddvai = Meddygon Myddfai*. Cribyn, Lampeter: Llanerch Press, 2008.

Reusing, Andrea. *Cooking in the Moment: A Year of Seasonal Recipes*. Toronto: CNIB, 2012.

Rogak, Lisa. *Death Warmed Over: Funeral Food, Rituals, and Customs from around the World*. Berkeley: Ten Speed Press, 2004.

Schreiber, Charlotte. *The Mabinogion*. London: Fisher Unwin, 1902.

Serith, Ceisiwr. *A Book of Pagan Prayer*. Newburyport: Weiser Books, 2018.

Swanhart, Kenzie. *Paleo in 28: 4 Weeks, 5 Ingredients, 130 Recipes*. Berkeley: Sonoma Press, 2015.

Swift, Jonathan. *Poetical Works of Jonathan Swift: With a Life (Classic Reprint)*. N.a.: Forgotten Books, 2016.

Symon, Michael. *Michael Symons Carnivore*. New York: Clarkson Potter, 2012.

Wolkstein, Diane, and Samuel Noah Kramer. *Inanna Queen of Heaven and Earth*. New York: Harper & Row, Publishers, 1983.

Woolf, Virginia. *To the Lighthouse*. Middlesex: Penguin Books, 1964.

Zakroff, Laura Tempest. *The Witch's Cauldron: The Craft, Lore & Magick of Ritual Vessels*. Woodbury: Llewellyn Worldwide, 2017.

Index

A

Airmed, 103

Aja, 103

Altar, 39, 79, 120, 132, 145, 154–156, 171, 182, 183, 212

Ancestors, 1, 3, 4, 8, 31, 46, 47, 56, 66, 77, 110, 126, 128, 131, 136–138, 144, 150, 154, 163–166, 175, 195, 199, 211, 212, 239, 241–243

Anglo-Saxons, 52, 55–57, 237

Aphrodisiac, 86, 87, 92, 107, 247, 250

Aphrodite, 86, 92, 183, 250

Apicius, 42–44

Apollo, 103

Apples, 3, 16, 18, 89, 102, 103, 108, 115, 117, 143, 151, 155, 156, 164, 175, 194, 222, 225, 234–236

Archestratus, 27

Arugula, 20, 230, 248, 249

Athame, 80, 156, 171, 174

Athena, 26, 27, 34–36

Athenaeus, 27

Awen, 176, 178, 204

B

Baba Yaga, 175, 203

Bacchus, 115

Barley, 15–17, 19, 21, 28–30, 32, 33, 53

Bay Leaf, 35, 121, 122, 149, 174, 194, 195, 220, 221, 239–241

Beans, 16, 44, 53, 62, 74, 82, 116, 155, 175, 182

Beer, 3, 12–20, 23, 53, 55, 71, 80, 92, 143, 144, 146–148, 160, 199, 213

Black Pepper, 107–110, 121, 174, 186, 220, 241, 248

Blackberries, 53, 155, 232

Book of Shadows, 77, 172, 174

Bowls, 20–23, 29, 33, 35, 36, 39, 43, 48, 54, 56, 63, 64, 67, 72, 73, 78–81, 88, 90, 95, 97, 105, 108, 110, 112, 118, 122, 132, 133, 136, 149, 154, 169, 172, 183, 185, 192, 193, 197, 198, 204, 206,

213, 221, 223, 226, 229, 231, 235–243, 249–252, 254

Bread, 16–18, 21, 23, 24, 26–28, 30, 31, 35, 36, 47, 53–56, 63, 76, 80, 81, 94, 95, 102, 104, 110, 111, 115, 122–126, 145, 148, 153–155, 157–160, 162, 190, 192, 221, 228, 229, 236–238, 240, 241

Breakfast, 3, 28, 29, 37, 51, 63, 75, 98, 103, 138, 181, 184, 231, 241, 246, 248

Brigid, 82, 103, 228

Broth, 19, 20, 23, 118, 121, 122, 152, 179, 192, 194, 196, 218, 219, 234, 235, 242, 243, 246

Brown Sugar, 175, 185, 197, 198, 213, 214, 225, 235, 236

Butter, 13, 14, 20, 93, 104, 105, 162, 166, 173, 185, 197, 198, 219, 228, 229, 232, 233, 239, 240, 245, 246, 248, 252, 253

C

Cabbage, 52–54, 110, 111, 165–167, 222, 223

Cakes and Ale, 3, 143, 144, 146–148, 199, 213

Campfire, 8, 16, 53, 187

Candle, 3, 35, 36, 57, 93, 97, 98, 109, 127, 148, 149, 168, 174

Cardamom, 16

Carin McKay, 139–141, 163

Carob, 16, 186, 252

Cast Iron, 20, 105, 174, 177, 178, 242, 248

Cauldron, 3, 53–56, 66, 67, 108–110, 119, 172, 176–179, 204

Ceres, 147, 150

Cerridwen, 103, 176, 178, 192, 204

Cheese, 26, 28–30, 39, 45, 62, 74, 87, 88, 92, 98, 104, 132, 148, 152, 155, 156, 158, 162, 206, 222, 230, 231, 236–238, 244–246, 254

Chicken, 8, 54, 82, 118–122, 158–161, 168

Chicken Soup, 118–122

Chili Powder, 107, 110, 186

Chocolate, 17, 86, 89, 90, 98, 252–254

Cinnamon, 19, 23, 55, 106, 107, 110, 121, 186, 213, 214, 218, 219, 228, 229, 252, 253

Cloves, 19–21, 94, 105, 106, 117, 121, 140, 175, 194, 213, 214, 218, 220, 222, 225, 239, 245

Coffee, 21, 22, 28, 69, 76, 77, 91, 94, 133, 181, 182

Coriander, 16, 20, 21, 23, 43, 110, 121, 174, 218–221

Coven, 5, 65–67, 69, 76, 80, 99, 120, 134, 136, 143–148, 158, 159, 161, 168, 195, 205, 209

Cucumbers, 2, 16, 26, 39, 92, 116, 222, 223, 254

Cumin, 16, 20, 21, 23, 43, 109, 110, 121, 174, 218–221, 225

Cuneiform, 12, 13, 15, 18, 19, 42

Curcumin, 106

D

Dates, 16, 17, 21–23, 25, 26, 30, 95, 157, 254

De Re Coquinaria, 42

Death, 19, 30, 37, 38, 42, 131–134, 202

Demeter, 30, 31, 33, 36, 222

Devotion, 2, 18, 36, 37, 48, 60, 78, 144, 184

Diane Wolkstein, 13–15

Diet, 16, 26, 30, 31, 37, 53, 58, 86, 101, 107, 134, 146, 148, 151, 152, 160, 190, 192, 206, 222

Dining, 19, 23, 27, 39, 45, 48, 64, 67, 71–73, 77, 78, 80, 93, 99, 111, 136, 137, 149, 163, 234

Dinner, 16, 18, 19, 27, 28, 30, 31, 37, 44, 45, 48, 56, 65, 98, 103, 132–135, 138, 146, 160, 164, 181, 205, 217, 234, 241

Dionysus, 36–39, 211, 220, 224

Dopamine, 87, 89–91

Doreen Valiente, 36, 86

Drink, 12–15, 17, 18, 24, 28, 31–33, 37, 38, 41, 46, 70, 71, 78, 86, 94, 97, 108, 135, 144, 152, 183, 184, 188, 194, 196, 200, 202–209, 211–213, 221, 235, 236, 241, 254

Duck, 12, 16

E

Ebers Papyrus, 106

Ecstasy, 37, 38, 60, 74, 200

Eggs, 19, 30, 39, 62, 76, 77, 79, 80, 91, 104, 151, 182, 185, 228–233, 248, 249, 252, 253

Elements, 8, 61, 74, 112, 113, 127, 128, 130, 151–154, 159, 178

Eleusinian Mysteries, 13, 31, 32

Enchantment, 37, 57, 68–70, 156

Enki, 13–15, 192

Exercises, 2, 5

F

Farmer's Market, 62, 91, 98, 102

Fennel, 104, 105, 250, 251

Fermentation, 110, 111, 115, 124

Feta Cheese, 39, 87, 88, 222, 223, 254

Figs, 8, 16, 21, 23, 28, 30, 48, 52, 55, 87, 88, 92, 102, 118, 132, 159, 176, 186, 190, 192, 194, 224, 254

Fire, 9, 16, 47, 51, 53–55, 61, 109, 112, 114, 119, 126, 128, 130, 145, 152, 154, 169, 171, 176–178

First Law of Affinity, 87

Fish, 11, 16, 25, 30, 41, 53, 92, 105, 112, 152, 180, 192, 193, 251

Flatbread, 21, 23, 124

Food Magick, 2, 3, 5, 59, 62, 67, 163, 173, 191, 197, 215, 227

Food Safety, 196, 251

Frigg, 55

G

Garlic, 16, 20, 21, 23, 94, 105, 108, 116–119, 121, 140, 141, 175, 186, 194, 195, 218–223, 225, 226, 237–240, 245, 246

Ginger, 4, 108, 140, 141, 175, 184, 239, 240

Goat, 12, 26, 37–39, 71, 104, 220, 221

Goddesses, 3, 13, 15, 16, 18, 23–25, 31, 33, 34, 36, 46, 47, 62, 63, 66, 76, 86, 103, 111, 112, 147, 150, 184, 196, 199, 206, 228, 230, 242, 243

Gods, 3, 5, 13–16, 18, 19, 25, 26, 30, 34, 36–39, 41, 46, 55, 56, 58, 60, 62, 74, 76, 77, 86, 103, 111, 112, 130, 143–145, 150, 154, 174, 176, 177, 183, 184, 186, 187, 192, 196, 197, 199, 211, 213, 215, 217, 220, 241, 242

Gooseberries, 53

H

Harvest, 3, 31, 46, 67, 69, 112, 146, 150, 155, 156, 159, 187, 232, 237, 239

Healing, 60, 101, 103, 108, 118–120, 127, 135, 136, 169, 176, 179, 183, 186, 212

Hearth, 16, 29, 47, 48, 119, 138

Herbs, 44, 53, 58, 67, 77, 87, 98, 103, 106, 112, 113, 116, 118–120, 123, 127, 147, 149, 155, 169, 174, 175, 178, 186, 192, 199, 204, 237, 238, 243

Hestia, 47

Honey, 17, 22–24, 28–30, 33, 39, 49, 76, 87, 88, 108, 140, 192, 193, 197, 198, 204, 208, 209, 212, 213, 221, 234–237, 254

I

Imbolc, 145, 228

Inanna, 13–16, 23, 24, 31, 138, 190, 218, 219

Inflammation, 118, 124

Intention, 67, 74, 91, 92, 96, 97, 99, 118, 136, 149, 158–160, 171, 178–180, 183, 185, 197, 198, 205

Invoking, 150–154

Iran, 13, 17

Iraq, 11, 41, 138

Israel, 8, 41

J

Jean Bottero, 16, 17, 19

K

Kitchen Witch, 2, 5, 102, 146, 163, 169–173, 176, 178, 179, 182, 183, 187, 191, 215, 255

Kykeon, 31–33

L

Lamb, 16, 20, 23, 26, 28, 218–220, 244, 245

Lares, 46–48

Lavender, 16, 17, 19, 137, 149, 174, 184, 202–204

Leeks, 3, 16, 19, 20, 53, 54

Leftovers, 24, 54, 62, 63, 114, 133, 147, 181–183, 217, 223, 228, 244, 246, 250

Lemon, 4, 33, 39, 108, 140, 155, 174, 181, 184, 192, 193, 197, 198, 204, 206, 208, 211–214, 225, 226, 232, 233, 239, 240, 248–251, 254

Lentils, 16, 30, 44, 140, 141, 175, 222, 223

Leptin, 87, 89, 91

Lunch, 28, 30, 37, 55, 62, 74, 77, 92, 98, 138, 163, 241, 246

M

Marjoram, 116, 225, 239, 240

Mead, 55, 76, 220, 221

Menthe, 208

Milk, 26, 33, 39, 45, 58, 63, 64, 71, 90, 104, 114, 140, 141, 148, 162, 164, 185, 197, 198, 213, 228, 229, 239, 240, 245, 246

Milk Sop, 63, 164

Mint, 33, 96, 140, 141, 208, 222, 223

Myths, 3, 25–28, 36, 38, 138, 164, 174, 176, 178, 193, 202, 209

N

Ninkasi, 17, 18

Nowruz, 230

Nutmeg, 109, 228, 229

Nutrition, 4, 102

O

Oatmeal Stout, 19, 20

Oats, 17, 19, 20, 53, 54, 75, 211

Odyssey, 28

Offerings, 2, 3, 5, 15, 16, 28, 31, 35–37, 46–49, 76, 80, 112, 113, 120, 144, 146, 147, 150, 154, 155, 181, 182, 186–188, 192, 197, 200, 211, 213, 217, 231

Olive Oil, 29, 34–36, 39, 43, 88, 108, 140, 167, 192, 193, 218–222, 225, 234, 237, 238, 241, 242, 248, 249

Olives, 26, 30, 34–36, 39, 222, 223, 254

Onions, 16, 19, 20, 23, 26, 53, 73, 109, 116–119, 121, 140, 141, 162, 167, 175, 182, 186, 194, 195, 218, 219, 222, 223, 225, 226, 234–236, 239–243, 245, 246

Orange, 3, 19, 76, 107, 152, 203, 209, 213, 214, 240

Oregano, 116, 149, 174, 225, 237, 241

Oysters, 86, 152, 250, 251, 254

P

Pagan, 2–4, 46, 53, 58, 61, 80, 103, 131, 132, 134, 138, 143–145, 147, 164, 175, 187, 188, 199, 202, 215, 227, 230, 232, 241

Pancakes, 28, 29, 76, 107, 185, 186

Pantry, 5, 47, 62, 112, 124, 140, 145, 157, 165, 174, 190

Parsnips, 53, 150

Peas, 3, 16, 53, 155, 182, 245, 246

Penates, 46–48

Persephone, 31, 36, 202, 208

Pickle, 110, 111, 113, 115–117, 156

Pickling, 110–112, 114, 115, 117, 136, 175, 254

Pig, 45, 190

Pistachios, 22, 23, 39

Plates, 1, 5, 17, 21–23, 31, 45, 56, 65, 73, 79, 80, 89, 91, 93–95, 97, 105, 121, 132, 133, 135, 149, 150, 154, 155, 157, 168, 176, 182, 185, 187, 188, 198, 209, 219, 224, 226, 235, 236, 242–244, 249, 253, 254

Plums, 53

Polytheist, 3, 46

Pomona, 206, 207

Pork, 45, 53, 74, 105, 135, 164, 190, 234–236

Porridge, 16, 44, 45, 47

Pot Roast, 178, 241, 242

Potatoes, 33, 47, 56, 62, 69, 74, 82, 93, 109, 118, 121, 125, 150, 152, 165–167, 180, 186, 220, 230, 231, 241–246

Potions, 86, 161, 174, 176, 178, 179, 183, 184, 199

Potluck, 3, 65, 148, 158–160, 162

Pottage, 53–56

Prawns, 42

Preserving, 27, 53, 111, 112, 123

Prosperity, 42, 109, 186

Protection, 8, 47, 48, 108, 174, 176, 186, 197, 251

R

Rabbit, 53, 54

Raspberries, 53, 184, 225, 232

Recipe, 1–5, 12, 15, 16, 18–21, 23, 27, 31, 32, 42, 43, 54, 66, 67, 75, 81, 82, 85, 88, 90, 96, 98, 103, 105, 109, 113, 117, 119–121, 138–140, 144, 162, 164, 172, 173, 176, 178, 179, 181, 182, 185, 186, 189, 190, 192, 194, 200, 205, 206, 209, 213–215, 217, 218, 220, 222, 224, 225, 227, 230, 234, 237, 239, 241, 243, 244, 246–248, 250–252, 254, 255

Ritual, 2–5, 7–9, 23, 30, 32, 34–36, 38, 48, 57–61, 66, 69, 71, 74, 76, 80, 97, 109, 112, 114, 124, 127, 131–133, 138, 143–151, 153–156, 159, 161, 164, 168, 170, 171, 174, 177, 183, 187, 197, 199, 200, 211, 217

Roasted, 16, 17, 19, 28, 34, 52, 55, 56, 94, 158–161, 164, 168, 190, 195, 220, 221, 235

Roman, 41, 42, 44–47, 57, 147, 206, 213, 224, 243

Rome, 41, 44, 45

Rosemary, 116, 117, 149, 174, 220, 221, 248

S

Saffron, 16, 106

Salad, 9, 78, 79, 92, 135, 138, 158, 159, 193, 222, 223, 248, 249

Salt, 16, 20, 21, 29, 30, 34, 38, 43, 47, 48, 53, 54, 64, 82, 87, 93, 94, 96, 104, 105, 108–116, 118–121, 124, 140, 141, 151, 152, 162, 163, 166, 167, 172, 174, 185, 186, 192, 194, 195, 209, 218–223, 225,

226, 228–231, 234, 235, 237, 239–242, 245–249, 254

Samhain, 131, 136, 241

Semele, 36, 37

Semolina, 16, 20

Sex, 45, 85–87, 91–93, 95, 96, 99, 128, 129, 252, 254

Sheep, 12, 15, 19, 30, 31, 39, 45, 52, 104, 176

Shellfish, 9, 53, 72

Smoking, 53, 105

Soup, 64, 73, 98, 118–122, 128, 138–140, 173, 179, 194, 239, 240

Spell, 58, 66, 67, 69–71, 74, 75, 77, 87, 91, 92, 95–97, 99, 106–110, 112, 118, 120, 126, 132, 147, 149, 154, 161, 171–174, 178–183, 185, 186, 191, 192, 194–199, 204, 206, 208, 209, 241, 255

Spices, 19, 21, 23, 41, 43, 55, 58, 63, 78, 93, 106, 107, 112, 117, 119–123, 163, 172, 180, 185, 186, 190, 192, 213, 218, 222, 237, 240, 245, 255

Spirits of Place, 46–48, 83, 128, 181–183, 186, 211

Spoon, 33, 45, 51, 77, 80, 81, 95, 105, 109, 117, 122, 154, 169, 173, 174, 176, 186, 193, 196, 198, 208, 219, 223, 233, 235, 236, 238, 240, 246, 248, 250, 251, 253

Statue, 13, 34, 35, 47, 80, 224

Stew, 19, 20, 53, 54, 61, 75, 114, 173, 177–179, 243

Stock, 27, 54, 80, 114, 119, 121, 177, 194, 195, 214, 239–242, 245, 246

Strawberries, 1, 89, 90, 156, 184, 209, 232, 254

Sumer, 11, 12, 17, 18, 42, 111

Sumerians, 12–20, 25, 41, 64, 78, 93, 112, 190, 192, 197, 218

Supermarket, 2, 91, 102, 104, 175, 179, 190

Syria, 41

T

Tabernae, 44

Tea, 2, 61, 70, 71, 75, 77, 170, 171, 183, 184, 198, 212, 214, 238

Tea towel, 170, 171, 238

Tiganites, 28, 29

The Charge of the Goddess, 36, 62, 86

The Physicians of Myddfai, 103

Thor, 76, 220, 221

Thyme, 16, 54, 113, 174, 241, 245, 246

Transformation, 4, 8, 113, 152, 204

Tuh'u Broth, 20, 23, 218

Turmeric, 16, 43, 54, 106, 108, 121

Turnips, 53, 109, 150, 241, 242

V

Vanilla, 62, 183, 186, 197, 198, 228, 229

Vegetables, 16, 17, 20, 30, 31, 42, 44, 53, 54, 56, 58, 61–63, 65, 67, 75, 82, 83, 91, 93, 102, 107, 110, 112, 113, 116, 118–122, 127, 129, 135, 145, 150, 155,

163, 165–167, 172, 177, 190, 194–196, 221–223, 230–232, 234, 235, 239–241, 244

Vegetarian, 2, 30, 31, 101, 138, 146, 190, 222

Vinegar, 43, 108, 110, 115, 117, 140, 167, 175, 193–195, 221–223, 225, 226, 235–237, 248–251

W

Wine, 27–30, 37–39, 41, 43, 44, 48, 55, 76, 92, 98, 105, 107, 110, 111, 115, 117, 122, 167, 199, 203, 204, 211, 213, 214, 218–222, 225, 226, 234–236, 241–243, 245, 246, 248, 250, 251

Woden, 55

Wonderwerk Cave, 8, 154

Worcestershire Sauce, 162, 194, 195, 241, 245, 246

Z

Zeus, 28, 36, 37